HIGH-LIGHTS OF THE BIBLE

A Bible Commentary for Laymen/Genesis to Nehemiah
BY RAY C. STEDMAN

Regal Books A Division of G/L Publications
Ventura, CA U.S.A.

The foreign language publishing of all Regal books is under the direction of Gospel Literature International (GLINT). GLINT provides financial and technical help for the adaptation, translation and publishing of books for millions of people worldwide. For information regarding translation, contact: GLINT, P.O. Box 6688, Ventura, California 93006.

Second Printing, 1981

Published by Regal Books
A Division of GL Publications
Ventura, California 93006
Printed in U.S.A.

Library of Congress Catalog Card No. 79-65423
ISBN 0-8307-0656-9

Contents

A Teacher's Manual and Student Discovery Guide for Bible study groups using this book are available from your church supplier.

Invitation to a Journey

The Bible is easily the most fascinating book in the world. Granted, it doesn't often appear as such to many. Some have even thought it to be dry, and even boring. But that is surely because they have not spent much time with it. It is a book of wonderful variety. There are beautiful love stories which reflect the tenderest and most delicate of human passions. There are stories of political intrigue and maneuvering which rival anything we know today. There are stories of blood and thunder which chill the heart. There are poetic passages which soar to the very heights of ecstasy. There are narratives of intense interest and intricate plot, and there are strange and cryptic passages filled with weird symbols and allegories which are difficult to penetrate and comprehend.

THE BIBLE'S THEME

Yet through all this variety there runs one coherent theme. Despite the diversity of human authorship and the vast span of time over which it was written (which surely precludes all possibility of collusion), this book has but one message, tells one story, moves to one point, and directs our attention to one Person: it is the glorious story of how God became flesh, the Immortal became a mortal, the Eternal One became a temporal being like ourselves that we may know the truth concerning ourselves.

The ultimate theme which makes the Bible of eternal fascination is essentially the story of your life and mine. It reveals the secrets I need to know about myself. It is the book that goes with man, as an instruction book goes with every major appliance. The Bible explains man. It instructs us, exhorts us, admonishes us, corrects us, strengthens us, teaches us. In the story which unfolds throughout the book God has incorporated all the truths we need to know about ourselves to discover the beauty and glory He had designed for man in the beginning.

The more you understand of the Bible's truth the more thrilling it becomes. I have been studying this book for over four decades and it has grown more fascinating, more mysterious, more marvelous in its implications, as my apprehension of it has increased.

A physicist friend once said to me, "Studying the Bible is like my study of the physical universe. At first it seems rather simple and easy to grasp. But the more deeply I probe into the makeup of the universe, the more complex and challenging I find it to be, till at last it blows all my mental fuses and I have to admit to myself that it is beyond me. So is Bible study. It is relatively simple to read, somewhat more difficult to understand; but once understood it is mind blasting in its implications." That ought not to surprise us, seeing that one God is behind both the universe and the Bible.

Even the story of how the Bible came into being is one of sheer fascination. The apostle Peter tells us the Bible was written by men who were "moved by the Holy Spirit" (2 Pet. 1:21). No one has ever been able to analyze that process. How was it that ordinary men like ourselves, some from the most common callings of life, could have been so led by the Holy Spirit in recording what they thought and felt that they would succeed in capturing in human words the thoughts and attitudes of God Himself? We do not really know. It is an amazing miracle. All we can know is that is what did happen, and if it had not, the Book could not have come into being.

When we hold it in our hands, sooner or later we ask ourselves: Why was it written? What is the ultimate aim of the Book? What does God want to accomplish by giving us a book like this, and giving us also the Holy Spirit to interpret it and make it real in our experience? The questions are surely to the point for nothing exists that does not have a purpose. The Bible was written by men moved of the Holy Spirit, and it has been kept and preserved through the centuries in strange and providential ways. It comes to us with its pages wet by the blood of martyrs. Surely God would not have gone to all this tremendous trouble to record His words in written form and preserve them through centuries of attack without some overwhelming purpose in view.

THE BIBLE'S PURPOSE

The Bible itself gives us the purpose. It can be found in a number of places, but one of the clearest is found in Paul's letter to the Ephesians. Paul states that the Lord Jesus, having finished His work here on earth through the cross and the resurrection, ascended to heaven and gave gifts to men. "And He gave some as apostles, and some as prophets, and some as evangelists, and some as pastors and teachers, for the equipping of the saints for the work of service, to the building up of the body of Christ; until we all attain to the unity of the faith, and of the knowledge of the Son of God, to a mature man, *to the measure of the stature which belongs to the fulness of Christ*" (Eph. 4:11-13, italics added).

God's purpose in giving us the Bible, is that we might know what it takes to become a "mature man." According to the *Amplified Bible*, the definition of mature manhood is "nothing less than the standard height of Christ's own perfection." Amazing! This verse says that the whole universe in its physical and moral dimensions, and the entire biblical record of God's actions among men exist in order that you might fulfill your manhood or your womanhood in Jesus Christ. That is God's purpose. That you and I might fulfill the possibilities God has hidden in our humanity. The true measure of that humanity is the measure of the manhood of Jesus.

At one time in my ministry I met regularly with five young high school boys. On one occasion I said to them, "Fellows, tell me this. What is your idea of a real he-man?"

One of them answered, "Well, I think a real he-man is a guy with a lot of solid muscle."

There happened to be a young man in that high school who had a tremendous body—lots of muscle, and especially between the ears! So I said, "Do you mean so-and-so?"

He thought for a moment and said, "No, I guess not. He's really not too much of a man."

So I went on. "Obviously, manhood is not muscles. What is it? What does it mean to be a real man?"

They all thought for a bit, then another replied, "I think a real he-man has guts." We started making a list and wrote "courage" at the top. They named other qualities: considerateness, kindness, integrity, honesty, and so on. After a while we had quite a long list. I said to them, "You know, guys, isn't it amazing that you could go anywhere in the world to any man in any city, open countryside or jungle—rich or poor, high or low, black or white or red or yellow—and ask him the question, 'What do you think it means to be a man?' you would eventually get the same answers you've given me! All men everywhere want to be real men. All women want to be women. The ideal they hold in their hearts is exactly the same. There may be small variations in standards but not in the general qualities."

They looked disbelieving until I asked: "Do you know anywhere on earth where courage is regarded as a vice and cowardice a virtue? Does any man want to be known as a coward and is proud that he is widely regarded as such?"

They all shook their heads.

I said, "Right. Everywhere, cowardice is despised; courage is admired."

Then I said to these fellows, "Do you know anyone who has fulfilled his idea of manhood? How are you doing yourselves?"

One of them rather cockily said, "Well, I think I make it about 30 percent of the time."

The others jumped on him right away and said, "No you wouldn't even make five percent!"

I questioned further. "Do you know anybody who has done it 100 percent?"

For a moment they looked blank. Then their faces lit up and they said, "Of course! It was Jesus!"

They were right! There is God's perfect man. In Him we see humanity in its fullest flower.

As a boy I ran across a copy of Rudyard Kipling's poem "If." When I read it I put it up on the wall of my room, for it seemed to describe exactly what I understood a real man to be. The opening verses read:

If you can keep your head when all about you
    Are losing theirs and blaming it on you;
If you can trust yourself when all men doubt you,
    And make allowance for their doubting too;
If you can wait and not be tired by waiting,
    Or being lied about, don't deal in lies,
Or, being hated, don't give way to hating;
    And yet don't look too good, nor talk too wise;

If you can dream, and not make dreams your master;

If you can think, and not make thoughts your aim;
If you can meet with Triumph and Disaster,
  And treat those two impostors just the same;
If you can bear to hear the truth you've spoken
  Twisted by knaves to make a trap for fools,
Or watch the things you gave your life to, broken,
  And stoop and build them up, with worn-out tools;

These admonitions describe character where it counts. Anyone who has seriously tried to do them knows that they are tough demands—too tough for me. I've broken them scores of times. In a concluding stanza Kipling says:

If you can talk with crowds and keep your virtue,
  Or walk with Kings—nor lose the common
  touch,—
If neither foes nor loving friends can hurt you,
  If all men count with you—but none too much;
If you can fill the unforgiving minute
  With sixty seconds' worth of distance run,
Yours is the Earth and everything that's in it,
  And—which is more—you'll be a Man, my son!

THE BIBLE'S PERSON

Who fulfills the glory of Manhood? In the course of human history, only one Person had the qualities that describe precisely the aim God has in mind in giving us His book of revelation.

Let us think about Ephesians 4:13 again. It says that we must come to mature manhood and that the steps toward that end are two. First, we are to come to "*the knowledge of the Son of God.*" There is no possibility of achieving manhood, as God intends man to be, if there is no experiential knowledge of the Son of God. We must be born again.

The step that flows from this knowledge is that "*we all*

attain to the unity of the faith." We share the same life
(the life of Jesus) because we have "come to the
knowledge of the Son of God" in the new birth. We
discover, then, that we belong to one another and are
gradually growing into a mutual understanding of the
teaching of truth. This means we need each other to
achieve the maturity that God desires. It is impossible to
move to maturity unless we are sharing truth with each
other. What the Presbyterians know should be shared with
the Pentecostals, and what the Baptists know is to be
shared with the Episcopalians, and vice versa. Those who
know the Son of God in any denomination may help in the
building up of other such believers wherever they encounter them, till the whole church universal attains an
increasing unity of faith. We need each other, to the end
that we may continue growing in the knowledge of the
Son of God. Thus the knowledge of Christ both begins the
Christian life (in the new birth) and characterizes it
throughout its duration. The apostle Peter exhorts the
Christians to whom he writes: "Go on growing in the
grace and in the knowledge of our Lord and savior Jesus
Christ" (2 Pet. 3:18, *JB*).

This is why the Bible was given to us. It is, from
Genesis to Revelation, all about Jesus Christ. In symbol,
in narrative, in marvelous prophetic vision, in history, in
poetry, it all points to Him—the true center of the universe
of God. He is the secret of the book. But, as we have
already implied, in learning about Him we discover that
we are learning about ourselves also. We discover our true
nature as human beings when we see it reflected in Him.
We understand our problems and our reactions to them as
we see Him at work both in the Old and the New Testaments. We will find all our needs fully met in Him.

Major Ian Thomas has well stated of Jesus: "He had to
be what he was in order to do what he did." He had to be
the Son of God in order to be the Saviour of the world. No

other could have done it. He had to be God, manifest in the flesh—the Eternal, Immortal One—yet dying upon a cross. He had to be what He was in order to do what He did.

But Major Thomas goes on: "He had to do what he did in order that we might have what he is." That is the true glory—the good news—of the gospel. It is not particularly good news to be told that our sins are forgiven by the shed blood of Jesus if then we must struggle on through this life doing the best we can, falling and failing, struggling and slipping, going through periods of doubt, despair, discouragement and defeat, until at last we get over on the other side and find the release we crave. That has an element of hope about it, but it is not really the good news. The truly good news is that not only does final fulfillment await us over there, but right now, where we are in this present life, we may have all that our Lord Jesus Christ is! He had to do what He did in order that we might have what He is.

But still further: "We must have what he is in order to be what he was." What was He? As we have seen, He was perfect man. He was God's ideal man, man as God intended man to be. For more than 33 years, right down here on this sin-drenched planet where you and I live, in the very circumstances and under the same pressures, up against the same problems, the same "contradiction of sinners against himself" that you and I face every day, He lived that perfect life. If God's intention is that we too may learn how to live like that, to be "mature" as He was, then it clearly follows that: "We must have what he is in order to be what he was."

THE PROCESS

We don't come to the knowledge of the Son of God without learning to do so, without a process. We require a gradual, deepening understanding of God's truth. Someone once said to a Christian, "Will your God give me a hundred dollars?'' His reply was, ''He will if you know Him well enough.'' George Müller, man of prayer, and founder of the world-famous Bristol Orphanages in England, knew Him so well that God gave him millions of dollars. He will give you whatever you need to serve His purposes—if you know Him well enough.

We learn to know God through the pages of Scripture, as interpreted and taught by the Holy Spirit and put into actual practice in our lives. We cannot separate the Word and the Spirit. The Bible without the Spirit leads to dullness and intellectual pride, to a dead Christianity. The Spirit without the Bible leads to fanaticism and folly. It takes both the Spirit and the Word.

And we need the entire Bible. The story of man before the Fall is necessary in order that we might know what God intended when He made man, and what we can expect to come to in our relationship with Him. We must also know the story of the fall of man, to study it, to search out its secrets, in order that we may have an explanation for the strange reactions which arise within us, often unbidden, that make it easy to be bad and difficult to be good. We need to know the Law in order to see what God expects of us, and to learn our guilt and our helplessness before Him.

We must know, too, the stories of the men and women of faith throughout the Bible, to see how God meets them, strengthens them, delivers them, teaches them, and ultimately brings them to glory. What an encouragement these lives are to us! As we read our Bibles we see that Abraham, Moses, Isaiah, Jeremiah, David, Ruth, Daniel, Mary, Paul, Peter and others, all went through many of the same experiences we do, and we understand that God recorded these experiences that we may learn how to handle our problems and find the way through them.

We must read and understand the Prophets that we might see the whole picture to the end, and come to a certainty that God knows what He is doing and can work all things out. We must learn God's thoughts and ways, which are different (and higher) than ours. Especially must we learn what Paul refers to in 1 Corinthians 2:7 as the "mystery, the hidden wisdom, which God pre-destined before the ages to our glory." We must be brought by the Spirit into the proper attitude to learn that hidden wisdom, for Jesus once said to His Father, "I thank Thee that Thou hast hidden these things from the wise and understanding and revealed them to babes."

The four Gospels, Matthew, Mark, Luke and John, next demand our attention in order that we may see the perfect life of Jesus—that remarkable, magnificent dis-play of God in humanity—which is totally different from anything we can learn outside the Word of God. We must then know the Epistles of the apostles in order to apply the great truths we learn in the Gospels to the everyday circumstances of our lives. It is the business of the writers of the New Testament letters to explain truth in logical and clear fashion and to translate these truths into practical daily lessons.

Finally, we need to know the book of Revelation, be-cause in hours of crisis (both as individuals and nations) we will find in Revelation the assurance that the darkness shall ultimately pass, the futility will be ended, man's present bondage shall cease, and Jesus Christ shall be fully and completely manifested throughout the universe as King of kings and Lord of lords. Then "the kingdoms of this world shall become the kingdom of our Lord and of his Christ."

Thus the whole of the Bible is needed to convey us to the maturity which God desires for us, and to which He has called us. The Testaments are not divided into two portions so that we may choose the one that best appeals to us.

THE PREPARATION

There is a good reason why our Bibles are consistently

divided into two major portions: the Old Testament and the New Testament. Some may reason that the division is because of the 400-year gap between the Testaments. It is true that some 400 years of human history lie between the close of the writing of the Old Testament and the beginning of the New, during which time no prophet spoke for God and no new truth was added to the revelation of God to men. Though many religious books were written during that period, and several helpful books of the history of God's people came into being, none of them ever found their way into the sacred canon as authentic words from God. However these "silent years" are not the only reason for the two Testaments.

Another thought is that the Old Testament was written almost entirely by Jews; the New Testament was written wholly by Christians (though most of them were Hebrew Christians). Yet the differences of outlook between Jews and Christians are not the only reasons why the Bible consists of two books.

A third idea is that each Testament is intended to do a separate and distinct thing. Both help in bringing us to the maturity God desires but in two quite different ways. Thus it would be folly to use one to the exclusion of the other.

Dr. W.H. Griffith-Thomas has suggested that if we were to approach the Old Testament for the first time and read it through we should doubtless become aware of certain remarkable predictions that pointed forward to Someone who was coming. The predictions would begin in the early chapters of Genesis and, as the text moves along, the predictive element grows in detail until, in the Prophets, it breaks out into glowing, marvelously flaming colors of description giving us detail after detail of the One who was to appear. When we finished our reading at Malachi we would be abundantly aware that the Old Testament is a book of *unfulfilled prophecy*.

Then, if we read it through again, noticing this time all

the strange and bloody sacrifices which begin in Genesis
and are mentioned in increasing volume throughout the
book with thousands and multiplied thousands of animals
whose blood was poured out in unending rivers of death,
we would close the book again at Malachi with a realization that here is a book of *unexplained sacrifices,* as well
as one of unfulfilled prophecy.

Yet once again, if we read through the Old Testament,
this time noticing the prominent personages who appear
on its pages, we could hardly escape seeing the longing
they express for something more than life was offering
them. Abraham sets out to find a city whose builder and
maker is God. Moses leads his people out of Egypt with
the hope of finding a promised land of rest and hope, and
yet when at last the people enter Canaan they do not find
the satisfaction they seek. Men and women are on a
pilgrim journey all the way through the book. There is a
continual cry from thirsty souls, longing after something
which has not yet been realized. Again we would end the
book at Malachi with the realization that it was a book not
only of unfulfilled prophecies and unexplained sacrifices,
but also a record of *unsatisfied longings.*

But the moment we opened the New Testament the
first words we would read would be: "The book of the
genealogy of Jesus Christ." Reading on we would soon
discover that He is the one who fulfills the prophecies,
who explains the sacrifices, and who satisfies the longings
of human hearts. Thus the Old Testament has fulfilled its
role of awakening us to the full and deep meaning of the
life and work of Jesus of Nazareth. It has prepared us to
understand Him in richer and more incomparably pro-
found ways than a reading of the New Testament narrative
alone would have done.

Dr. G. Campbell Morgan puts the same truth in a
slightly different way. He divides the Old Testament into
three major divisions: A sigh for a priest; a cry for a king;

and a quest for a prophet. The first five books, the books of Moses, are a sigh for a priest, an expressive plea for the ministry of one who can successfully stand between man and God. The books of the historical section are a cry for a king. They gather up in a unified declaration the desires of men for a voice of final authority. The didactic books, the teaching books of the Old Testament—Job, Psalms, Proverbs, the Song of Solomon, and the Major and Minor Prophets—are a quest for a prophet; a reaching out for one who can expertly analyze human problems, offer insightful commentary on the passing scene, and anticipate accurately what is coming. Yet again, when we open the New Testament, we find all this fulfilled in one magnificent person: Jesus Christ, the Priest, the King, the Prophet.

This indicates clearly for us the nature of the Old Testament. It is a book intended to prepare us for something. Every successful process requires an adequate preparation. Why else should a farmer take all the trouble to plow and disc his fields and get them ready for planting? Why doesn't he just sprinkle seed over the hard and rocky ground, hoping that it will grow? Because every farmer knows that though the seed is the most important single item in raising a crop, yet it will never take root unless there has been adequate preparation of the ground.

So the Old Testament enables us to grasp the teaching of the New Testament with a cogency and power quite impossible otherwise. Paul says in Galatians 3:24: "The law was our schoolmaster to bring us unto Christ" (*KJV*). I am confident that something will forever be lacking in our lives if we try to appropriate Jesus Christ without living for a while with the Ten Commandments. We shall never be able to find the release we desire unless, like Paul, we have wrestled with the demands of a rigid, unyielding law which makes us cry out, Oh "wretched man that I am! Who will set me free from the body of this death?" (Rom. 7:24).

I have read the book of Romans for years, especially chapters 6, 7 and 8. I even taught it, rather frequently. But I never grasped with real understanding the truth it contains, never let its mighty, liberating power come through to my own heart and experience until I had lived for a while out in the wilderness on the back side of the desert with the children of Israel, and felt the burning desert heat and shared the barren, fruitless, defeated life they experienced. When I had been there too and saw how God delivered them then I was able to understand for the first time what God tells us in Romans 6, 7 and 8.

There is no book in the New Testament which asks the same deep, soul-searching questions you will find in Isaiah or Job in the Old Testament—questions which are forever recurring in the hearts of men. There is no place in the New Testament where you find gathered up in brief pungent phrases the deep, deep searchings of mind and heart when confronting the problems of injustice and cruel twists of fate such as you find in the prophets. There is no book like the Psalms to put in graphic, precise terms those troublesome attitudes we find so frequently bothering us today. It is only there we can find these attitudes so accurately put into words that we can say, "That's exactly how I feel" and then go on to find the answer for the problem as well.

The opening words of the book of Hebrews state: "God, after He spoke long ago to the fathers in the prophets in many portions and in many ways, in these last days has spoken to us in His Son, whom He appointed heir of all things, through whom also He made the world" (Heb. 1:1,2).

In these words you have the two Testaments side by side. The Old Testament: "God. . . spoke. . . in many portions and in many ways," in the New Testament: "In these last days [He] has spoken to us in His Son." The phrase the writer employs describing the Old Testament is

very significant: "In many portions and in many ways."
As we read the Old Testament through, we can see how
true this is.

The Old Testament is God's utterance of syllables of
truth which are sometimes almost impossible to understand by themselves, but when merged together the whole
produces meaning, preparing us for that marvelous
expression of the fullness of truth given to us in God's
Son.

In the New Testament, all the many voices from the
Old Testament merge into one voice, the voice of the Son
of God. Remember that marvelous scene in the book of
Revelation in which John sees the Lamb and hears His
voice "as the sound of many waters"? That voice then
sounds out, catching up in itself all the rivulets and creeks
and streams of a thousand rivers, flowing together in one
great confluence of sound—the voice of the Son of God!

Some of you may be feeling, "Well this may all be
very good, but why not turn directly to the New Testament
and listen directly to the final voice of the Son. Why
bother with the Old Testament at all?" The answer is that
not only does the Old Testament properly introduce the
New; it is also true that without the preparation of the Old
no one can fully and properly understand the meaning of
the New.

Remember the statement of Abraham in that parable
Jesus told about the rich man and Lazarus in Luke 16. The
rich man had died and gone to Hades. There he besought
Abraham to send Lazarus back to his five brothers to warn
them of their fate unless they should repent. Abraham said
Lazarus could not do this and added, "They have Moses
and the prophets; let them hear them." The rich man
pleaded that if someone would just go to them from the
dead and tell them the truth, then they would believe. But
Abraham replied, "If they do not hear Moses and the
prophets, neither will they be convinced if someone

should return from the dead." That is, even though someone should return from beyond the river of death with a
report of all he has seen and heard, those who refused to
believe Moses and the prophets will also reject the one
who returned from the dead. Having failed to hear Moses
and the prophets they are no longer able to believe truth
though it come from beyond the grave. It is simply true
that in this, as in many other relationships of life, we
cannot short-circuit the processes of learning.

Let us then turn to the Old Testament and allow it to
set our hearts aflame with the anticipation that Someone is
coming who can supply to us all that we need.

CHAPTER ONE

The Beginnings of Mankind

GENESIS 1—11

It's no exaggeration to say that there are no writings more important for the proper understanding of history and man than the first chapters of Genesis. Here is hidden the secret of man's sinfulness, that terrible mystery of evil and darkness which continually confronts us in this modern world. In this section is the key to the relationship of the sexes, the proper place of man and woman in marriage, the solution to the problem of mounting divorce rates and other marital issues that abound in modern society. Here, also, is the explanation of the struggle of life and here great light is thrown on the problems of work and leisure. In these opening chapters of the Bible is the first and fundamental revelation of the meaning of divine redemption and grace, and here the essential groundwork is laid for the understanding of the cross of Jesus Christ. Therefore, it is clear that this whole section is unprecedented in its importance.

INCOMPLETENESS OF MAN

Genesis is the book of beginnings. That is what the word itself means, and it takes us back into the very dawn of human history. It traces the story of man from his beginnings within the natural world and follows his history in a continually narrowing process down to the story of four great men of the past: Abraham, Isaac, Jacob, and Joseph. These men are not mere mythical figures of the past, but are living, breathing, flesh and blood personalities whom we can all relate to. This marvelous account preserves accurately for us not only the facts of these men's lives but the color and depth and the tone of life in their days.

But Genesis is not only history, it is also a book with a single message, and a message which can be declared in one brief statement. It reveals to us the need of man for God. That is the whole purpose of the book and as such, it strikes the keynote for all subsequent revelation concerning God and man throughout the Bible. Genesis reveals that man can never be complete without God, that he can never discover or fulfill the true meaning of his life without a genuine and personal relationship with an indwelling God.

Throughout the book this incompleteness is revealed to us in three realms—realms in which each of us personally and daily live.

First, our incompleteness is revealed in the realm of natural relationships, that is, the area we call the natural sciences. These consist of cosmology (the study of the universe, its origin and makeup); geology (the structure of the earth itself and its major features); and biology (the study of life in all its divisions and manifestations). These natural relationships circumscribe our lives with regard to the physical world around us, and yet within them man is seen to be inadequate without God.

The second area is the realm of human relationships. This would include the sciences we call today sociology, psychology, anthropology, demonology, etc. The beginnings of all these are traced in the opening chapters of Genesis and again man is set forth as inadequate to function within them without a relationship with God.

The third area is that of spiritual relationships, encompassing the studies of theology, philosophy, soteriology, angelology, etc. The beginnings of all these themes are explored in Genesis and yet the one message of man's inadequacy apart from God echoes throughout the book like the sound of a bell.

UNIVERSALITY OF MANKIND

Genesis opens with an awareness of the greatest material fact in all human life; a fact that we are all subconsciously aware of almost every waking moment, that is, that we are living in a universe. We quickly become aware that we are living on a planet shared with millions of other human beings like ourselves. As we come to know more about modern science we become aware that our planet is part of a solar system. In some strange, mysterious way this mass of earth upon which we live is winding its way on a prearranged path about the sun circling continuously and precisely on schedule.

We are also told by astronomers that the whole solar system itself—the sun with all its planets—is making its way through a great whirling body of stars called a galaxy, a vast almost incredibly immense system of stars some 300,000 light years across. Then this galaxy itself is moving at incredible speed through the vastness of space in conjunction with millions (and some astronomers say even billions) of other galaxies like ours. It is precisely at that point that the Bible opens in a majestic recognition that man is part of a universe. "In the beginning God created the heavens and the earth" (Gen. 1:1).

What a strange conjunction—to put all the vast heavens on one side and our tiny planet Earth on the other. But the book moves right on to tell us that man—insignificant man—this tiny speck of life living on a minor planet in the midst of this unthinkably vast universe, is the major object of God's concern.

One of the marvels of the Bible is that it uses language that communicates with people of the most primitive and limited understanding, while at the same time it has significance and is inexhaustible in its meaning to even the most erudite and learned of men. It addresses itself with equal ease to all classes of mankind. This universality is evident in the phrase ''the heavens and the earth.'' That has meaning for a savage in the jungle when he simply perceives the land on which he lives and the sky over his head. He would describe it as ''the heavens and the earth.'' On the other hand, a modern astronomer looking out into the far reaches of the universe through a great telescope would also use the phrase, ''the heavens and the earth.'' Thus the Bible consistently remains true to the most complex discoveries of science at the same time retaining a simplicity of statement that the most uneducated can understand, even though it is not the intention of the Bible to be a textbook on science.

God has deliberately made the physical universe to reveal and manifest an inner spiritual reality. There is a direct correspondence between the two. This correspondence between the outward physical reality and its invisible spiritual counterpart is fundamentally the reason why ''All Scripture is inspired by God and profitable for teaching, for reproof, for correction, and for training in righteousness; that the man of God may be adequate, equipped for every good work'' (2 Tim. 3:16,17). Since the world is made for man it constantly reflects truth to him. This is, without doubt, why Jesus found the world of nature such an apt instrument to teach men spiritual realities, as His parables reveal.

Dr. F.A. Filby, senior lecturer on inorganic chemistry at an English technical college, has put this very accurately: ''The material world is designed to produce parallels—parables—of the spiritual. There is indeed a spiritual law operating in the natural world and God put us on a planet where light is separated from darkness for our spiritual education as well as for our physical needs. There is a spiritual as well as a physical reason for the pattern of creation, and he who divorces science from true religion will never be able to come to a real understanding of the world.''

Granting this to be true, then the first truth God would suggest to us, manifested in a material universe all around us, is that there is a heavenly as well as an earthly life. There is a difference between the heavenly life of God and the earthly life of man. The supreme subject of the Bible will be how to move from the level of earth to the life of the heavens. This difference is declared by Isaiah where God says, '' 'For My thoughts are not your thoughts, neither are your ways My ways,' declares the Lord. 'For as the heavens are higher than the earth, so are My ways higher than your ways, and My thoughts than your thoughts' '' (55:8,9). That is the great truth with which, symbolically, the Bible begins.

THE CREATION

We have seen that the greatest observable fact known to man is the existence of the universe, "the heavens and the earth." To this, verse 1 links the greatest fact made known by revelation: the existence of a God who creates. There is thus brought together at the beginning of the Bible a recognition of the two great sources of human knowledge: nature (including human nature), discoverable by the five senses; and revelation, which is discoverable only by a mind and heart illuminated and taught by the Spirit of God. Both of these sources of knowledge originate with God and each of them is a means of knowing something about God and man. The scientists who study nature are searching ultimately for God. One great Christian scientist declared, "I am thinking the thoughts of God after him." That is an excellent way to describe what science basically is doing. So also those who seek to understand the Bible are likewise in search of God. Nature is designed to teach certain facts about God, but revelation is designed to bring us to the God about whom nature speaks. The two are complementary and are not contradictory in any sense.

Verse 2 adds the information that the earth began as a planet covered by an uninterrupted ocean which was itself wrapped in darkness. Revelation says that it was "formless and void," that is, without life. There was no land, there were no promontories, nothing to catch the eye. It was simply one great, vast deep of water covering the whole world with no life in it. With that picture science fully agrees. But revelation adds a key factor that many scientists do not acknowledge. Revelation says, in addition, "the Spirit of God was moving over the surface of the waters." God was at work in His universe interacting and interrelating with it. Notice that in these verses of the first chapter there is a moving toward order out of disorder and form out of formlessness. Something comes out of nothing. God is moving. The Spirit of God is producing an intended end. He brings light out of darkness, shape out of shapelessness, form out of formlessness.

The first step God took, according to the record, was to create light, " 'Let there be light'; and there was light." Light as we know now is absolutely essential to life of any sort. Without light there can be no life. With the advent of light we are now ready for the record of the six days of creation. Each of the days, except for the seventh, includes an evening and a morning and each, except for the seventh, records a progressive order of creation.

How are we to view these days? Are they 24-hour days, constituting one literal actual week, or do they represent long and indefinite ages of time as science would claim today? It is my conviction that the controversy which has endlessly raged upon these questions has been largely responsible for missing the real purpose for which God gives to us this first chapter of Genesis. It should be clear to anyone upon reading the passage that the chapter does not focus upon the question of time. Important as this may seem to us it is not the focus of God, and if we center upon it we shall miss the point that He intends to make. God is moving toward a goal which He has clearly in mind from the beginning and toward it all the physical universe is moving. The steps God takes to accomplish this goal are recorded as several great creative acts occurring in certain progressive stages which logically succeed one another. It does not all happen at once. God did not bring the world and the universe into being with a snap of His fingers or with one sentence from His lips. He chose to do it in stages and these stages are very clearly evident throughout this passage.

Each of the days of creation include an evening and a morning and the evening comes first. This suggests a period of incompleteness moving toward completeness, of gradualness coming at last to completion. Furthermore, let us remember that these physical things which God makes are reflections of an inner greater reality. God made the physical universe to reflect spiritual realities so that as we look around us and observe and assimilate with our senses we are constantly to be reminded of the great things that are to take place within us in the invisible kingdom of spiritual truth.

If this be the case then Genesis 1 becomes a kind of table of contents, if you like, for the rest of Scripture. It introduces in physical symbolism the great themes which will be amplified throughout the rest of this amazing book. In other words, there are great lessons which God has deeply etched in nature in order to remind us of corresponding realities in our lives which the physical processes around us are designed to picture. Let us go through the creative days from this point of view and we will see what I believe to be the real point of this passage.

Day one describes the creation of light and darkness. The light is said to be good and the darkness by implication is not good. Both these words, light and darkness, are used subsequently in Scripture to picture good and evil. There is good in the universe but there is also that which is "not good," which is darkness. Thus a fundamental fact we must continually bear in mind is that throughout our lives we will need to discern between good and evil, right and wrong, truth and error. We are reminded of it every day and night.

On day two we learn of the firmament which separates the waters below from the waters above, and this firmament is called heaven. Physically this is a description of the creation of the atmosphere around the earth which supports great quantities of water in evaporated form above the earth and separates it from the oceans below. This ocean and sky, divided asunder, picture for us the reality of human physical life (elsewhere frequently symbolized by water), and a subsequent heavenly life. There is a life now and a life to come and one passes into the other. Human existence is not complete when this earthly life is fulfilled. The two levels of human existence are tied together with invisible but very real links and one merges into the other as oceans, by evaporation, move into the waters of the air.

It is striking that it is the forgetfulness of these two facts, revealed in the first two creative days, that is the root cause for the violence and moral decline of our day. Men no longer seek to distinguish between good and evil, between light and darkness. Though every 24 hours these reminders come to us, we continually blind our eyes to them and seek to blur these distinctions. It is also increasingly evident that men no longer want to think about the life to come. We want everything now. Instant happiness! That is what the world is seeking. We do not wish to anticipate a future or to prepare for a life to come. But we must remember that this present earthly life will find its culmination and fulfillment only when the intended lessons are learned here below and then all God's great provisions for man will be available to him. That is what God is teaching us in the first two creative days.

Day three is a different kind of day from the first two. It is a double day in which there is first the emergence of the land from the oceans and second, the first appearance of life upon the earth in the form of plants, trees and vegetation. As we have seen, on the physical level this is but a manifestation of a parallel spiritual and moral reality. We are to learn that human life on earth between the period of birth and death is itself divided, pictured by the land rising up out of the oceans. Thus, there will be land which is capable of producing fruit surrounded by vast oceans which are incapable of doing so. The truth God wants us to learn from this is that there is an old humanity which by nature is incapable of bringing forth what God desires, but there is also a new humanity, called out of the old, which will be capable of producing the fruit God envisions. In the second part of the day, that fruit actually appears and is pronounced by God to be good. It appears in three divisions: general vegetation, seed bearing plants, and fruit trees. Perhaps this reflects the divisions of the apostle John who describes Christians as "little children, young men and fathers" (see 1 John 2:13). At any rate, this fruit is pleasing to God and is a result of the activity of the Spirit upon the barren waters of humanity.

Day four describes the creation of the sun and moon and the stars, and the placing of them as lights and signs to govern the seasons of earth. The sun clearly pictures Jesus Himself (called in Mal. 4:2 "the sun of righteousness") as the light of the world; and the moon, reflecting the brightness of the sun and shining in the darkness of the night, is a symbol of the church shining in the moral darkness of this world. The stars are used repeatedly in Scripture as symbols of individuals who shine with great moral influence upon others.

The fifth day describes the creation of birds flying in the heavens above the earth and great living creatures that swarm through the waters of the seas. Since the atmosphere above depicts the heavenly kind of life and the waters, as we have seen, are a picture of unregenerate humanity, this created day symbolizes to us the possibility of living triumphantly in either an alien or a hostile environment. Both birds and fish are used symbolically of believers in the Bible. The spiritual life is alien to natural man but by the redemption of God he can "mount up with wings like eagles" (Isa. 40:31). The world is a hostile environment to him but he can learn to live in it as effectively as a fish learns to swim in the sea.

MAN'S UNIQUENESS

There is a sense of heightened anticipation as we come to the sixth day of creation, for it is on this day that man makes his appearance. This sixth day is parallel in some respects to the third day in that it is also a double day. It has, as do all the days, an evening and a morning, and during the first part of the day God created the land animals—from the larger beasts (called "the cattle") to the creeping things, including the world of insects, reptiles, etc. It is quite obvious that all this is aiming toward the creation of man and is in exact accordance with the fossil records. Man makes his appearance last in the order of life. But there are some distinctive things said of him that are never said of any of the animal creation.

First, God holds a divine consultation about Him saying, "Let Us make man in Our image, according to Our likeness" (Gen. 1:26). This divine conversation clearly is the first hint given to us that God consists of more than one person. This revelation is given only in connection with the emergence of man upon the earth for only man can understand and enter into an experience with a triune God and is seen also as the link between God and the rest of His creation. The first man, Adam, is a mediator between God and the animal world just as later the last Adam (Jesus Christ) will be seen as the mediator between fallen man and God. The first Adam was made to reign over the world of nature as the last Adam also makes it possible for those who are in Christ to reign in life through Him as Paul puts it in Romans 5:21.

The key phrase about man as created on the sixth day is the ''image'' and ''likeness'' of God. That image is found not in man's body or his soul, but in his spirit. For, as Jesus told the woman at the well in Samaria, ''God is spirit; and those who worship Him must worship in spirit and truth'' (John 4:24). But what is godlike about our spirit? If the spirit is made in the image of God, then it can do things that God can do but no animal can. Three things are suggested throughout Genesis 1 which God alone does: first, God creates; second, God communicates; and third, God evaluates, pronouncing some things good and others not good. It is here that the image of God in man appears. Man can create. Inventiveness clearly marks him off from the world of beasts. Further, man communicates as no animal can possibly do, sharing ideas which affect (and infect) others. Finally, man is the only creature that has a moral sense, recognizing some things as good and others as bad, feeling the impact of conscience upon his own actions. Thus, man shares the image of God.

However, though he has retained the image, he has now lost the likeness of God. Image is the capacity to be godlike, but likeness is the proper functioning of that capacity. Adam, formed by the creator, stood before God as a spirit dwelling in a body and exercising the functions of a soul. He had the ability to be creative, to communicate, to make moral choices, but he not only had that ability, he was actually doing it. He was exercising the function of God-likeness. The secret, as we learn from the rest of Scripture, lay in an inner dependence that continually repudiated self-confidence.

The seventh day is clearly quite different from all the preceding six. It is a day without an evening or a morning. There is no movement within, no advance from incompleteness to completeness. It is, instead, a day characterized by rest; God ceased from His labors, intending it to be a picture of what is called later in Scripture "the rest of faith." Hebrews 4:10 declares "For the one who has entered His rest has himself also rested from his works, as God did from His."

Here is pictured a revolutionary new principle of human behavior on which God intends man to operate, and which was His intention from the very beginning of history. It is from this principle that man fell and it is to this in Jesus Christ that he is to be restored. It is the principle of human activity resting upon an indwelling God to produce extraordinary results. The weekly observance of a Sabbath day is but a shadow, Paul says in Colossians 2:17, of this principle of activity, resting upon God's willingness to work in and through what we do. He who learns to labor on those terms is keeping the Sabbath as God intended it originally to be kept.

Chapter 2 finds man walking in the Garden in communion with God, functioning as a spirit living within a physical body and manifesting the personality characteristics of the soul. At this point, God gives him a research project, to investigate the animal world in search for a possible counterpart to himself. God knew that man would not find what he was looking for but in the process man discovered at least three marvelous truths.

First, he learned that woman was not to be a mere beast of burden as the animals are, because that would not in any way fulfill his need for a helper and companion.

Second, it became evident that woman was not to be merely a biological laboratory for the producing of children. This is what the animals use sex for, but that was not sufficient for Adam's needs. Sex in mankind, therefore, is different from that among the animals.

Third, Adam learned that woman was not a thing outside himself—she is not something to be used at the whim of man and then disposed of. Women are to be helpers, fit for him, corresponding to him.

So, in a remarkable passage we are told that Adam fell into a deep sleep and God took a rib and from it made a woman and brought her to him. This period of Adam's unconsciousness strongly suggests what modern psychology also confirms, that the relationships of marriage are far deeper than mere surface affection. They touch not only the conscious life, but the subconscious, even the unconscious as well.

Chapter 2 ends with a marvelous statement of the principles God intends for marriage. The first and most fundamental is that marriage involves a complete *identity* of the partners. The two are to become one. This is not an immediate act of magic happening during or immediately after a wedding, but takes place as a couple lives together, blending their psyches, merging their lives, and creating a single history.

The second principle is that of *headship* which marks the role of man as the leader in determining the direction in which a home should go and the woman's responsibilities to support and sustain that leadership. The third factor emphasized is that of *permanence*. Men and women are to cleave to one another—he is to stay with her and she with him, because marriage is a permanent bond. The fourth factor is revealed in the verse, "And the man and his wife were both naked and were not ashamed." This speaks clearly of openness and free *communication*.

MAN'S LIMITATIONS
In chapter 3 of Genesis we have the explanation for

over 100 centuries of human heartache, misery, torture, blood, sweat and tears. Remove this chapter from the Bible, and the rest of it is beyond explanation. But the most striking thing about it is that we find ourselves here. The temptation and the fall are reproduced in our lives many times a day. We have all heard the voice of the tempter and felt the drawing of sin and we all know the pangs of guilt that follow. This is why many have called this story a myth. In one sense this is true. It happens continually because it did actually happen once to our original parents and thus we, their children, cannot escape repeating it.

Many biblical scholars feel that the tempter in the Garden was not a snake, but a "shining one" which the Hebrew word means. Snakes were undoubtedly created to represent the punishment that fell upon this being when he brought about the fall of man by his cunning and his deceit. It is clearly the devil, in his character as an angel of light, who now confronts the woman in the Garden of Eden. His tactic with her is to arouse desire. First he implanted in her heart a distrust of God's love, "Has God said, 'You shall not eat from any tree of the garden'?" (Gen. 3:1). Next, he dares to deny openly the results that God had stated will occur, "You surely shall not die" (v. 4), he says. Then he clinches his attack with a distorted truth, "God knows that in the day you eat from it your eyes will be opened, and you will be like God, knowing good and evil." All the devil wishes to do is to leave Eve standing before the fruit, hanging there in all its luscious fascination, tantalizing her, offering her an experience she never dreamed would be possible.

Now the mind comes into action. Without Eve's realization she has already experienced an arousing of her emotions so that she longs for the tantalizing fruit before her. Thus, when her mind comes into action it can no longer do so rationally. Already the will has secretly determined to act on the facts as the emotions present them and thus the mind can only rationalize. It must twist the facts so that they accord with desire and the result was that Eve took the fruit and ate.

But there was still hope for the race. Adam had not yet fallen, only Eve. A battle has been lost, but not the war. But in the innocent but ominous words, "she gave also to her husband with her, and he ate" (v. 6), we face the beginning of the darkness of a fallen humanity—what the Bible calls "death" immediately follows.

The first sign is that Adam and Eve knew they were naked. This is the birth of self-consciousness, and the immediate result is an attempt to cover up, which is the invariable psychological reaction of mankind to self-exposure ever since.

The second mark of death is the tendency to hide. It reveals the fact of guilt—that inner torment we are all familiar with which cannot be turned off no matter how hard we try.

The third mark of death at work in human life is the beginning of blame—the passing of the buck from Adam to Eve and from Eve to the serpent. Behind both excuses is the unspoken suggestion that it is really God's fault. Thus man attempts to turn guilt into fate and make of himself a mere innocent victim suffering from a breakdown in creation for which God is responsible.

The fourth mark of death is the divine establishment of the limits of life: pain, sweat and death. Adam and Eve must learn the hard cruel facts of life lived apart from dependence upon God. At this point of repentance, God then clothes them with animal skins as a picture (as all animal sacrifices are, a kind of kindergarten of grace) to teach us the great truth that ultimately it is God Himself who bears eternally the pain, the hurt and the agony of our sins. This is followed by banishment from the garden, not as we so often imagine, to keep man from coming to the tree of life, but as the text specifically states "to guard the way *to* the tree of life" (v. 24). There is a way to the tree of life, but it is no longer a physical way. In the book of Revelation, we are told that the tree of life is for the healing of the nations (see Rev. 22:2). It is surely to this that Jesus refers when He says, "I am the way." Spiritually and psychologically (in the realm of emotions and mind) we are to live in the presence of God because a way has been opened back to the tree of life.

We can thus summarize chapter 3 in the process it follows: beginning with temptation; followed immediately by death; leading to repentance and grace taken by an act of faith; and resulting in a public acknowledgement on God's part of acceptance; and ending at last in healing.

In chapters 4 through 11, relating early human history, we also see the underlying threads of all human society for all time. Without doubt there was a real Cain, there was a genuine 40-day deluge, there was a solid gopherwood ark and there was an actual tower of babbling confusion. There is no need to question the historicity of these events, but they are recorded so as to teach us graphically the principles on which man has built his society and the inherent flaws in those principles.

History, as we know it, is the chronicle of man's progress from the use of the primitive ax to machine guns, napalm and nuclear explosions. It is the story of wars, battles and the bloodshed of mankind. The key to this 20 centuries of dilemma actually lies in the story that took place at the dawn of history—the story of two brothers: Cain and Abel.

The focus of the story is in the two offerings which these brothers brought to God. It is clearly indicated that there was a prescribed time for the bringing of an offering, and a prescribed place for the offering of it; but Abel's offering of a lamb is accepted and Cain's offering of grain is rejected. Surely the commentators are right in indicating that God's reason for rejecting Cain's offering was that it was a bloodless offering and, therefore, could not take away sins, for "without shedding of blood there is no forgiveness" (Heb. 9:22). But it is not clear that Cain understood that.

What is clear is that Cain was angry at God's action, and when given opportunity to repent refused to do so. Thus, when later opportunity finds him in the field with his brother, Abel, Cain's jealousy takes over and the murderous ax rises and falls and Abel sinks to the ground with a smashed skull, murdered by his brother's hand. Thus the roots of human warfare are seen to lie in the jealous and envious spirit in the heart, in the unwillingness to forgive and forget and the ease with which we utter Cain's contemptuous words, "Am I my brother's keeper?"

The blood of Abel cries from the ground for justice and God answers by cursing the ground in which Cain took such great pride and joy. Cain has lost his green thumb; the ground will no longer release its fruitfulness to him and he will therefore be forced to wander from place to place as the crops fail wherever he goes. To protect Cain from excess punishment, God set a mark upon him. It is not a mark of shame, as many interpret it, but a mark of grace by which God is saying, "This man is still my property; he is guilty, he is a murderer, but he is still mine, and don't forget it in your dealings with him."

EXPANSION OF CIVILIZATION

The next element we trace in Genesis is the beginnings of culture, or civilization, and especially the part city life plays in the shaping of human society. To Cain is born Enoch, who builds his city on ground that is yet red with the blood of Abel.

The city Enoch builds is certainly a most imposing one. Within it are found all the ingredients of modern life: travel, music and the arts, the use of metals, the organized political life, and the domestication of animals. These things look impressive, but they are all built on shaky ground. Polygamy appears with Lamech and his two wives. Violence and murder are justified on the grounds of self-defense. The state begins to replace the family as the focus of human interest. The trend toward urban over rural life is evident and increasing toleration of sexual excess appears.

But in the midst of this deterioration God has another plan ready. Adam knew his wife again and she bore a son and called his name Seth (which means appointed), and through Seth the redemptive work of God is traced in chapter 5 in a most remarkable sequence of names. There is difference among authorities as to the meaning of these names, but one authority gives an interesting sequence of meanings. *Seth*, as we have seen, means "appointed"; *Enoch*, his son, means "mortal," and his son, *Kenan*, means "sorrow." His son, *Mahalalel*, means "the blessed God"; he names his boy, *Jared*, which means "came down," and his boy, *Enoch*, means "teaching." *Methuselah*, the son of Enoch, means "his death shall bring"; *Lamech*, Methuselah's son, means "strength," and *Noah*, the end of the line, means "comfort."

When this is all put together, it tells the story of grace: It is appointed that mortal man shall sorrow, but the blessed God came down teaching that His death shall bring strength and comfort. The focus of the chapter is Enoch who learned to walk with God. Thus, a brilliant but wicked age ends with a single man having learned to walk in fellowship with God in the midst of a godless and violent generation.

Who are the "sons of God" who are mentioned in Genesis 6 as coming in and marrying the daughters of men and producing a race of giants? Of many explanations, the best seems to be that of Jude who suggests that these are angels who "abandoned their proper abode" (Jude 6) and, presumably, took up improper dwelling places. Human bodies in Scripture are called dwelling places. This would then imply that fallen angels (evil spirits) possess the bodies of men and these demon-possessed men married women and produced a race of strange beings called the *Nephilim*. The word means "the fallen ones," and thus explains the race of giants which are frequently referred to in mythical accounts as half men and half gods. But God immediately sets a limit to their existence of 120 years during which time Noah became a preacher of righteousness. Thus, the first mark of an imminent collapse of civilization is the appearance of demonic powers which manifest themselves in open and unchecked violence. The outward wickedness rests upon a deeper corruption within—"every intent of the thoughts of his heart" (Gen. 6:5). Thus, demonic control, outward violence and inward corruption become the marks of a civilization so decayed it can no longer be tolerated.

God announces to Noah that He intends to judge the world and commands Noah to build an ark of safety which will be his means of deliverance from the coming catastrophe. When the ark is completed, Noah is invited to enter it with all his family, bringing also two of every kind of animal and seven of clean beasts. Noah demonstrated his faith by entering the ark in obedience to the word of God against the ridicule and contempt of his age.

The distinction between clean and unclean animals is an artificial distinction drawn in order to teach men a needed truth. As soon as the lesson was clearly evident in the work of Christ, the distinction disappeared. By certain functions of animals that were designated as clean, corresponding spiritual qualities which God loves are indicated; while the absence of those functions in unclean animals is intended to teach that God disapproves of their corresponding character in the lives of men. So the flood comes with the fountains of the great deep bursting forth and the windows of the heavens opening. The whole earth is covered to the tops of the mountains and all life perishes except the handful of humans in the ark and those marine animals which could survive in the waters. The rain continues for 40 days and nights and then ceases. At the end of 150 days the waters begin to abate and on the seventeenth day of the seventh month, the ark comes to rest on the mountains of Ararat.

This seventeenth day of the seventh month is the same exact day of the year when, centuries later, Jesus rose from the dead. After the exodus from Egypt God changed the beginning of the year from the seventh month (in the fall) to the first month (in the spring) when the Passover was eaten. Jesus rose on the seventeenth day of the first month, which would be the same as the seventeenth day of the seventh month in the old reckoning in this passage in Genesis. Thus, clearly, the emergence of Noah from the ark is intended to be a picture of the new beginning of life which every Christian experiences when he enters into the resurrection life of Jesus Christ by the new birth.

GOD'S INTERVENTION

Chapter 9 of Genesis records one of the major covenants of the Bible—a covenant made with Noah, but beyond Noah with all humanity. This covenant is the basis for all human government today. It contains God's provision for the ordering of human life.

First, nature is made to be dependable, secured by the promise of the rainbow from universal catastrophe. Then man's rule over the animal world through fear is disclosed and animals are given to man as food along with plant life.

Next, human life is seen to be so sacred that only God has the right to take it, but He uses the state as His instrument and a foundation is thus laid for police work and capital punishment. Once again, the command is given to multiply and populate the earth. All this is to be lived under the constant reminder that "the intent of man's heart is evil from his youth" (Gen. 8:21).

The strange story of the drunkenness of Noah and the curious action of his son, Ham, toward his father, followed by the cursing of Canaan and the blessing of Shem and Japheth contain much of great significance. Many scholars feel that Ham committed some homosexual act; at the very least it is clear that Ham looked upon his father in his exposed condition with a leering glance that had sexual connotations.

It is also noteworthy that Shem and Japheth would have nothing to do with their brother's lewd delight. They exemplify in action the verse in the New Testament, "Love covers a multitude of sins" (1 Pet. 4:8). Literally, they covered their father and refused to look upon his shame, thus they honored their father and won the approval and blessing of God. If this is the case, then Noah knew that Ham's tolerance of perversion would break out in an intensified form in at least one of his children.

Thus, guided by divine wisdom, Noah unerringly selects the one boy of Ham's four sons in whom this perversion will find outlet and expression. So a curse is pronounced upon Canaan. That curse is not a black skin as many have mistakenly stated, but a tendency toward homosexuality which was clearly evident in the Canaanite tribes that inhabited the land of Palestine when Israel came into it, and which has broken out in human society in many places since.

In the prophetic words uttered by Noah concerning his sons, we have a key to the dispersion of mankind throughout the earth. Shem is given religious primacy and the Semitic people are responsible under God to meet the spiritual needs of mankind. It is most striking that the three great religions of earth all come from the Semitic family: Judaism, Islam, and Christianity.

Japheth was promised enlargement and the Japhetic people are in general the peoples of India and Europe. It is largely from this family that Americans come and it is most interesting that history has recorded their geographical enlargement. The entire western hemisphere of our globe is settled by Japhetic peoples and the Indians of Asia are of the same stock.

Ham is given the role of a servant in relation to the other families of earth, but not in the sense of enslavement. The sons of Ham fulfill a servant relationship as the practical technicians of humanity. The Egyptians, the Babylonians, the Mayans, the Aztecs all were Hamitic people, and they are the great inventors of mankind.

In chapter 10 God narrows the flow of history down to the Semitic races. In chapter 11 He will narrow it still further to one man—Abraham. From there it begins to broaden out again to take in Abraham and all his descendants, both physical and spiritual. The rest of the Bible is all about the children of Abraham physically and spiritually. We have, then, in these two chapters one of the most important links in understanding the Bible.

The atmosphere of this time is one of movement, migration. People are thrusting out from a center like spokes of a wheel radiating out into the corners of the earth. One branch of the Hamitic family settled in the land of Shinar or Babylonia. They soon discovered they could invent their own materials for building and they were fired with desire to build two things—a city and a tower. A city reflects the need of man for social intercourse where the hungers of the soul can be satisfied for beauty, art, music, commercial and business life. A tower, on the other hand, reflects the need to satisfy the spirit of man.

Archeologists have now found that the Babylonians built great towers called ziggurats which were built in a circular fashion with an ascending spiral staircase terminating in a shrine at the top around which were written signs of the zodiac. Obviously, such a tower is a religious building. Unquestionably there was a plaque somewhere attached to each which carried the pious words "Erected in the year——to the greater glory of God." But it was not really for the glory of God. It was a way of controlling God, a way of channeling God by using Him for man's glory. This is revealed in what the builders said, "Let us make a name for ourselves."

The reaction of God is one of exquisite irony. God takes note of their unity and their creativity and comes to a startling conclusion, "Nothing that they propose to do will now be impossible to them." Thus, for man's sake, to keep him from destroying himself by ignorant ambition, God confused their language and man is scattered over the face of the earth. It is God's way of preventing the ultimate catastrophe. When man at last gets together again, and under the illusion of technical ability thinks he can master all the great and intricate mechanisms of life, we will have achieved the ultimate disaster.

CHAPTER TWO

The Need of Mankind

GENESIS 12—50

Imaginative writers of our day seek continually to depict what kind of world this would be after an atomic holocaust had completely wiped out all life as we know it. What would it be like to be the first people to start out in such a world? Noah and his family knew, for that is exactly what happened after the flood.

Physically and materially they began again to fulfill the original divine command to "be fruitful and multiply, and fill the earth." Spiritually, having been on both sides of the flood, Noah becomes a picture of regeneration. He went through the waters of judgment, being preserved in the ark, and came out into a new world and a new life, as a Christian passes from death into life in Christ.

Genesis 12—50 traces three great truths that belong to this new life. In the lives of four men—Abraham, Isaac, Jacob and Joseph—Genesis reveals what man is always seeking:

Righteousness, the sense of being right. Man dislikes the feeling of guilt or unrighteousness and wants always to be seen as acceptable by whatever standard he views as relevant. We see the fulfillment of this need in the life of Abraham.

Peace, a sense of inner well-being. Man is ever seeking a certain calmness and inner confidence which can only be described as peace. The story of Isaac and Jacob, who portray sonship and sanctification, are in themselves the secret of peace of heart.

Joy, a sense of gladness and happiness out of life. This is so evident as to require no documentation other than life itself. Joseph manifested the truth of glorification.

These three virtues are the unseen, almost unconscious goals of life everywhere. But where are they truly to be found? Romans 14:17 says, "The kingdom of God is not eating and drinking, but righteousness and peace and joy in the Holy Spirit." Only God can impart these things to men, and this is the story of the rest of Genesis.

MAN SEEKS RIGHTEOUSNESS (Gen. 12—25)

Abram appears first as called by God to exemplify in his entire life story the process of achieving righteousness by means of faith, or as the New Testament calls it, "justification by faith."

God appeared and conversed with Abram on seven occasions, beginning with Abram's call in Ur and ending with his offering of his son Isaac in obedience to God's command. Out of this relationship with God Abram learned eight lessons of faith. The parallel to all these is found in the life of every believer today. For this reason, Abraham is known as the father of the faithful and is called "the friend of God." He depicts forever the friendship which God desires to have in intimate communion with everyone who is made righteous by faith.

The first lesson faith must learn is that of obedience. It is not faith to simply say "I believe"; it is necessary also to add "I obey." In his first encounter with God, Abram is sent out on a march without a map to an unknown destination, but with the promise that God will go with him and show him the way. The promise includes seven specifics: (1) I will make of you a great nation; (2) I will bless you; (3) I will make your name great; (4) you shall be a blessing; (5) I will bless those that bless you; (6) I will curse them that curse you; (7) in you shall all the families of the earth be blessed. Though Abram was 75 years of age when this call came to him, his obedience was immediate. He left Ur and went to Haran where his father Terah lived. There, after his father's death, he came into the land of Canaan in obedience to the call of God. The spiritual parallel of this in today's believer is found in a willingness to turn from the natural claims of family and friends, and to recognize the right of God to lead and direct his life.

In the land of Canaan God appears to Abram for the second time. He promises to give the land to Abram's seed, despite its present possession by the Canaanite tribes. Abram's life in the land is immediately characterized by two meaningful symbols: a tent and an altar. Whenever Abram is walking in faith these two symbols are always present. The tent is the symbol of the pilgrim character of his existence. He is never to own the land outright but is to be a sojourner in it, looking for that "city which has foundations, whose architect and builder is God" (Heb. 11:10). The altar is the symbol of fellowship and communion with a living God. It is the secret of the ability to endure in a land possessed by enemies. Every believer must have such an altar, a personal time alone with God, for Bible reading and prayer, that he might endure in a hostile world.

The second lesson Abram learns in the life of faith is that of the sufficiency of faith to meet all human need. Abram's faith was tested by a famine in the land. He trusted God enough not to return to the land of Haran, but he does attempt to flee the famine by going down to Egypt. During his time in Egypt, there is no record of either the tent or the altar. His weak faith led Abram to resort to a lie to defend his wife's honor and finds himself a recipient of Pharaoh's rebuke (see Gen. 12:10-19). Thus, through failure, Abram learns the necessary truth:

God is able to supply his need, even in the midst of pressure and circumstantial difficulty. Humbled and repentant, Abram returns to the land and once again the tent and the altar appear.

Abram's third lesson of faith is that of humility, to learn to take second place. Abram and his nephew, Lot, illustrate different principles of Christian living: Abram was following God; Lot was following Abram—he was a tag-along believer. When a dispute arose between the herdsmen of the two men over the use of the land, even though Abram was the older and had the God-given right of first choice, he exhibited the humility of faith and allowed Lot to choose first. Lot chose his land on the basis of human measurements and ended up in Sodom. However, even though he obtained, he did not truly possess the land, because God gave Abram all the land, including that which Lot had chosen for himself (Gen. 13:14-18). In this lesson of Abram's we see that God's children are called to risk the obedience of faith, believing that God will take care of them even though they apparently are giving up their rights.

Abram's fourth lesson was to exhibit the boldness of faith. Chapter 14 records the historic invasion of the valley of the Dead Sea by the five united kings from the east. Lot was captured and, through this, Abram learned this fourth lesson. Though greatly outnumbered, Abram gathers his servants about him and with a company of 318 he pursues the united armies as far north as Dan and overcomes them in a great battle.

On his triumphant return he is met by Melchizedek at the King's Vale (now known as the Kedron Valley outside Jerusalem). Melchizedek appears as the type of an eternal priesthood, to strengthen Abram to meet the most subtle encounter of his career so far: the offer of the king of Sodom to make him rich. Strengthened by the bread and wine which Melchizedek gave him (forerunner of the

Lord's Table established centuries later), Abram refuses to be made rich except by God Himself, thus manifesting the fifth quality of faith.

Faith is independent of all natural resources. Chapter 15 is the account of the fourth direct appearance of Jehovah to Abram. Abram had now passed through several testings of his faith and the divine voice declares that He is Abram's shield (for his protection) and his exceeding great reward (as Abram's ultimate resource). Abram's intimacy with God had grown to the point where he can now share the temptation to doubt that was in his heart. God's response is to promise him an heir from whom would come a progeny as numerous as the stars of the sky.

Despite his age Abram believed in the promise of a coming son and for the first time in Scripture we read the great sentence, "his faith was reckoned to him for righteousness" (see Gen. 15:6). Abram is now the friend of God, not by his own merit but on the basis of his faith. Jehovah renews the promise of the land as Abram's inheritance and confirms it with a sign at Abram's request. The sign is a vision of a smoking furnace and a lamp, indicating the furnace of affliction Abram's descendants would go through in Egypt before the land was granted to them. Here Abram begins to learn the sixth quality of faith.

Faith endures and has patience. Chapter 16 is the account of Abram's second major deflection from faith. After 12 years of waiting for God to fulfill His promise of a son, Sarai and Abram resort to a human expediency to help God along. Hagar, Sarai's maid, is given to Abram as a wife and from her is born Ishmael. No tent or altar appears in this chapter and Abram reaps the harvest of his folly by continual strife between Sarai and Hagar and the eventual exclusion of Hagar from the household. Thus the man of faith of chapter 15 becomes the man of flesh of chapter 16 and the far-reaching result is visible today in the strife between the Arabs (of Ishmael) and Israel (of Isaac). Yet God tenderly cares for Hagar and sends her back to her mistress with a promise of divine support.

God then appears to Abram for a fifth time and an everlasting covenant is made, symbolized by the change of names from Abram to Abraham and from Sarai to Sarah. This is clearly what the New Testament calls "the new covenant," by which God undertakes Himself to be the total resource of the believer for daily activity. This is confirmed by a new revelation of God's name, that of El Shaddai, which means "the God who is sufficient." The sign of this new covenant is that of circumcision, which involves the cutting off of the flesh. It was the outward sign of an invisible inward truth. Abraham's faith falters slightly in seeking to bring Ishmael before God for blessing, but Jehovah patiently explains that he cannot be the heir of the promises since his birth does not rest upon faith, as does Isaac's. (The apostle Paul will base a great argument upon this difference in the letter to the Galatians—3:15-18.)

The next chapter records the sixth appearance of God to Abraham, during which God announces the imminent birth of the promised son, and reveals to Abraham His plan to destroy Sodom and Gomorrah. The encounter grows out of Abraham's warm hospitality toward three strangers who appear to him as he sits in the door of his tent. As he shows them hospitality there gradually dawns upon him the realization that it is the Lord Himself who thus comes, accompanied by two angels.

Sarah, listening behind the tent door, hears the announcement that she would bear a son within a year. She laughed when she heard it. But God graciously meets her with a divine revelation upon which her faith may seize and rest. He asks the question, "Is there anything too difficult for the Lord?" (Gen. 18:14). Sarah doubtless meditated on that for the intervening months, and by the time her son was born she was strong in faith, even as Abraham her husband.

Then Jehovah reveals to Abraham, His friend, the second purpose of His coming, that of the imminent destruction of the cities of the plain for their extreme wickedness and unbelief. This introduces a most helpful manifestation of the authority of faith, exercised in prayer by Abraham out of concern for Lot and his family and the inhabitants of Sodom. With obvious reverence Abraham intercedes with God on behalf of the doomed cities. This intercession is based upon Abraham's awareness of the character of God: "Shall not the Judge of all the earth deal justly?" (v. 25). It would be a mistake to view Abraham's prayers as reflecting more mercy than does God. We learn from the New Testament that it is the Spirit of God who prays within the believer, urging him to the specific requests that are made. Thus it is God's mercy, expressed through Abraham's prayers, that limits and tempers the justice and wrath of God. The sequel shows that God goes beyond anything we ask. Abraham stopped at ten righteous persons, but God saved the two or three in whom there was any recognition of Himself.

Chapter 19 records in vivid detail the sequel of the two angels' visit to Sodom and Gomorrah. Lot himself is righteous, as the New Testament makes clear, but his righteousness has been compromised by his conformity to much of Sodom's ways and he finds himself unable to influence his city, even his own family, toward righteousness. The homosexuality practiced in Sodom reflects the curse of Canaan upon these Canaanite tribes, and the ugly story of Lot and his incest with his daughters reveals the degree to which such practices may pervert those who maintain only an external pattern of righteousness.

Again, for the third time, we see a weakness in Abraham's faith (Gen. 20). Surrounded by the men of Gerar (who afterward were known as the Philistines) Abraham again lies concerning his wife Sarah. Once again the man of faith is censured by the man of the world as Abimelech, the heathen king, rebukes him for his lack of complete honesty. These deflections in Abraham's faith are never in the great things but in the smaller details of his life. Clearly they illustrate for us the danger we face in trivial matters where we feel no compulsion to act in confidence and trust in the living God.

At long last Sarah's laugh of incredulity is turned into the laughter of realization. As Isaac, the child of promise grows, conflict breaks out with the son of bondage, Ishmael. Eventually Abraham must make a choice between the two and in simple obedience he sent forth the child and the bondwoman, and leaned back on the gracious provision of God to fulfill His promise.

Chapter 22 records the last great lesson of faith, the intimacy of faith. In this chapter we also find the seventh and last appearance of Jehovah to Abraham. A gap of perhaps 20 years is evident between chapters 21 and 22. Isaac has grown to young manhood and, as the pride of his father's heart, God asks that he be offered up as a sacrifice to Him whom Abraham serves. It is Abraham's greatest test and must have proved a stunning and desolating trial to him. But faith enables him to triumph as he rests upon the character of God and feels that God is able even to raise the young man from death. Thus, as Hebrews (11:17-19) tells us, in a figure of resurrection Abraham received his son back from the dead. It is most striking that, according to biblical scholars, the mountain on which Isaac was offered is the same mountain upon which the Temple was later built and upon whose summit, many centuries later, Jesus Himself was offered as the Lamb of God which takes away the sin of the world.

This last experience ended the testing of Abraham's faith. He had learned his faith lessons and there are no more failures of faith on his part. The testing however is followed by the repetition of God's great promises to Abraham, with the addition of a promised seed, as numerous as the sands of the seashore (22:17). It is clear from this that Abraham is to have two lines of descendants: a heavenly line, symbolized by the stars of the heavens; and an earthly line, symbolized by the sands of the seashore. Thus the writer of Hebrews will later reflect upon a heavenly Jerusalem which is above, and an earthly Jerusalem which is below. Those who by faith are the children of Abraham, whether Jew or Gentile, are of the heavenly seed. Those who belong to the earthly Jerusalem are the physical descendants of Abraham, the Semitic nations of today (see Rom. 4:9-16; 9:6-8).

Chapters 23 through 25 record the death of Sarah and Abraham's sorrow at her passing. For her burial Abraham purchases the cave of Machpelah from the Hittites. Thus Abraham's first actual possession in the land is a grave.

In the story of Abraham's servant, Eliezer, sent to find a bride for Isaac, we have a beautiful Eastern idyll, picturing in accurate terms the sending of the Holy Spirit from the Father to seek the church as a bride for His own dear Son. Running throughout the account is the theme of the sovereign call of God. This alone accounts for Rebecca's willingness to leave her home and family to join a man she has never seen, in a land to which she has never been before. She finds Isaac waiting for her, meditating in the fields at evening time. Abraham's faith is rewarded by seeing the union of his son with a woman of his own kindred, who, though they are of two different temperaments, would walk together in the fulfillment of the divine purpose.

The final years of Abraham's life are gathered up for us in chapter 25, following his marriage to Keturah. From this union there came six more sons who also fathered tribes that later appear in the record of Israel. They form no part of the heirs of the promises made to Isaac, but are nevertheless given, by God's grace a place to dwell and made to flourish as nations.

Finally, at the age of 175 Abraham dies and is buried by his two sons Isaac and Ishmael in the cave of Machpelah, beside Sarah his beloved wife. Throughout the rest of the Bible, the figure of Abraham looms as preeminently the man of faith. By his experiences with God, and even by his failures, he has been taught the ingredients of righteousness which come by faith alone. These, as we have seen, may be summarized as: the obedience of faith, the sufficiency of faith, the humility of faith, the boldness of faith, the independence of faith, the authority of faith, and finally, in the sacrifice of Isaac, the intimacy of faith.

MAN SEEKS PEACE

Isaac symbolizes the condition of those who are the sons of God by faith in Jesus Christ. He dwells in the land in the midst of God's blessing and is refreshed by a continual supply of water in the wells that he digs in various locations, despite the opposition of his enemies. This truly depicts one who has found peace.

There is another aspect to Isaac: the principle of sonship. While his father was alive Isaac was the darling of his father's heart, and after Abraham's death he becomes the heir of the promises to Abraham and of the blessings of God. But Isaac's sonship also reflects the weaknesses of his father. For in the land of Gerar he repeats his father's sin: he lies about his wife Rebekah. Abimelech—not a proper name but the title of the kings of the Philistines— was the man of the world who rebuked Isaac.

As the heir of the promises, Isaac is given authority to pass these along to his posterity. When he was an old man, nearing the end of his life, he called his sons before him to give them his blessing. Before his twin sons, Jacob and Esau, were born, God told their mother Rebekah that the elder would serve the younger. Even though Isaac must have been aware of this prediction, when the sons appeared for their blessing Isaac sought to reverse the divine command. He intended to give the greater blessing to Esau, the firstborn.

Through a series of deceptions, masterminded by Rebekah, Jacob appears before his blind father in the guise of Esau, and receives the blessing of the firstborn. When Isaac found out that he had been tricked, he dares not alter the blessing he has pronounced. Instead he confirms to Esau the fact that he must serve his brother, but assigns to him the role of rebel and proud overthrower of his brother's yoke.

When Isaac died, the story centers on Jacob. Isaac has been a man of peace, quite content to enjoy his close relationship with his father and to experience his own spiritual relationship with God, distinct from those of Abraham or Jacob. He has learned how to pray and receive God's answer and to obey God's word and experience His blessing. In the brief record of his life we learn the secret of being a son and enjoying the inheritance of a great and glorious father.

Just as the life of Abraham vividly illustrates what is involved in the teaching of justification by faith, and that of Isaac, his son, portrays the meaning of sonship, so the life of Jacob describes and illustrates for us in exceedingly helpful ways the doctrine of sanctification by faith. Jacob's story is that of the struggle of two natures within him. His natural disposition was one of cunning and self-centered shrewdness. When he was born he emerged from the womb with his hand upon his brother Esau's heel and thus was given the name Jacob which means "heel-catcher" or "supplanter," one who seeks to take another's place. But Jacob had another bent within him which Esau, his twin brother, seemed totally to lack. Jacob had a hunger for spiritual relationships. He valued his brother's birthright which he took from him by trickery. He had a strong personal faith, was a hard worker and an intensely loving person. The story of Jacob, therefore, is the story of how God so dealt with a man of like passions with ourselves that He taught him how to rise above his lower nature and to become a man of God and a man of respect and dignity in his own generation.

Jacob's life can be seen in three clear stages. The first stage is his early years at home when he was basically a deceiver of others, living up to his name. In the second period of his life he learns what it is like to be deceived. Finally, Jacob learns to live as a man devoted to the word and will of God.

Jacob, the Deceiver

Esau, the older of Isaac's twin sons, was a man of the field, a skilled hunter, hairy and of ruddy complexion; he was also called *Edom,* which means red. Jacob, his brother, on the other hand, was a quiet lad and content to live in the tent around his mother. As the firstborn, Esau had the right to the blessing of Isaac, but God had told Rebekah that the ''elder shall serve the younger.'' So Rebekah was determined that Jacob would receive the inheritance.

One day, in a moment of hunger, Esau traded his birthright to Jacob for a mess of pottage. The Bible said that ''Esau despised his birthright.'' So when the time came for her sons to receive their father's blessing, Rebekah decided to make sure that Jacob would get the firstborn blessing. Isaac, old and blind, had sent Esau out to the field to hunt game ''and prepare a savory dish'' for his father. While he was gone, Rebekah told Jacob to dress in Esau's clothes. She covered his hands with hair. Then she prepared a savory stew of goat meat and sent Jacob to his father with the food. When Jacob entered his father's room he said, ''I am Esau your first-born; I have done as

you told me. Get up, please, sit and eat of my game, that
you may bless me'' (Gen. 27:19). Isaac was a little doubt-
ful at first, but finally gave Jacob the blessing.

When Esau returned from the field, he also prepared a
savory stew from the game he brought. He approached his
father to receive the blessing. As Isaac learned of the
deceit practiced upon him he fell into a violent fit of
trembling, undoubtedly caused by his consciousness of
the sovereign overriding of God. Isaac, aware of the
divine prediction which he had sought to evade, gave
Esau a lesser blessing.

Rebekah, fearing what Esau would do, convinced
Isaac to send Jacob to Laban, her brother, to find a wife.
Isaac sent Jacob off with his blessing.

Jacob, the Deceived

It was 600 miles from Jacob's home at Beersheba,
southwest of the Dead Sea, to Haran in Mesopotamia,
where Rebecca's family lived. Jacob spent his first night
in lonely homesickness at a spot which he later named
Bethel. There God appeared to Jacob in a dream of a
ladder reaching up into heaven upon which angels ascended and descended. The ladder symbolized the continual communication open between him and God. This
was followed by God's renewal of the promises which He
made to Abraham, now extended and confirmed to Jacob.
Thus God's first step in the process of sanctifying Jacob
was not to scold him or punish him or rebuke him, but
rather to reveal to him His love and faithful concern.
Jacob was shown that the way was open between himself
and God and was given a promise upon which his faith
could rest and which he could pass on to this descendants.

Jacob had thought he was alone and uncared for, but
he found that God was with him, loving him and seeking
to help him. In response, Jacob erected a great stone,
anointing it with oil, and named the place Bethel—the

house of God. To this place Jacob returned again and again, gaining from each visit a renewed awareness of God's faithful love and sure promise. So the sanctifying process in each believer today will consist of returning again and again to the faithful promises of God and the reminders of His love and care for us.

The rather lengthy account in chapters 29 through 31 of Jacob's life in Haran is the story of God's loving discipline of a favorite son. It is a record of God's careful mingling of blessing and chastisement so that Jacob's spiritual fiber is toughened and strengthened while his heart is kept from discouragement by the love of Rachel, one of his wives, the fertility of Leah, another wife, the birth of sons, and by his growing prosperity even under the exacting hand of his uncle Laban. The scene when Jacob arrived at Haran and met Rachel beside the well is reminiscent of the story of Rebecca and the servant of Abraham many years before. Jacob fell in love with Rachel at first sight and, having been welcomed initially into Laban's family, felt that all was working out well for him, for he was promised his beloved Rachel for his wife after seven years of service to his uncle.

But Jacob must learn the harvest of deceit, and at the end of seven years he found himself tricked into marrying Leah, Laban's older daughter, instead. When Jacob protested, Laban offered to let him have Rachel for yet another seven years' servitude. So great was Jacob's love he consented to this as well. Fortunately for him, Rachel was given to him immediately and he had her love and companionship throughout the second seven years of service.

During this time a total of 11 sons were born to Jacob's wives and their handmaids who became his concubines. This was in accordance with the customs of the day and before the written law made such practices clearly wrong. When Rachel gave birth to a son after many years of barrenness she named him Joseph. At that point Jacob decided that the time had arrived when he should return to Canaan.

But God was not yet through with Jacob's training. He must again experience the deceitfulness of his uncle in the matter of obtaining flocks and herds to take on his journey. After 14 years of service Jacob had learned much of the need for straightforward honesty and integrity and so he offered to make a deal with his uncle. He would take only the speckled and spotted sheep and goats while Laban would retain all those who were totally white, which was certainly a predominance of the flock. To this Laban readily agreed but secretly separated the spotted and speckled sheep and goats and put them under his sons' care at a distance of three days' journey. Jacob was left with nothing but white sheep and goats. He resorted to what he felt would be a stratagem to overcome his uncle's deceit. He tried a method that we would consider an "old-wives-tale" to insure that he would have sheep and goats to take with him. What he did not know was that God, who understood the laws of genetics since He Himself had called them into being, was using the invisible, hereditary genes for color in the white sheep to produce offspring which were spotted and speckled. The result was a spectacular increase in Jacob's flocks.

At this point God appeared to Jacob again in a dream and commanded him to return to the land of promise. To escape from Laban's wiles Jacob left in the middle of the night with his wives, children and flocks, and though Laban pursued him and caught up with him, God intervened to keep him from harming Jacob any further. Instead Jacob and Laban made a covenant of peace with one another and Laban returned to his own home. Despite Jacob's suffering during all these 20 years there was no trace of bitterness in his attitude, but one of praise to God for His blessing. Jacob had grown spiritually in tremendous ways during the 20 years of his servitude, but he would reach his true potential only after he had wrestled with God and his human strength was broken completely.

Jacob, Man of God

As Jacob came to the ford of the river Jabbok he learned that his brother Esau was on his way to meet him with 400 armed men. Immediately his reaction was to resort again to wiles and stratagems of his own. He divided his household into two groups and planned to send them on before him to try to appease the wrath of Esau with gifts before he must encounter him personally. While he waited alone, an angel in the form of a man, met him and began to wrestle with him through the long night. As the day broke the angel sought to disengage himself but Jacob clung with stubborn persistence. The angel touched Jacob's thigh and threw it out of joint; but still Jacob clung in helplessness to the divine messenger, refusing to let go until he was blessed of God. Then the divine being changed the name of Jacob to Israel which means "he who prevails with God." As the sun rose, Jacob limped off to meet Esau with a totally different attitude in his heart. He no longer feared man but was confident that God would fight his battles for him. When Esau arrived his own heart had been strangely altered and instead of attacking he fell upon Jacob's neck and embraced him. Thus Jacob learned the great principle of sanctification: that God was his strength and his refuge and is fully capable of working out all the problems with which he may be confronted.

As the result of an incident involving Jacob's daughter Dinah, God appeared again to Jacob and sent him back to Bethel to dwell there with a tent and an altar, as his grandfather Abraham and his father Isaac had done before him. There God renewed His promises to Jacob and there Jacob's beloved wife, Rachel, gave birth to her second son Benjamin, and died in childbirth. Jacob traveled on to Mamre where he found his aged father on his deathbed and he and Esau joined together in burying Isaac with honor and reverence. The record then traces in one chapter (36) the extent of the sons of Esau and the nation of Edom which came from his loins. From here on, in Scripture, Jacob and Esau will forever stand for conflicting and opposite principles, the Spirit versus the flesh. The spotlight of Genesis now turns to Joseph and his sons.

MAN SEEKS JOY

With Joseph we come to the last of the four great patriarchs who symbolically present to us the great truths of redemption. To justification by faith, exemplified in Abraham; to sonship, shown in Isaac; and to sanctification, revealed in the life of Jacob; we now add the truth of glorification, set forth in the story of Joseph. He cleaarly appears as the forerunner, sent into Egypt to prepare the way for the coming of the 12 tribes into that land, and as such he pictures our great Forerunner who has gone on before us, even Jesus our Lord, to prepare the way for all His own to come into glory with Him and to share that glory together. In line with that emphasis, the character of Joseph is presented to us with almost unblemished consistency. He is often regarded as a type of Christ since he was beloved of his father but rejected by his brethren, sold into slavery for 20 pieces of silver, and, in the view of his father Jacob, died and eventually was brought to life again as a triumphant king instead of a suffering servant. Like our Lord he also forgave his brothers for their treatment of him and was used to save them from death and preserve the family line.

Beloved by His Father, Rejected by His Brothers

We have already learned that Joseph was born in

Haran while Jacob was serving Laban, his uncle. In chapter 37 we discover him at the age of 17 working as a shepherd in his father's home in Hebron. Joseph was the obvious favorite of his father Jacob, who had bestowed on him a princely coat as a special mark of his favor. Therefore, he was the object of bitter hatred by his brothers. When, further, they learned that God had given Joseph two special dreams which predicted his elevation above his brothers, their hatred took a murderous form and they sought a way to kill him. Like his father Jacob, to whom God also spoke in dreams, Joseph seems to have had a special spiritual quality which God would greatly use in the years that lay ahead.

When Jacob's sons delayed returning from Shechem where they were feeding their flocks, Jacob sent Joseph the 50 miles from Hebron to Shechem to check on his brothers. Upon arriving at Shechem he found his brothers had departed for Dothan and he trudged on another 20 miles further north to find them there. Seeing him coming from afar, and recognizing the hated coat, his brothers plotted together to kill him, throw him into a pit, and tell his father that a wild beast had destroyed him. The oldest of the 12, Reuben, objected and persuaded them to leave him to die in a pit.

One can imagine the agony and fear of the 17-year-old boy who was thus roughly treated by his own brothers and tossed into a pit to die alone. While his brothers were in preparation for their journey home, they saw a caravan of Ishmaelites traveling by and hit upon a scheme to sell Joseph to them as a slave, but to tell their father that he had been killed.

Sold for 20 Pieces of Silver

Thus for 20 pieces of silver they sold Joseph to the Ishmaelites. Then they brought his coat, dipped in goat's blood, back to their father with the report that Joseph had been killed by a wild beast. Once again, Jacob who had deceived his own father Isaac, is now most truly deceived by his sons. But God's strange purposes were at work to bring about a quite different turn of events.

Chapter 38 records an incident to show why God found it necessary to remove the chosen family into Egypt for a period of time. Judah the fourth son of Jacob, married a Canaanite woman. Their marriage led to a series of events that indicates the degradation of Canaan. To prevent them from being absorbed by a heathen culture, God was moving in ways that would eventually put the family out of Canaan.

Meanwhile, Joseph was sold to Potiphar, an officer in the army of Egypt. The excellence of Joseph's character soon elevated him to a place of trust and responsibility and he was put over all of Potiphar's household. Surely he must have felt that the prediction of his dream was soon to come to pass. But a loving heavenly Father saw his need for being made perfect through suffering (see Heb. 2:10) and events quickly took another turn.

Because Joseph was handsome and good-looking, Potiphar's wife attempted to seduce him. Joseph resisted until one day she found him alone and lay hold of his garment, attempting to drag him into her bed. Crying out, "How then could I do this great evil, and sin against God?" (Gen. 39:9), Joseph fled from her presence leaving his garment behind.

Potiphar's wife reported the incident to her husband as though Joseph had attempted to assault her. Potiphar cast Joseph into prison. In all this there is no hint of bitterness or resentment on Joseph's part, but a quiet trust that God was working His way. Joseph's kindliness and skill soon won him a position as trusty over the other prisoners, because "the Lord was with Joseph." Whatever he did, the Lord made it to prosper.

Once again, dreams play a large part in Joseph's story.

This time Pharaoh's butler and baker, who were cast into prison, were the dreamers, and Joseph was the interpreter. The dreams were fulfilled as Joseph said. The baker went to his death and the butler was restored to Pharaoh's household, but soon forgot his promise to remember Joseph when he was released. But another dream got Joseph out of prison two years later.

From Suffering Servant to Triumphant King

Pharaoh had a dream. He commanded his seers to interpret the dream for him. When they could not the chief butler remembered Joseph and told Pharaoh of his interpretative skill. Joseph was hastily hauled from the dungeon and brought before Pharaoh. There he interpreted Pharaoh's dream, predicting the seven years of good harvest followed by seven years of drought and famine. Pharaoh, impressed not only by Joseph's interpretative skills, but also by the wisdom with which he suggested ways to meet the coming crises, put his signet ring upon Joseph's hand, arrayed him in garments of fine linen, put a gold chain about his neck and made him at the age of 30 years the second ruler in all the kingdom. Thus the stage was set for the coming of Jacob and his sons down to the land of Egypt.

Meanwhile, back at the ranch in Canaan, Jacob and his sons were experiencing terrible famine which settled upon the land. Jacob sent all his sons but the youngest, Benjamin, into Egypt to buy grain for their cattle. When the brothers came before Joseph he recognized them immediately, but did not reveal his knowledge. Instead he treated them roughly and accused them as spies come into the land. When they protested he ordered that they leave one of the brothers behind as a hostage and return to Canaan and bring back Benjamin, the youngest, as proof of their integrity. In discussing this among themselves, Reuben, the eldest, reminded them that this was a divine retribution for their treatment of Joseph many years earlier. Simeon, the second oldest, remained behind and the brothers returned to Canaan. Jacob at first was adamant that he would not let Benjamin leave. But the famine forced him to relent.

Upon reaching Egypt, Joseph entertained the brothers in his own home, much to their bafflement and uncertainty. When they left he commanded that the money they used to buy the grain be put back in their bags, and his own private cup be hidden in Benjamin's bag. A short way out from the city he sent his servants after them who accused them of stealing the cup. Protesting their innocence they vowed that the man in whose bag the cup should be found would immediately be put to death. But when the cup was found in Benjamin's bag they were overcome with sorrow and were brought back to Joseph's presence.

There, in a most moving plea, Judah privately recited the whole story in Joseph's ear and begged of him that Joseph would permit Judah to remain as hostage and let Benjamin go. Upon hearing this Joseph could not control himself any longer, and ordering all the Egyptians from the room, in a most moving scene he made himself known to his brothers. Upon Pharaoh's command the brothers returned to Canaan with the good news, and at last Jacob was persuaded to come with them into Egypt. Once again God appeared to Jacob in a vision of the night and reassured him that it was right for him to go into Egypt, for there He promised to make of his sons a great nation and to bring them again to the land of Canaan.

The remainder of the story is quickly told. The Israelites settled in the land of Goshen with Pharaoh's permission and became the herdsmen and keeper of Pharaoh's cattle. As the famine continued, the Egyptians sold first their cattle and then their land to Pharaoh, and at the end of the drought Joseph gave them seed to plant their land and retained the fifth part for Pharaoh's possession.

As the aged Jacob neared his death, Joseph brought his two sons Manasseh and Ephraim before him to be blessed of him. Joseph stood Manasseh, the older one, at Jacob's right hand and Ephraim, the younger, at Jacob's left hand, but when the old patriarch, sitting on the side of his bed, blessed them he crossed his hands so that the blessing of the firstborn fell upon Ephraim the younger and Manasseh, the elder, was given the secondary blessing. Once again the right of the firstborn was withheld from the one born first, and, by means of a cross, was transferred to the younger son. It was God's reminder that the right of the firstborn, which belonged to Adam, was now transferred to the last Adam (Jesus) that He might be "the firstborn of all creation."

In a great predictive chapter, Jacob called his sons before him and in poetic style foretold their destinies. When he had finished charging his sons "he drew up his feet into the bed, and breathed his last."

The final chapter recounts how Joseph brought the body of his father, in a great procession, up to the land of Canaan and buried him with Abraham in the cave of Machpelah. Joseph then returned to Egypt where he lived till the age of 110 and himself died, having made his brothers swear that they would bring his bones into Canaan when at last God brought the nation out of Egypt into the Promised Land (see Exod. 13:19).

Thus Genesis, which began with the creation of the heavens and the earth, ends in a coffin in Egypt. But behind the sad reality there burns the bright promise of El Shaddai, the God who is sufficient to bring about the fulfillment of all His promises by means of the process of justification, adoption, sanctification, and ultimately, glory.

CHAPTER THREE

God's Answer to Man's Need

EXODUS

As we have already abundantly seen, Genesis is the book that reveals the need of mankind. It is all about man—the creation of man, the sin of man, the world in which he is placed, and his slow journey through time groping after God. Its very last phrase, ''a coffin in Egypt,'' is a revelation that the most you can say about man when you have said all there is to say is that he lives in the realm of death.

But Exodus is all about God. Exodus is God's answer to man's need. God's supply for man's sin. It commences immediately with God's activity in the preservation and call of Moses, and throughout the whole of the book we will see God mightily at work. The theme of the book is redemption, God's activity to restore man from his sin, his degradation and misery. It contains many instructive lessons for us, especially what constitutes redemption in our own lives. We shall understand what God is doing with us when we see what He did with Israel in the book of Exodus.

The book centers around four great events which are easy to keep in mind for they focus on four experiences in the lives of the people of God in any age.

The first event is *the Passover*, chapters 1-14, which climaxes in that great event. The second significant event is *the crossing of the Red Sea*, described for us in chapter 14. The third great event is *the giving of the Law* at Sinai, chapters 19 and 20. The fourth event is *the construction of the Tabernacle* and its accompanying regulations for the camp of Israel.

The first two events relate closely to each other. The Passover and Red Sea are but two aspects of one great truth: the deliverance of God's people from the bondage of Egypt. They portray in Christian experience one great truth which we call conversion or regeneration—the deliverance of an individual from the bondage of the world. If you want to understand what God did with you when you became a Christian, study the Passover and the crossing of the Red Sea.

The other two events likewise tie together. The giving of the Law and the construction of the Tabernacle are absolutely inseparable. The pattern of the Tabernacle was given by God to Moses on the mountain at the same time that the Law was given, and we must understand from this book why these two are inextricably linked together. We shall do so as we move into this study. The Law requires the Tabernacle and the Tabernacle exists because of the Law.

OBSERVING THE PASSOVER

When man wants to change history he usually uses a battle or a ballot, but when God wants to change history He begins with sending a baby.

The opening chapter informs us that a new king had arisen over Egypt who did not know Joseph—Exodus opens some 300 years after the close of Genesis. The original 70 Israelites had multiplied to a great multitude of nearly two million. The new Pharaoh greatly feared the power of this developing nation in Egypt, and gave orders that all male Hebrew children should be cast into the river at birth. Against this dark background, Moses was born.

The story of his first 80 years is given to us in one brief chapter (chap. 2). In a delicate twist of irony that is wonderful to observe, God moved in such a way that despite the decree of Pharaoh to put all Hebrew male babies to death, Moses was not only saved but Pharaoh hired Moses' own mother to care for her baby. This is surely one of many delightful manifestations of the humor of God.

Moses was reared in the court of Pharaoh and had access to all the learning of the Egyptians. As Stephen will tell us many centuries later (see Acts 7:17-22), Moses was trained in the best university of the biggest empire of the world in that day. He was the foster son of the Pharaoh, and every privilege and every advantage were his.

But when Moses came of age, he realized, evidently from his mother's instruction, that he was destined to be the one who would deliver Israel from the bondage of the Egyptians. He attempted this in his own wisdom and ended up murdering a man and having to flee into the wilderness to escape the justice of Pharaoh. There in the wilderness of Midian he spent the next 40 years herding sheep for his father-in-law, Jethro. What a sense of failure and humiliation Moses must have had! All his dreams of glory fading away, he saw nothing in the future but the life of a sheepherder in a barren desert. But all this was necessary in God's disciplinary training of his faithful servant. What Moses could not learn in Egypt, he must learn in the quietude of the desert. In Egypt he had learned the wisdom of man; in the desert he was to learn the wisdom of God.

It was here that God appeared to Moses in the remarkable confrontation of the burning bush. That bush was to become a symbol of Moses' own life. As the bush burned with great brilliance and power yet was not consumed, so Moses would become a man of tremendous power so that when he died at the age of 130 years "his eye was not dim, nor his vigor abated" (Deut. 34:7). The power was not from Moses but from God.

Moses' response to God's call was to doubt himself. "Who am I?" he cried out (Exod. 3:11).

To this God replied, "I will be with you."

Again Moses doubted, based on his awareness of his ignorance of God. "What do I know about you?" is the essence of his query.

The answer was the reminder of the meaning of the divine name, "I AM WHO I AM." In its full intent, this is the name, the Lord "who is and who was and who is to come, the Almighty," as found in Revelation 1:8.

Yet again Moses doubted, and this time his doubt is based upon the people of Israel. "What if they will not believe me, or listen to what I say? For they may say, 'The Lord has not appeared to you' " (Exod. 4:1). God understood this fear and granted him three signs: the rod which could become a serpent; the hand which could become leprous and cleansed; water which could become blood on the land.

All Moses' fear had been met by the revelation of the grace and power of God, but still Moses doubted and retreated to his first argument, asking that someone else be sent in his place. At this the Lord became angry, for Moses in effect was saying, "I can't do this and I don't think you can do it either." God answered Moses' faltering faith by giving him Aaron as a mouthpiece. Here, as in many other instances in the Bible, God accommodated Himself to man's unbelief and yet at a cost of sorrow to that man's own heart, for Aaron proved to be an unreliable companion in times of crisis.

A further flaw in Moses' obedience is dealt with when at a lodging place enroute to Midian the Lord met Moses and sought to kill him. For some unrecorded reason (probably due to the opposition of his Gentile wife) Moses had failed to carry out the divine instructions concerning circumcision. The circumcision rite being taken care of, Moses and Aaron met the people of Israel, performed the signs God had given them, and were encouraged by the reception and obedience of the people.

In chapters 5-11 is found the record of Moses and Aaron's confrontation with a repeatedly obdurate and stubborn Pharaoh, and God's breaking of his power by the presentation of nine miraculous plagues. This is a most dramatic encounter, and the drama is clearly designed to reveal the redemptive power of God against the satanic power personified in Pharaoh.

Moses and Aaron appeared before Pharaoh and demanded in the name of the God of Israel that Pharaoh let God's people go. As predicted, Pharaoh defiantly refused, and actually increased the burden of the people by requiring that bricks be made of straw which the people must themselves supply. Jehovah encouraged Moses by reminding him of His promises of judgment until the Egyptians should know that He is the Lord. Subsequently, in the king's presence, the sign of the rod was employed, but when Aaron's rod became a serpent and swallowed up the rods of the Egyptian magicians who performed the same feat, Pharaoh's heart was still unmoved. These miracles by Egyptian magicians were undoubtedly manifestations of evil powers such as those manifest today in occultism.

Then began the series of nine plagues, to be culminated in a tenth, the death of the firstborn of the land and the celebration of the first Passover. The plagues came in series of three and were all directed against the gods of the Egyptians. The first plague was that of turning the water of the Nile River into blood so that the fish died and the Egyptians found little water to drink. Before the second plague Pharaoh was given opportunity to repent, but hardened his heart instead, and the land was filled with the frogs of the second plague. The Egyptian magicians had imitated both the first and second plagues, but when the third plague struck, with gnats covering the land on both man and beast, the magicians confessed their inability to imitate and declared it to be the finger of God.

Again Pharaoh hardened his heart, and so the judgment of God continued and we have the first of the second cycle of plagues. Swarms of flies filled all the houses excepting in the land of Goshen where the people of Israel dwelt. Thus Pharaoh was to be impressed by the immunity of Israel, that they are truly the people of God.

Pharaoh attempted to compromise by suggesting the people sacrifice in the land of Egypt, but Moses would have none of this. Pharaoh then seemed to give way, declaring his willingness to let them go, but not far away. At this sign of turning on Pharaoh's part, divine mercy turned toward him and the flies were removed from the land. But Pharaoh broke faith and again God warned him, and the next day sent the second plague of the second cycle. All the cattle of the Egyptians died, but none of the cattle of the people of Israel died. Still Pharoah was unrelenting; so without warning, the sixth plague struck. Ashes which Moses and Aaron tossed into the air became boils on the Egyptians, both man and beast throughout the kingdom.

The third cycle of three plagues began with hail. In the midst of a terrible thunder and lightning storm, heavy globes of hail struck down everything in the land of Egypt, sparing the land of Goshen. When Pharaoh seemed to repent the hail ceased, but again we are told Pharaoh calloused his own heart and God responded by hardening His own. Pharaoh attempted another compromise but Moses rejected it and called for the plague of locusts to cover the land. Pharaoh was now beyond reason and God did not reason with him. Instead He sent a ninth plague, a terrible darkness to be felt throughout the land of Egypt for three days. In the midst of the darkness Pharaoh made his fourth and last attempt at compromise by suggesting the cattle be left behind. When Moses refused,

Pharaoh said he did not want to see his face again.

Chapter 11 describes the conversation between Jehovah and Moses in which the final plague, the death of the firstborn throughout Egypt, is predicted and Israel is commanded to ask of the Egyptians gold and silver and jewels that they might leave with abundance when the hour strikes. This brings us to the central act in the redemptive program of God, the feast of the Passover. Jehovah now made this the beginning of the year and gave detailed instructions how the Passover lamb should be taken and killed and the blood placed on the doorposts of the houses, followed by the eating of the unleavened bread.

At midnight, in a most solemn account, the Lord smote the firstborn in the land of Egypt, from Pharaoh on his throne to the captive in his dungeon, as well as the firstborn of all the cattle. In that very night the Egyptians urged the Israelites to leave, thrusting their gold and silver upon them, "six hundred thousand men. . . aside from children. And a mixed multitude also went up with them" (Exod. 12:37,38) of those who had married Egyptians.

Every Israelite was commanded to teach the meaning of this Passover to his children.

Centuries later when John the Baptist would meet Jesus of Nazareth at the River Jordan, his announcement, "Behold, the Lamb of God who takes away the sin of the world!" (John 1:29), would be understood by every Hebrew present. The Passover feast is clearly the anticipation of the cross of Christ where the judgment of God was vented against all that is of the flesh within man and only those are saved who rest under the protecting blood of the Lamb.

Following the Passover is the feast of unleavened bread described in chapter 13. This was to be a perpetual memorial to the necessity to abstain from anything and everything which causes defilement in the individual life.

As the Israelites began their journey God went before them in a pillar of cloud by day and a pillar of fire by night, to guard them on the way.

CROSSING THE RED SEA

Immediately after the Passover and the feast of unleavened bread, the people of Israel left the safety of their homes in Egypt and went out into the wilderness, coming at last to the shores of the Red Sea. Looking back they saw 600 Egyptian chariots hot upon their trail; looking ahead they saw only the waters of the Red Sea. The case looked hopeless to them, and they began to cry out to Moses and ask him why he had brought them here to die in the wilderness.

Moses' answer is wonderful. He said, "Do not fear! Stand by and see the salvation of the Lord" (Exod. 14:13). It was a great cry of faith, and God's word came immediately, saying, "Lift up your staff and stretch out your hand over the sea and divide it, and the sons of Israel shall go through the midst of the sea on dry land" (14:16). The pillar of cloud moved between Israel and the Egyptians and throughout the night a great east wind drove back the waters of the sea. The next day the people marched through the sea safely, the waters standing as a wall on either side. When the Egyptians attempted to do the same, the waters of the sea returned upon them and they all perished. "Thus the Lord saved Israel that day from the hand of the Egyptians" (Exod. 14:30).

In 1 Corinthians 10:2 we are told that all the people "were baptized into Moses in the cloud and in the sea." The meaning of that is they were made one, they became a nation when they passed through the Red Sea. When Moses went down to Egypt the people of Israel were not a nation. They were a disorganized mob. But when they came out of the sea they were a unit. This is a beautiful reflection of the truth that every Christian must discover.

Before he became a Christian he was simply an individual struggling to make his way through life. But when he has gone through the experience of the Passover, when he has seen the blood of the Lamb nailed to the cross for him and has rested in the security of that fact, and when he has passed through the Red Sea experience, moving forward into an openly Christian stand, he will understand fully that he has now become part of a Body, the Body of Christ, and is joined together in a living unit with all other Christians.

The Red Sea typifies a break with the world. Egypt is now on the other side. Once Israel passed through the Red Sea they were then in the wilderness, but they were out of Egypt. The river of death now rolled between them and the place of bondage; and exactly that same river of death rolls between the Christian and the world when he claims Jesus Christ as Lord. Here is perhaps the reason why many professions of Christian faith never seem to go anywhere. There are people who are willing to sit under the Passover blood, willing to receive Jesus Christ as Saviour, but they are not willing to walk through the waters of the Red Sea. They never take that step which brings them to the other side and cuts them off from the world. In their mind and thinking they are still back in Egypt. They will not move forward through the waters of death, and until that happens they are still under the bondage and control of the world.

The first thing Israel did as they walked through to the other side of the sea was to break into song. There had been no song in Egypt. That was a place of unrelenting bondage and heartache, misery, toil and danger. But when they came onto the far shore of the Red Sea they began to sing. Real deliverance always brings a song, reflecting joy in the greatness of God. The song they sang acknowledged the sense of dread that falls on the men of other nations who hear the story of the triumphal crossing.

Annie Johnson Flint has written a beautiful poem reflecting the truth of the Christian crossing of the Red Sea.

> Have you come to the Red Sea place in your life,
>   Where, in spite of all you can do,
> There is no way out, there is no way back,
>   There is no other way but—through?
> Then wait on the Lord with a trust serene,
>   Till the night of your fear is gone,
> He will send the wind, He will heap the floods,
>   When He says to your soul, "Go on."
>
> And His hand will lead you through—
>   clear through—
>   Ere the watery walls roll down,
> No foe can reach you, no wave can touch,
>   No mightiest sea can drown;
> The tossing billows may rear their crests,
>   Their foam at your feet may break,
> But over their bed you shall walk dry shod
>   In the path that your Lord will make.
>
> In the morning watch, 'neath the lifted cloud,
>   You shall see but the Lord alone,
> When He leads you on from the place by the sea
>   To the land that you have not known;
> And your fears shall pass as your foes have passed,
>   You shall be no more afraid;
> You shall sing His praise in a better place,
>   A place that His hand has made.

We have also in chapter 15 the story of the waters of Marah, the place of bitterness. In order to cure these bitter waters, Moses cut down a tree which the Lord showed him and threw it into the water and the water became sweet. This is a clear symbol to us that the cross, that great tree on which the Lord Jesus hung, is God's answer to the bitterness of life. When we have experienced the security of the Passover and passed through the Red Sea, cutting ourselves off from the world, we discover that the cross is forever the answer to the bitterness that sin may have brought into our lives, both past and present. To accept that cross as the will of God is to find the waters of life sweetened.

In the record of chapters 16-18 we have the account of Israel's first experiences in the wilderness. They provide a continuing contrast between the murmuring, unbelieving people and the patient mercy of God. It becomes increasingly clear that Jehovah was attempting to wean them from their craving for the material and the immediate, to a realization of the value of the spiritual.

Their first supernatural provision was the gift of manna, the bread from heaven. They were given clear instructions to gather each day for five days and on the sixth enough for that day and the following Sabbath. The people had difficulty in obeying, even as today. We also find it difficult to trust God for His deliverance in the midst of impossible situations. Again their faith was tried when they came to a barren desert, wherein there was no water at all; but again Jehovah patiently met their murmuring unbelief by providing water out of the rock for them.

They encountered a third trial when they suddenly found themselves under attack from Amalek. This was their first experience with war after leaving Egypt. The principles of divine conflict were revealed in that Joshua led the men in actual fighting while Moses, assisted by Aaron and Hur, prayed on the mountainside. The Israelites, through this experience, taught that faith requires obedient action, combined with dependence on God. Here again the eternal conflict between Jacob and Esau reappears. Amalek was a tribe that descended from Esau and represents always the flesh in eternal battle against the spirit. Here a great victory was gained, which Moses commemorated by raising an altar which he named The Lord is My Banner. It was to be a continuing encouragement to any who would have to battle Amalek, with whom Jehovah declared Himself to be at war from generation unto generation.

In chapter 18 an interesting interlude occurred when Jethro, Moses' father-in-law, brought Moses' wife and his two sons from their home in Midian. Even though Jethro was a priest of *Midian*, upon hearing Moses' recital of God's activity in delivering Israel from Egypt, Jethro acknowledged Jehovah as supreme and offered to Him a sacrifice. Purely as a matter of common sense, he offered advice to Moses on the delegation of authority within the camp of Israel. The fact that Moses acted on this advice is clear evidence that he recognized God speaking through Jethro. The advice probably saved Moses from an early death from sheer exhaustion, and is excellent counsel for those who have not learned to share their work load with others.

From chapter 19 through the remainder of the book, the record concerns itself with the last two great events of the book of Exodus.

GIVING OF THE LAW

The 10 words of God are introduced to us in a scene of fearful solemnity and majesty. God called Moses and announced to him the purpose for Israel: They shall be to Him "a kingdom of priests and a holy nation." When Moses repeated these words to the people their easy and superficial response was, "All that the Lord has spoken we will do" (Exod. 19:8). It is clear that the people have no true consciousness of what these words mean. Jehovah, therefore, directed Moses to separate the people from the mountain and to consecrate them for three days that they might be able to endure the sights they were soon to see.

On the third day there were thunderings and lightnings and a thick cloud upon the mountain and a piercing trumpet blast which made the whole camp of Israel tremble. As the trumpet blew louder and louder and the mountain shook continually, Moses and Aaron were summoned to the mountain and Moses alone was called into the very presence of God. There the voice of God delivered to him the words which we call the Ten Commandments.

The first five of the commandments deal with the relationship between God and man and especially guard against the violation of God's Person. The first warns against polytheism. The second against idolatry. The third proclaims the righteousness of God and warns against profanity. The fourth guards the worship of God against secularism, and the fifth requires the honoring of father and mother as representatives of God, guarding against irreverence to authority.

The second five concern the relationships between persons, guarding the sanctity of life, the sanctity of marriage, the sanctity of property, the sanctity of character and sanctity of the inner thought-life.

Immediately instructions were also given as to the nature of worship, and it is significant that the only altar which God will honor was to be made of simple, unadorned stones devoid of any human workmanship in which the heart of man might boast. Thus the people were instructed in two essential matters: the law which describes the character and holiness of God and the system of sacrifice by which a sinful and lawbreaking people may yet draw near to a holy and righteous God, and find Him merciful and gracious toward them.

As yet the words of the Law were not written upon the stones, but Moses had simply repeated them before the people. He proceeded to give them certain ordinances which apply the principles of the ten words to life. The first section deals with the rights of persons, regulating slavery, wrong done to one's fellow man, and injuries brought about through neglect or carelessness. The second section deals with the rights of property covering theft and dishonesty. The third section (22:16—19) touches upon matters which directly affect worship, including seduction, sorcery, bestiality and idolatry.

Great concern is shown for the rights of strangers, indicating that God hears the cry and avenges the sorrows of many who are oppressed. Warnings are given against reviling God and cursing rulers, and the rights of God concerning the firstborn are reiterated.

Finally, matters of justice are detailed, and the three great feasts which Israel was to keep each year are described. These are the feast of unleavened bread, associated with the Passover; the feast of firstfruits, later associated with Pentecost; the feast of harvest at the end of the year.

These divine admonitions conveyed by Moses to the people conclude with God's great promise to send His angel before them to guard them and to bring them to the place that God had prepared. This angel of the Presence is surely to be identified with Him who eventually became flesh and dwelt among us. He would insure God's blessing to the people and drive out all their enemies.

Following these ordinances, Moses and Aaron and 70 of the elders of Israel were called apart and Moses in their presence repeated all the words of the Lord, reading them as they were written in the Book of the Covenant. Taking blood from the altar he sprinkled the people as they responded, ''All that the Lord has spoken we will do, and we will be obedient.''

At this solemn point, the elders of Israel were invited to ascend the mountain further where they saw the glory of God described in words which recall the vision of the apostle John, recorded in the fourth and fifth chapters of the Revelation. Here they entered into some mystic communion in which "they beheld God, and they ate and drank" (Exod. 24:11).

Following this, Moses alone was called to the top of the mountain where he waited for six days, and on the seventh he disappeared into the cloud of glory which, in sight of the people of Israel, was like a devouring fire on the top of the mountain. There he remained for 40 days and 40 nights.

CONSTRUCTING THE TABERNACLE

From chapter 25 through chapter 31 we have the account of the explicit directions given to Moses for the construction of the Tabernacle, the dwelling place of God among the people. It begins not with the building itself, but with the three articles of furniture which were to be at the heart of the worship of Israel. The first was the Ark of the Covenant with its covering cherubim over the mercy seat, symbolizing the place of the dwelling of God. The next instructions describe the table for the bread of the Presence. In Eastern imagery the table is the symbol of fellowship, and thus the people were reminded of their constant need for communion with God and with one another. The golden lampstand follows, symbolizing the revelation these people were to receive and the testimony they were subsequently to give to the outside world.

These three pieces of furniture were to be the center of all national life and worship: (1) The meeting place with God on the basis of propitiation; (2) the table for fellowship between God and His people; (3) the lampstand of testimony, symbolizing the work to which they were called.

Following this, the divine details of the curtains and coverings in the Tabernacle are specified. The 10 curtains of fine-twined linen contain white (the color of purity), blue (the color of heaven), purple (the color of royalty) and scarlet (the color of blood), as foregleams of the Person and work of Him who would fulfill the symbolism of the entire building. This is also true of the Tabernacle coverings, the boards, the veil and the door screen, which are next described. The veil which separates the holy place from the holy of holies is interpreted in Hebrews 10:20 as the flesh of our Lord. When Jesus died the curtain of the Temple was torn in two and a new and living way was opened up into the presence of God, by Jesus' death.

Exodus 27 brings before us the court surrounding the Tabernacle, and once again the description begins from the inside. We are given first the brass altar on which the animal sacrifices were to be burned. It was to be set within the outer court of the Tabernacle in front of the entrance to the holy place. The outer court was to be enclosed with curtains of finely twined linen, set in sockets of brass and capped by crowns of silver, suggesting purity resting upon the strength of government and crowned with the symbol of redemption.

The screen before the entrance to the court was similar to that before the holy place, and in turn was somewhat like the veil before the holy of holies. As we have seen, intertwined colors picture the person of Christ. Thus no man might pass within the court save through the symbol of mediation. Likewise there could be no entrance into the holy place of fellowship and testimony but through the same gateway. And none might reach the inner chamber of the presence of God without participating in the very body and blood of the mediator.

Oil was also commanded to be brought for the continuing light of the lampstand. This clearly symbolized the Holy Spirit who gives the light of revelation in the midst of the darkness of human knowledge.

Following the revelation to Moses of the precise pattern of the Tabernacle, he was then shown the divine mind concerning the priesthood. The priesthood in Israel was to be vested in Aaron and the sons of the tribe of Levi. Aaron as the high priest foreshadowed the work of Christ as confirmed by the book of Hebrews. The garments of the high priest were to represent the glory and beauty of Christ as our High Priest. The vestments of the high priest with their colors of gold, purple, scarlet and white, spoke eloquently of the Person and work of Jesus. The shoulder pieces, each adorned with two onyx stones, engraved with the names of the 12 tribes, symbolized the office of burden-bearing. On the heart was the glorious breastplate embellished with precious stones containing also the names of the 12 tribes. At the center of this were the strange Urim and Thummim (Lights and Perfections) which indicated in some mystic manner the work of the priest in discovering the divine mind and will.

The robe of the ephod was entirely blue, suggesting the heavenly matters with which the high priest was to be engaged. The alternating bells and pomegranates on the skirts of the robe spoke of testimony and fruitfulness necessary to priestly intercession. Attached to the golden mitre on the head was a plate bearing the words "Holy to the Lord," indicating the exquisitely balanced perfection of the priestly office.

The consecration of the priests to their office is described in chapter 29, consisting of a threefold function: washing, dressing and anointing. The washing symbolizes the forgiveness of sin; the dressing symbolizes imputation of righteousness; the anointing speaks of the enduing of the Holy Spirit. The offerings which follow are repeated in more detail in the book of Leviticus. They emphasize anew the truth that Jehovah wants always to be before His people, that God could meet with them only through sacrifice and the cleansing of sin. The priests alone are to feed upon the meat of the offerings as a symbol of the necessity of understanding all that is involved in the work of redemption, that by these means and these alone would a living God be able to dwell among a sinful people.

At this point the altar of incense which is supremely the altar of priesthood is introduced. It completes the furniture of the holy place and speaks of the offering of praise and adoration unto God. The bronze laver is then described, which stood before the entrance of the holy place within the outer court.

Finally, we have instructions concerning the use of anointing oil and incense. The whole is symbolic of the fact that only those who had given the half-shekel of redemption, had been cleansed at the bronze laver, and anointed by the fragrant oil could truly offer the worship of prayer and thanksgiving typified by the incense. The Lord who gave these complicated instructions was able also to call and equip certain workmen to construct the Tabernacle and all its furnishings. Two men, Bezalel of Judah and Oholiab of Dan, were filled with the Spirit of God in order to provide the skilled labor necessary to this work.

Then the Sabbath was brought in as essential to all, typifying that the energy by which they labored was to be that of those who have entered into God's rest and have ceased from their own labors. As we have seen before, the Sabbath is forever the symbol of restful activity, dependent upon the Spirit of God.

While these careful instructions were being given to Moses on the mountaintop, the people at the bottom of the mountain were already falling into grievous sin. The people who had so wondrously been redeemed from Egypt and led through the waters of the Red Sea and fed miraculously by manna from heaven and refreshed by water from the rock, now manifest a great wickedness in making and worshiping a golden calf. In a scene reminiscent of Abraham pleading with God for the salvation of

Sodom and Gomorrah, we see Moses pleading before God on behalf of this people. As with Abraham, it was God Himself who was using Moses to call upon His mercy and allay His wrath. Moses pleaded not so much for the people but for God Himself. He reminded Him that His honor is at stake and pleaded the covenant made with Abraham, Isaac and Jacob. He thus became the instrument to turn aside the divine wrath.

On coming down from the mountain with the tables of stone, and surveying the scene of idolatry and debauchery, Moses angrily threw the plates to the ground, breaking them at the foot of the mountain. He ground the golden calf to powder and compelled the people to drink of the water into which it was thrown. He called, ''Who is for the Lord?'' In response, the Levites gathered to him and he sent them throughout the camp with a sword in every hand and 3,000 of the worst offenders were slain. The next day he returned to the presence of God and there confessed the sin of the people and pled that they might be spared even if he himself must be blotted out of God's book. God responded by sending him back again to lead the people and promising the angel of the Presence to go with him. Though the angel of the Presence will go before the people to Canaan, nevertheless Jehovah indicated that He would not dwell among them in their sinful state. This remoteness is indicated by the tent of meeting (the predecessor of the Tabernacle) being placed outside the camp where God would commune with Moses.

Moses again interceded before Jehovah saying, ''If Thy presence does not go with us, do not lead us up from here'' (Exod. 33:15). With this God acquiesced and Moses asked for further display of the glory of God. Hidden in the cleft of the rock he saw the back parts of God but not His face. While man is yet on earth, God may be seen only by the results of His passing by; the vision of the face of God is reserved only for heaven.

Strengthened by this vision, Moses was called again to ascend the mount and to receive two other tablets inscribed by the hand of God. There on the mountaintop the Law and the covenants were renewed and the necessity to keep the feasts and the Sabbath was again decreed. After another 40-day stay with the divine presence, Moses came down the mountain with a shining countenance to greet the people. When he learned of his shining face, he put a veil upon his face that he might speak to the people unhindered. Later we learn from the apostle Paul that he kept the veil there that the people might not see the fading glory. This is to contrast the glory of the law with the superior glory of the face of Jesus Christ.

Chapters 35 to 39 contain the account of the actual building of the Tabernacle. Once again the Sabbath law is restated as emphasizing the need for all activity to be performed in the consciousness of the divine activity superseding the human. The offerings commanded in chapter 25 were brought by the people for the construction of the Tabernacle. The offerings were wholly voluntary, and the labor on the Tabernacle was to be done only by those who came with a willing heart. So abundant was the offering that Moses had to command the people to cease their giving.

First the curtains for the Tabernacle proper were set up, and then the beams for the building itself. These were overlaid with cloths of blue, purple and scarlet stuff, with fine-twined linen and cherubim skillfully worked in. The furniture of the Tabernacle was then constructed, beginning with the Ark of the Covenant with its cherubim overshadowing the mercy seat. This was followed by the table of showbread, the golden lampstand and the altar of incense. For the outer court the altar of burnt offering was made, with its horns and grating. Then the great laver of bronze was cast. Finally the curtains of the outer court were hung on each side and the screen for the gate of the court was embroidered in blue and purple and scarlet stuff with fine twined linen. Then the accounting was given of the worth of the materials of which the Tabernacle was made.

Full details are given concerning the holy garments of the priest which were made strictly according to the pattern shown to Moses. At last the statement is made, "Thus all the work of the tabernacle of the tent of meeting was completed; and the sons of Israel did according to all that the Lord had commanded Moses; so they did" (Exod. 39:32).

Moses blessed the people for their obedient labors and, according to the instruction of God, set up the furniture of the Tabernacle all in its proper place. When the work was finished and the Tabernacle stood exactly according to the pattern which God had shown Moses on the mountain, then the cloud covered the tent and the glory of the Lord came down and filled the whole of the Tabernacle. So splendid was this glory that Moses was not able to enter the Tabernacle. Moreover the cloud of glory remained over the Tabernacle as a permanent guide. Throughout the years of their wanderings it was to be a symbol to the people of the presence of God and the sign of the divine intent to move or to settle.

What shall we make of this amazing building and its precise God-given design? We have already seen that its intimate detail is a foreview of both the Person and the work of Christ, but in the Epistle to the Hebrews we are given a further hint as to its significance. There in chapter 3 verse 5 we are told, "Moses was faithful in all His house as a servant, for a testimony of those things which were to be spoken later; but Christ was faithful as a Son over His house, whose house we are, if we hold fast our confidence and the boast of our hope firm until the end." There the full meaning of the Tabernacle is stated plainly for us. It was the symbol of man himself. It was a symbol of Christ because Christ was the perfect man, but it was also the symbol of every believer in Christ who with his Lord shares the glory of the Son of Man.

As the Tabernacle in the wilderness was built in three parts—an outer court, the holy place, the holy of holies—so man is a threefold construction consisting of body, soul and spirit. The human spirit is intended to be the dwelling place of the Holy Spirit, and this is symbolized by the Ark of the Covenant with its mercy seat by which the living God can dwell within His people. The apostle Paul confirms this when he says, "You are a temple of God" (1 Cor. 3:16). The soul of man corresponds to the holy place, and the furniture within, that of the table of the bread of the Presence, the golden lampstand and the altar of incense, reflect the qualities of emotion (essential to fellowship), mind (encompassing knowledge which gives light), and will (making obedient choices which redound to the praise and glory of God).

The outer court symbolized the body of man with its exposure to the outside world. As Paul tells us in Romans 6, the body is the seat of sin and therefore the site of the altar of sacrifice. It is also the place of defilement and requires the cleansing work of the laver. But above all else, man is to be the dwelling place of God and the anointing of the Holy Spirit is to suffuse his being with the presence and power of God.

It has always troubled me to hear Sunday School teachers and others teach children that a building is the house of God. It is true that the Tabernacle of the Old Testament is called the house of God, but it was a mere shadow. The Temple in Jerusalem took its place, and it too was a shadow. When we come to the New Testament we never find a building designated as the house of God. The house of God in the New Testament is a human body. The apostle Paul declares in 1 Corinthians 3:16 "Do you not know that you are a temple of God, and that the Spirit of God dwells in you?'' When we teach that a building is the house of God, we make it very difficult for people to grasp the idea that their bodies are the temples of God. Nothing is more important than to realize that Jesus Christ Himself is dwelling in your body, which is His temple. Deep at the center of your life is the holy of holies, your human spirit, and in that place the Spirit of God dwells.

Sometimes we hear that the weakness of the Old Testament was that they were under the Law and did not know the grace of God. Nothing could be further from the truth. It is true, they were under the Law, but the Law was not given to them to be their Saviour. It was given to reveal their sin and to make them aware of how hopeless was their condition apart from God's redemptive grace. Their problem was not the Law, but the Tabernacle and its system of sacrifices. It was not sufficiently complete; it was not real enough. It consisted only of shadows, just kindergarten pictures, and could never really accomplish anything. Thus when we come to the book of Hebrews we learn that the shadows are done away because they are fulfilled in the great anti-type, the Lord Jesus Christ. We read: ''We have confidence to enter the holy place'' (Heb. 10:19). We need no longer fear to enter; for in the blood of Jesus, by means of the cross, God has set aside all that separates us from Him and has brought us near to Himself.

Thus the great message of the book of Exodus is that by means of the cross God has made it possible for a holy, righteous God to dwell with sinful man. The Tabernacle is the picture of God's dwelling with His people. The great truth for us is that God has so totally handled the problem of sin in the sacrifice of His Son that, as Paul says in Romans 8:1, ''There is therefore now no condemnation for those who are in Christ Jesus.'' We have perfect access to the Father through the Son, and God's indwelling Spirit will never leave us or forsake us. He has taken up His abode in our hearts.

CHAPTER FOUR

The Way to Wholeness

LEVITICUS

The book of Leviticus is probably most famous for being the place where many people stop in their reading through the Bible. It seems to be a book of strange ceremonies and sacrifices with many odd restrictions, problems of diet, and other difficulties which seem meaningless. But properly understood, Leviticus is one of the most beautiful books of the Bible. If you wish to understand Leviticus, one verse near the center of the book will help greatly, "You are to be holy to Me, for I the Lord am holy; and I have set you apart from the peoples to be Mine" (Lev. 20:26). That is the purpose of the book of Leviticus. It details the way by which man is made holy enough to live in the Divine Presence and to enjoy a relationship so close that God will delight to say, "You are mine."

Don't be turned off by the word "holy" in this passage. Most people associate holiness with some kind of grimness. They react as did the little girl who happened to see a mule looking over the fence at her. She had never seen a mule before and she said to it, "I don't know what you are but you must be a Christian—you look just like grandpa." To many of us, "holy" people are those who look as if they had been steeped in vinegar or soaked in embalming fluid. But the Scriptures speak of "the beauty of holiness" (Ps. 29:2, *KJV*). True holiness is therefore something splendidly attractive.

The original root from which the word holy is derived

is the same root from which a very attractive English word also comes. That word is "wholeness." Holiness, therefore, means wholeness, being complete. If you read "wholeness" in place of "holiness" everywhere you find it in the Bible, you will be much closer to what the writers originally meant. We all know what wholeness is. It is to have together all the parts which were intended to be there and to have them function as they were intended to function. Our modern expression "getting it all together" is very close to the root meaning of holiness.

The word "wholeness" has power to awaken desire within us. We long to be whole people. Who does not want to be what God made him to be, with all the ingredients of his personality expressed in perfect balance? That is what the book of Leviticus is all about. We are much aware of our own brokenness, of our lack of wholeness. We know how much we hurt ourselves and each other. We are aware of our inability to cope with life. We sometimes put up a facade and try to bluff our way through as though we are able to handle everything, but inside, most of the time, we are running scared. That is a mark of our lack of wholeness. We also know our diabolical power to irritate, to enrage and to inflame others—and even ourselves. But this great statement in Leviticus 20:26 declares that God knows all about human brokenness and hurt. He knows that we are that way. He sees it in sharp contrast to His own wholeness, and His love reaches out and says, "You shall be whole, for I am whole."

Leviticus, then, is the story of how God has determined to heal man's brokenness and make him whole again; and He knows how to do it, for He says, "I have separated you from the peoples." The reason we are so broken is because we are involved in a broken race. Our basic attitudes are wrong. Our vision of life is twisted and distorted. We believe in illusions and follow them as facts. We pursue phantoms and fantasies and delusions.

Therefore, God must separate us from such thinking. He must break us loose from conformity to the thought patterns and attitudes and reactions of those around us. When He has straightened out our thinking and set our minds and hearts aright and corrected our tangled, fouled relationships, then we shall be whole as He intended.

This is a process which takes infinite patience and love, because we are so slow to learn. That is why God gave us this book of pictures. He starts in kindergarten with us. He begins with shadows and pictures as a kind of visual aid in order to show us what is the meaning of what He eventually does in history. Therefore, all the ceremonies and offerings of the Old Testament are foreviews and pictures of Jesus Christ. Leviticus is full of Christ. As He Himself said, "I am the way, and the truth, and the life; no one comes to the Father, but through Me" (John 14:6). Thus, these Old Testament sacrifices and rituals are the means by which believers before the cross laid hold of the full value of the work of Jesus Christ on their behalf. These men and women before the cross were as hurt and broken and fragmented as we are. They, too, needed Christ, and through these shadowy anticipations He was available to them. They may not always have seen the fulfillment of these things in Christ, but God did! Any Israelite who obediently and sincerely offered these sacrifices found that the reaction of the Spirit was to bring him to the same joy and peace that we have today. Read the Psalms and see how much David understood of the presence and the grace of God in his life. Some of these men and women of old were so taught of the Spirit that they actually foresaw the person and work of Christ as the great anti-type of the shadows with which they were involved. Thus, Jesus could say in John 8:56, "Your father Abraham rejoiced to see My day; and he saw it, and was glad."

But there's even more to see in a book like Leviticus.

Since in Jesus Christ God took upon Himself the form of a man, and Jesus dwelt among us as a man—man as God intends man to be—therefore, everything that pictures Him also pictures us. Here in this book, therefore, we can understand our own humanity better than we can know it anywhere else. This book, then, becomes a penetrating study into human psychology, made all the more valuable because it is divinely guaranteed to be the truth about humanity.

The book itself falls into two basic divisions. The first part, chapters 1 through 16, reveals the fundamental needs of our humanity and God's provision. The last section, chapter 17 through 27, unfolds what performance God expects from us in response.

GOD'S PROVISION FOR OUR NEEDS

First comes God's provision and then the performance which results from that provision. Within the first division there are four elements traced which reveal the basic need of sinful humanity.

Need for Offerings

The first is the series of five offerings with which the book begins. These are the burnt offering, the meal offering, the peace offering, the sin offering, and the trespass offering. In these is found a basic insight into the fundamental nature of humanity. They describe in symbolic terms the two essentials for human existence: love and responsibility—that is, the need to be loved and to love in turn. Love is the absolutely essential ingredient in life. Nothing harms or disfigures or blasts a person more than to deny him love. Another essential for wholeness, self-respect and a feeling of worth, is that we must have a sense of our responsibility to love others.

The Burnt offering. Each of the five offerings follows a five-step pattern.

First a selection of the sacrifice must be made. In the case of the burnt offering, it must be a male without blemish. It could be a bull from a herd, or a sheep or goat from the flock, or if the offerer was very poor, it could be turtledoves or young pigeons. In any case, it must be male, for in the burnt offering God is dealing with man to remind him of his role as a king over all the earth.

The second step was the laying on of hands upon the offering. What does that mean? That is God's way of teaching the great truth of substitution, the fact that we human beings are tied together with each other, belong to one another, and share life together, and thus others can do things for us which we cannot do ourselves. This is the basis of fellowship among believers. But in the case of dealing with sin, the substitute must be a spotless, sinless person. Thus, Jesus Christ is the only adequate substitute and this is symbolized by the burnt offering.

The third step was to kill the animal involved. God never allowed any compromise on this. He did not say, "This is a nice little lamb and is innocent of any wrongdoing himself, so if you'll just drain a half pint of blood from him I'll be satisfied." God would never say such a thing because He desires to impress upon us the fact that the problem He is dealing with is so intense and so deeply rooted in our human lives that nothing but death itself can solve it. It cannot be palliated by some temporary expedient. It requires the pouring out of life itself.

The fourth step was either the sprinkling of blood or the burning of the sacrifice as an act of consecration and commitment to God. The instant one of these animals died it became fully acceptable to God. Death solved the problem of alienation and so the sacrifice could then be offered acceptably to God. In the case of the burnt offering, the animal was to be totally consumed. No one was ever to eat the meat of the burnt offering.

This burnt offering is the first of three sacrifices that

are said to be "a pleasing odor to God." It symbolized the great truth that in order to fulfill the dominion given to man he must himself be given wholly to God. Man was born to rule, but he was also made to be possessed. He was born to be king over all, but he was to be under the authority of God. The testimony of all history is that man is very unhappy until he is possessed by God. The most basic question of every life is to belong to someone, to have an identity, to be loved and accepted and owned by someone else. No sight is more pitiable or pathetic than someone who feels that no one loves him—that he belongs nowhere, and no one cares for his soul.

Thus, the purpose of the burnt offering is to remind us that in the death of Jesus Christ we can find the full satisfaction of that basic human longing. You can find a certain amount of satisfaction in being part of a family, you can find satisfaction in having an ancestry, but you will never satisfy your restless longing in these ways. The cry of your heart, the clamant hunger to be possessed and to belong, can be satisfied only by God through Jesus Christ coming into your life.

The final distinction of the burnt offering is given in chapter 6. In verses 12 and 13 we are told that the fire on the altar must be kept burning constantly and must never be allowed to go out. Every morning and evening, the priests were to offer the burnt offering; the fire would consume the wood and the meat all through the day and all through the night and thus the fire of the burnt offering never went out. This symbolized the truth that our basic identity before God is the fact upon which all the rest of life must rest. It must never be forgotten. If you start there, you have a basis upon which all the other relationships of life can be worked out. That is the burnt offering—the need to belong.

In chapter 2 it is the cereal offering which is brought before us. This is otherwise known as the meal offering, or in the King James Version, the "meat offering," from the Old English use of the word meat as meaning food. It is the one offering which has no meat in it, for it consists of grains, or loaves of bread, sometimes even simply flour, offered before the Lord. It is obvious that the essence of this offering was that it was bread; it was food, the staff of life. This is the key to the meal offering. Since it is bloodless it does not symbolize a death but rather a life, and the reason for all this becomes apparent when we remember that in the New Testament Jesus stood before the people and said to them, "I am the bread of life. . . . I am the living bread that came down out of heaven; if anyone eats of this bread he shall live forever" (John 6:48,51).

All this should indicate to us that the gospel consists not only of the death of Jesus but also of His life, made available to us. The really good news is that Jesus Christ died *for* you in order that He might live *in* you. The fine flour beautifully symbolized the perfection of humanity in Jesus. He was without coarseness or granularity or any roughness at all. So, if we permit Him to live in us, all that we do will also be balanced and without coarseness.

As we move through chapter 2 we note there are three things which always had to be included in the meal offering, and two things which never could be included. It is important to heed these. The three things always included were *oil, frankincense* and *salt*. The oil, which always typifies the Holy Spirit, was both mingled with the fine flour and poured on top of it. Thus it speaks of the indwelling Spirit who mingles with our humanity and also of the anointing of the Spirit which is to empower us. The second element to be always included was frankincense. This is said to be a delight to God and speaks of our praise and thanksgiving, which pleases Him. The third element is salt, which is a preservative. It speaks of a life which reaches out to touch others with good effect. It is our righteous influence. "Every grain offering," God said, "you shall season with salt."

There are two things, found in verse 11, which were to be excluded from the offering. There was to be no *leaven* nor any *honey*. First, leaven is yeast and is always a type of sin, because it has the power to puff up. By this God is saying, "When you come to offer your humanity to me there must be no ego in it: do not do this for your own glory." As He says elsewhere, "No man should boast before God" (1 Cor. 1:29).

Second, there must be no honey. Honey is natural sweetness; there are people, even non-Christian people, who have a natural, even temper and disposition about them. They are naturally sweet. But God refuses to accept this, for the only sweetness He will accept is the imparted sweetness of Jesus Christ in you.

It is significant, too, that the meal offering is listed next to the burnt offering. The practice among the Israelites was usually to offer the two together. This is very instructive since the burnt offering indicates God reaching out to man and saying, "You are mine." Therefore, this requires a response from man. God has reached out to us and we need to reach back to Him. That is what the meal offering signifies; we must come to Him and say, "Lord, here I am, here is my redeemed humanity with its oil and its frankincense and its salt, but with no leaven and with no honey. I want to be yours; I give myself to you." When that happens, you have offered the meal offering unto the Father just as the Son of God in the beauty of His life constantly offered His humanity, through the Holy Spirit and without spot or blemish, unto God.

After the burnt offering—representing our need to be loved—and the meal offering—representing our need to respond to God's love—*then comes the peace offering*, found in chapters 3 and 7. This does not refer to the peace of forgiveness. That will come in the sin and trespass offerings. It is not peace *with* God which is in view, it is the peace *of* God which this sacrifice depicts—the sense of calmness, of serenity, of the untroubled heart which was so continually manifest in Jesus. It is of this He speaks when He says, "Peace I leave with you; My peace I give to you" (John 14:27). Man is not made to function out of tension, pressure, restlessness, or continual anxiety. He is made to live and act out of a sense of peace and it is how this peace can come to us that this sacrifice speaks.

There are four distinctives about the peace offering which mark it as different from the others.

The first distinctive is that the offering can be either a male or a female. It could be from the herd or the flock, and the sex was not important. This indicates that in the peace offering we are not dealing with man in his generic relationships, but in his present condition, his existential relationship, the way he actually is. There it does not make any difference whether you are a leader or a follower; whether you are in a position of authority or not—what you need is peace in any case. That is the point.

The second distinctive mark is that all the fat of the peace offering was to be consumed upon the altar. This is repeated several times and in the seventh chapter it is developed even further. The striking sentence is, "all fat is the Lord's" (Lev. 3:16). In the Scriptures, fat is everywhere used as a symbol of the richness of life. Even today we think of fat meat as rich meat, and that is what this symbol portrays. Richness belongs to God, and as these Hebrews were told to take the fat and carefully remove it, especially the interior fat on the inner organs of the body, they were being taught that all the inner richness of life—everything that makes a person strong and delighted within—is from God, belongs to Him, and comes only from Him.

There is a third characteristic of the peace offering (7:28-34) which is extremely important. Only two portions of the peace offering animal were to be eaten; the breast and the right thigh. But before they were eaten, they were offered to the Lord. They were not burned upon the altar, for that would have ruined them as food for the priests. They were merely waved up and down before the Lord. The thigh, perhaps heavier than the breast, was heaved up and down before the Lord, rather than waved. This was a symbolic gesture that these portions were related to God. And then the priests were to feed on them.

Hidden in these symbols is the secret of how to have peace in the midst of trouble. The breast is always a symbol of affection and love; the thigh is the symbol of power and strength. Dependence upon the affection and the strength of Jesus Christ is the way to solve our problems and live in peace. His love is to steady us and remind us of His concern about us. His strength is to encourage us that He not only knows what to do but is able to do it. As Paul will say in Ephesians 2:14, "He Himself is our peace."

There is one final characteristic of the peace offering (7:15-18). We are told that an offerer could eat the flesh of the offering on the day he offered it if it was an offering of thanksgiving for some particular thing. Or if it was just a general expression of gratitude toward God, some of it could be saved for the second day. But under no circumstances were they ever to eat of the flesh of the peace offering on the third day—it must be burned with fire. What does this mean? It is a very beautiful way of saying that we must not rely upon the feeling of peace, but only upon the One who is its source. We cannot live continually on the feeling of peace that comes to us when we trust God. It must be renewed day by day.

In the sin offering we come to the way God deals with the problem of guilt. Having offered to mankind both love and peace, He now begins to deal with the problem of the alienation which prevents man from receiving God's grace.

The first distinctive of the sin offering is that it provided for both public and private sin. When the sin was that of a group or a public individual representing a group, then the offering always had to be a male. When it was an individual sin, the animal was a female. Thus for a sinning priest a young bull without blemish was the offering. For the sin of the whole congregation it was likewise a young bull (Lev. 8:14). But in the case of a ruler or king, it was a male goat and for the common people, a female animal without blemish. Thus distinction is made between those in authority and the individual acting on his own.

There were further provisions for those who could not afford an animal, for they were permitted to bring either two turtledoves, or, if they could not afford those, a handful of fine flour. In the latter case they were to put no oil or frankincense on it. For oil was the symbol of the Spirit-filled life and frankincense the symbol of the heart dedicated fully to God, which anyone guilty of sin was not able to claim until the sin offering had effected his restoration.

The second distinction of the sin offering is that it was frequently offered when the individual had sinned unknowingly. Thus this offering deals not so much with the act of evil but with the nature which prompts such acts. Another element of distinction in the sin offering concerns what was done with the blood of the animal. In the case of the sinning priest, blood was sprinkled seven times before the Lord, and put on the horns of the altar of incense which stood in front of the veil before the holy of holies, that is, right in the very presence of God. The same thing was required if the whole congregation sinned, but in the cases of the offerings for a ruler or for an individual the blood was put on the horn of the brazen altar which was in the outer court (Lev. 8:15). Clearly a special emphasis is being placed upon the blood as displayed before the presence of God. Only when the offering individual sees that

God looks not at his sin, but at the blood shed for it, is there a release from the sense of guilt.

A final distinction is made in the handling of the fat and meat of the offering. The inward organs and their fat were to be offered to God, as in the peace offerings, but the entire rest of the animal is to be taken outside the camp and there it was to be burned (Lev. 8:14-17). Here is a remarkable symbol which says that all the inward life of the believer, redeemed by blood, is now acceptable to God but the outer life—the body—is still unredeemed. In the book of Hebrews we are told that Jesus fulfilled this Himself when He went "outside the camp" (Heb. 13:11) of the city of Jerusalem to be crucified, and believers are likewise exhorted to "go out to Him outside the camp, bearing His reproach" (Heb. 13:13). Thus, though our inner nature is now changed and acceptable to God, nevertheless we are still living in the world. We must bear its reproach and suffer its rejection, just as Jesus did.

The sin offering dealt with the nature which causes us to sin, but in *the trespass offering we are dealing with the actual acts of evil we commit toward one another*, including not only acts of commission but those of omission as well. The unique characteristic of the trespass offering was that it required restitution. It was necessary to right the wrong which had been done as far as it could be corrected.

There were five different categories of sin covered by this offering. Three of these categories are grouped together by virtue of their type of sacrifice. The first was what we might call acts of guilty silence—to see a crime committed and to keep silent about it was a trespass (Lev. 5:1); the second category involved defilement from contact with unclean things—these touch upon matters which we now would regard as ecological violations, threatening a whole society (Lev. 5:2,3); a third category dealt with rash oaths or vows (Lev. 5:4). This was evil because in attempting the impossible the individual was pretending to be God and not man. Nothing has done more to wreak havoc among mankind than man's arrogant pretension to control the forces of nature.

For all three of these categories the sacrifice to be offered was the same. It was to be a female lamb or goat, thus indicating that we are dealing with man in his weakness and submission to the laws of nature. As with the sin offering, provision was made for the poor to bring substitutes if they could not afford an animal (5:7). But the one inflexible requirement was that the individual must admit the offense (5:5). There could be no forgiveness without that.

Two other classes of trespass sins are brought before us. The first category was that of religious offense, something done with "the Lord's holy things" (5:15). Though the sin was an "unintentional" sin (vv. 15, 17), nevertheless the individual is required to offer a trespass offering and to make restitution up to the value of the offering plus a fifth added to it (v. 16). Thus even something done with utter conviction at the time that it was the right thing, when discovered to be wrong, was to require sacrifice and restitution.

The last category of sin involved cheating, robbing or defrauding a neighbor, or any form of dishonesty such as removing someone else's property or reputation (6:1-3). Such a broken relationship must be restored and restitution made. This is surely what Jesus refers to when He says: "If therefore you are presenting your offering at the altar, and there remember that your brother has something against you, leave your offering there before the altar, and go your way, first be reconciled to your brother, and then come and present your offering" (Matt. 5:23,24). Clearly the trespass offering is given for the healing of all broken relationships and to give the offender a clear conscience before God and man.

How clearly these five offerings have shown the provision made in Christ for our human need of love, of the joy of response, of peace, of forgiveness before God and of right relationships with our fellowman.

Need for Priesthood

From chapters 8-10 we will see that the second element required for an adequate walk and worship before God is that of a priesthood. The priests were in a sense the psychiatrists of the Old Testament. They were the ones to whom people came when they had emotional problems. Priests were skilled in handling problems of guilt and fear, anxiety and hostility, and all the traumas and neuroses and psychoses which arose out of these. In the Old Testament the priesthood consisted of Aaron and his descendants; all the sons of Levi. That is where Leviticus got its name.

We have in these chapters the historical account of the actual consecration of the priests and the Tabernacle, and the beginning of worship within the sacred building. The entire congregation of Israel, some two million strong, were assembled in solemn convocation to witness the stirring ceremonies. Aaron's first act as high priest was to bring a sin offering and burnt offering for himself, and then the acts of the priests on behalf of the people are recorded. They began with the sin offering, then the burnt offering, then the meal offering, and finally the peace offering, indicating the proper procedure in approaching the living God. Then Moses (the prophet) and Aaron (the priest) came out of the Tabernacle and blessed the people and the glory of the Lord appeared to them all. The waiting throngs were stunned by the sudden appearance of fire from the Lord which consumed the offerings, and when the people saw it they shouted and fell on their faces (Lev. 9:24).

Following this impressive moment we have the account of the two sons of Aaron, Nadab and Abihu who offered strange fire before the Lord (10:1). It was evidently a form of incense other than the prescribed frankincense. For this they were destroyed by a supernatural fire. But the charge that followed, to abstain from strong drink, suggests the possibility that Nadab and Abihu had acted wrongly because of excessive use of wine. The whole account helps us see that priesthood is a serious matter involving both privilege and responsibility. We must always bear in mind, in reading these accounts, that there is no special priesthood today. All believers in the Body of Christ are made priests one to another (see 1 Pet. 2:5). Thus in the church, the Body of Christ, we are all to minister to one another, bearing each other's burdens, rebuking and reproving one another, and doing all in the recognition that One is our Master and we all are brothers.

Need for Standard

The third element of human need revealed in this first section of Leviticus is the revelation of a standard by which men may tell the difference between true and false, the phony and real, the helpful and the hurtful.

In this chapter appears various dietary laws and sanitary practices which were necessary to preserve Israel from diseases and epidemics rife in the nations around them. An excellent book available today, called *None of These Diseases* by Dr. S.I. McMillen, shows in a very charming way how many of the illnesses and ailments of our present life could be avoided if we simply follow some of these common sense regulations which God taught His people in the Old Testament.

But not all the regulations were for health reasons. There was nothing wrong with many of the animals that were prohibited to these Israelites as food. They were prohibited only to teach a symbolic lesson. There were four spheres in which food could be taken.

There were the animals which walked about on the earth, the natural food of man. Among these they were to eat only those which both chewed the cud and split the hoof. Surely this pictures for us the spiritual food upon which believers are to feed, the Word of God.

The first requirement is that we must meditate, which is pictured by the chewing of the cud.

The dividing of the hoof pictures the principle of discrimination, the need to distinguish between that which is from above and that which is from below. It means to take note of the fact that the Bible reports the lies of Satan and the confused thinking of man, as well as the revelation of the mind of God.

The Israelites were also to take food from the sea, which is used throughout Scripture as a symbol of the world, of society. From this area the proper food was to be distinguished by the possession of both fins and scales. Since fins are for progress and scales are for protection, this symbolizes our need to have both the capacity to penetrate a subject and yet to protect ourselves from any wrongful effect. We need both to understand and to discriminate, when feeding upon the knowledge of the world and its ways.

The third sphere from which food could come was the heavens. There all birds who fed upon flesh, all carrion eaters, and those that are omnivorous (that is, eat anything and everything), were forbidden. Also the winged insects were largely forbidden except those which leap upon the earth, as the locust, the grasshopper, and the cricket. Since the heavens are clearly the realm of the spirit we are dealing here with spiritual knowledge, especially in the realm of religion. We are clearly warned to reject all that is related to the flesh, that which is carnal in nature, arising out of the principle of self-sufficiency. Then we are to reject spiritual knowledge which is eclectic, that is, gathering ideas from all sources with an attempt to blend everything together. Next, those insects which crawl and fly, but are not able to leap upon the earth, were to be rejected. Thus ideas which accurately tie man's earthly life to his relationship with God may be acceptable, but we are to be careful in this area.

Finally, there was a sphere from which all food was to be rejected. Those creatures which were in constant contact with the earth, whatever swarms upon the earth, goes upon its belly or has many feet, are all to be rejected. This immediately suggests the story of the Fall in the Garden of Eden and the curse which came upon the serpent in that he was to crawl on his belly for the rest of his life. This is clearly then, knowledge based on satanic philosophy. It is wholly of the earth, relating only to this present life—its standards, its values, its pride and its glory. We are not to feed upon these or accept them as principles on which to live.

Chapter 12 deals with congenital depravity, reminding us that the race is sinful and that every child is therefore born in sin. Women who gave birth could be returned to their privilege of worship only by the presentation of sin and burnt offerings. These kept fresh in mind a sense of sin, but also the promise of restoration through expiation and cleansing.

Chapters 13 and 14 deal wholly with the subject of leprosy. The term not only includes a number of skin diseases, but even types of mold and fungi appearing on garments and in houses. Leprosy in garments was symbolic of relationships with others, and the possibility of these relationships becoming infected through destructive practices or habits. The cleansing of a leper involved the death of a bird and the release of a living bird, picturing both the death and the resurrection of Christ. This step was followed by the personal cleansing of the applicant and then, on the eighth day, he was to bring first a trespass offering, then a sin offering, then a burnt offering, and finally, a meal offering.

Finally, the fifteenth chapter of Leviticus relates to sexual pollutions associated with various secretions and issues. Some of these were normal and others were unnatural. It all is to remind us of the pollution of our nature at its very fountainhead, and the perpetual necessity for cleansing.

Need for Atonement

The great Day of Atonement, described in chapter 16, closes the first half of the book of Leviticus and details the provision God has made for dealing with all sin in His people, whether known or unknown. It was the one day of the year when the high priest would actually enter the holy of holies, dressed not in his garments of beauty and glory but in simple white linen undergarments, which spoke of humility and weakness. There he offered incense for himself, the blood of a bull for his priestly household and, finally, the blood of a goat as a sin offering for the people.

Upon the head of a second living goat all the sins of the people were confessed and symbolically placed, and the goat was led away into the wilderness. It is specifically stated that he was sent to "Azazel" which is one of the names for Satan. This pictures the act of faith of a believer in returning sin to its author, and recognizing the fact that he has no ground upon which to bring further accusation against those whom the Lord has justified.

MAN'S PERFORMANCE

Chapters 17-27 form the second section of this book and describe the performance which is possible on the basis of the provision God has made. Notice carefully the order: God never mentions performance until He has fully revealed His provision. He does not speak about behavior until He has made clear the power by which we are to act.

In this section there are also four elements set forth.

Basis for Wholeness

First, there is a need to understand the basis for wholeness; that basis is blood. Many are offended by the amount of blood involved in the Old Testament sacrifices, but by this means God is impressing us with a fundamental fact. He is telling us that the basis for wholeness (holiness) is a life given up, that we can never be whole on the basis of our natural life. We must have a new kind of life and to have it we must give up the old. Often the problem of the Christian life is that we keep trying to hang on to the old way of life and refuse to accept the new. For this reason the Israelites were forbidden to eat blood but must remember that it is the symbol of life and the constant reminder of the need for atonement.

Standards for Purity

The second element of this section is a series of practical guidelines for acting in love amid all the relationships of life. The book proceeds to give standards for purity, first in the family, and especially with regard to sexual morals: incest, marriage of close relatives, adultery, homosexuality and bestiality, along with the terrible practice of the Canaanites, that of child sacrifice.

There follows a section of general ethical prescriptions which God, as it were, signs His own name 14 times. This is intended not only to indicate authority but also to suggest resource. Here the various regulations are summed up in the admonition of 19:18: "You shall love your neighbor as yourself: I am the Lord."

To enforce the standards for purity, Leviticus gives certain prescribed punishment. The death penalty is required for child sacrifice, consulting with spirits, cursing parents, for adultery and homosexuality, and for intercourse with animals. We must understand that in Christ, though these penalties are mitigated, and opportunity is given for repentance and forgiveness, nevertheless the deeds are as wrong today as they were in Old Testament times.

The final category of standards concerns those for the priesthood. The priest must avoid all personal defilement, especially keeping himself from all contact with the dead. In his marriage he must not impair his ministry, nor could he serve if he had physical defects in his own body. These matters, of course, have symbolic application to the universal priesthood of today.

Enjoyment of God

The third element in this last section is the enjoyment of the presence and power of God Himself. Here we learn the meaning of the worship of Israel, and deadly peril of blasphemy, and, in chapter 25, the provision for the compassionate distribution of wealth through the institution of the sabbatical year and the year of jubilee.

The feasts of Israel were not mere holidays, to be observed on the nearest Monday in order to provide for a long weekend. Each was a symbolic occasion designed to teach a truth which God wants to impart to His people that is fundamental to human happiness. In their arrangement they constitute an outline of history.

First, the Sabbath is reiterated as indicating that rest is at the heart of everything God requires. The indispensable secret of our humanity is to learn how to operate out of rest. It is activity, growing out of dependence upon the work of Another, with the realization that the responsibility to achieve lies with Him.

The first of the set feasts was the Passover, occurring in the spring of the year, on the fourteenth day of the first month. It was God's graphic way of teaching that His work of redemption must rest upon the death of another on our behalf. The New Testament calls it justification.

Linked with the Passover was the feast of unleavened bread, which followed immediately. Two Sabbaths were always involved in this, including the weekly Sabbath. Its central feature was the exclusion of all leaven. This pictures the cleansing of life which must follow the act of justification.

Associated also with the Passover and the feast of unleavened bread was the feast of first fruits, which came on the morrow after the Sabbath. This would place it on a Sunday and therefore it was a fitting anticipation of the resurrection of Christ, the "first fruits from the dead."

Counting 50 days from the feast of first fruits there came what was called the feast of weeks. In the New Testament this is called Pentecost. It was characterized by two loaves of bread, baked with leaven, which were waved before the Lord. Thus it typifies the church, made of two bodies, Jew and Gentile. Both are sinners needing redemption but joined together into one body, the church.

On the first day of the seventh month came the feast of trumpets. This followed the long summer in which no feast was held. Its central feature was the loud blast of trumpets. Prophetically, this anticipates the prediction of Jesus that He will return "coming on the clouds of the sky with power and great glory. And He will send forth His angels with a great trumpet and they will gather together His elect from the four winds, from one end of the sky to the other" (Matt. 24:30,31).

This was followed by the great Day of Atonement, on the tenth day of the seventh month. It was characterized as a time of affliction of spirit and of mourning over the wasted opportunities of life. It will find fulfillment when, after long centuries of unbelief, Israel "will look on Me whom they have pierced; and they will mourn for Him, as one mourns for an only son" (Zech. 12:10).

Finally, the last feast was the Feast of Tabernacles, also called the feast of ingathering, for it marked the end of the agricultural year. It pictures time when, after Israel's restoration to their Lord and God, they will experience a lifting of the curse from nature and the blessing of the earth so that the desert shall blossom like the rose. It is the time of Messiah's kingdom, when all nations shall feast in joy before Him.

In the opening part of chapter 24 we have a marvelous description of the functions which went on in the holy place of the Tabernacle. It begins with the candelabra, fueled by oil brought by the people. As light is always the symbol of truth, this becomes a picture of truth made known to the mind of man by the Holy Spirit. The table of showbread was to be spread every Sabbath day with a freshly baked series of 12 loaves of bread, with frankincense spread beside them. The 12 loaves, made of unleavened fine flour, depicts the commonality of life within the family of God.

The frankincense, as we have seen, was to be burned on the altar of incense, the third piece of furniture in the holy place. This represents the obedient heart, responding to the beauty of God, and offering praise and thanksgiving unto Him.

The closing incident of chapter 24, concerning the young man of mixed parentage who blasphemed the name of God, is doubtless inserted to indicate that which threatens the intimate relationship of God's people with Himself. The subsequent death of the young man highlights the seriousness of such violation.

This brings us to the sabbatical year. Not only was one day out of seven a day of rest, but every seventh year Israel was to let the land rest for a year. They were not to sow crops or even to prune vineyards but to let the trees and vines grow without hindrance. This periodic rest of the land is an important principle of horticulture. Symbolically, it points to a recognition of dependence upon God's ability to bring fruitfulness (1) in social life, (2) interpersonal relationships, and (3) even in governmental matters.

With this is linked the Year of Jubilee, which came every fiftieth year, as an intensification of the sabbatical year. Characteristic of the Year of Jubilee was the proclamation of liberty to all the inhabitants of the land. The mark of liberty is to regain a lost inheritance and to have broken relationships restored. There is no record that Israel ever actually experienced the Year of Jubilee. In all their history they never trusted God enough to try it out to see what He would do and so they never saw God's full supply. This becomes the reason, ultimately, for the 70 years of captivity in Babylon, for in the 490 years of their history God had been counting up the years, and at the end of that time God sent the people off to Babylon that the land might have its rest.

Preserved in Righteousness

The final section of the chapter consists of the necessity to give the poor a chance to recover from their poverty and restates the fact that no Israelite was to be a slave. The final lesson is summarized in the great statement "the life of the land is preserved in righteousness."

As the book draws to a close, the divine Voice recalls the people to two of the Ten Commandments: the warning against idolatry and the call to keep the Sabbath (26:1,2). In a passage of infinite beauty and light God promises six blessings upon the people if they would walk in faithfulness before Him, utilizing the provisions for cleansing which He had instituted. The first promise is for fruitfulness (v. 4); the second, for full supply (v. 5); the third, for security (vv. 6-8); the fourth, for increase (v. 9); the fifth, the fellowship of the living God (v. 12); and sixth, the promise to make the people "walk erect" as men and women ought to walk and live (v. 13).

But, in anticipation of Israel's actual future, God moves on to set forth the cursings which will follow failure to walk in the divine ways. These punishments would include: disease, conflict, drought, wild beasts, invasion, and break-up of family life, and finally, captivity. All of this now stands written in history, but the wonderful thing is that through it all God has a redemptive, constructive goal toward which He aims. If there is repentance and return, there is also the promise of recovery and restoration.

This is the story of the inflexibility of love and the ruthlessness of grace. It is an inevitable rule of life that if you reject light then you must endure darkness; if you will not receive the positive then you must experience the negative; if you will not go in then you must stay out—until the time comes when you are ready to go in. There are no other choices. Thus the last element dealt with in this book is the awareness of the issues at stake and the decision that is expected of us.

The final page of the book deals with the matter of vows. Vows are voluntary obligations which are promised to God, usually on the ground of some blessing from Him. They include here, vows concerning persons, animals, and objects. The point is that it is not necessary to make vows but if they are made they must be observed. If for any reason the one making a vow desires to be set free from it, he must pay its full value, plus something more, according to the appraisal of the priest. Doubtless God uses such vows to draw us out and to help us grow in the discipline of grace. It is significant that the book which calls us preeminently to worship closes with regulations on how to handle the voluntary commitments of our awakened hearts.

CHAPTER FIVE

The Incomplete Life

NUMBERS

Numbers takes its title from the census with which it begins and that with which it ends. It opens in the wilderness of Sinai, in the second year after the Israelites had left Egypt, and closes at the edge of the Promised Land, 40 years later. In between is a long and sad record of the failure of Israel to believe in God's provision and power during the wanderings in the wilderness.

Numbers is a dramatic setting for what is perhaps the hardest lesson a Christian must learn—to trust God instead of his own reason. The book forms a commentary on two verses from the Proverbs. Proverbs 3:5 states, "Trust in the Lord with all your heart, and do not lean on your own understanding." That is the truth God had vividly taught His people in the book of Leviticus. But another verse in Proverbs describes the way the people actually responded. Proverbs 14:12 says, "There is a way which seems right to a man, but its end is the way of death." Numbers is the record of the discipline of God in the life of those whom He deeply loves and continually cares for, but who stubbornly resist the way of spiritual progress and thus delay their experience of victory and the joy of fellowship with a living God.

The book easily falls into three divisions. The first 10 chapters summarize God's ample provision for Israel's guidance and warfare. The major part of the book, from chapters 11 through 21, is a description of the continual murmuring and rebelling of the people. The latter part, from chapters 22 through 36, is a remarkable record of the protection of Israel despite their failure.

GOD' PROVISION

The book opens with the divine command to number, from the 12 tribes, the men of war from 20 years old and upward and gives us a census of the fighting men of the nation. The total amounted to 603,550 (Num. 1:46). The Levites were omitted as being dedicated to the service of the Tabernacle. So their place was made up by dividing the tribe of Joseph into two tribes, named for Joseph's sons, Ephraim and Manasseh. It is instructive that only those who had a clear pedigree could go forth to war. The lesson for the Christian is clear: only those who are certain they belong to the family of God can effectually do battle in the spiritual warfare to which we are called.

The camp is then set in order, with three tribes placed at each of the four points of the compass (chap. 2). The Levites gathered around the Tabernacle, which is clearly to be the center of everything in the national life. Every man had his own appointed place in the great army of Israel, just as the apostle Paul reminds us that each member of the Body of Christ is placed according to the mind and will of God.

In place of the firstborn of every family, whom God had claimed for Himself, the entire tribe of Levi is substituted. There were 22,000 acceptable Levites. But since there were 22,273 firstborn sons, for the extra 273 firstborn sons above the number of Levites, God accepted redemption money which went to maintain Aaron and his family (Num. 3:39-43). Though the Lord Jesus, centuries later, was not of the tribe of Levi He was a firstborn and so, according to the original provision, He was rightly a priest.

Each of the families of Levi is then assigned its special

role in the work of caring for the Tabernacle (chap. 4). The family of Kohath was responsible to carry the holy furniture. The curtains and the tents were given into the care of the Gershonites, and the foundations of the Tabernacle were committed to the Merarites. The special care given to the symbols of divine relationship suggests how important are the divine provisions for maintaining a strong spiritual life.

Further arrangements were made for maintaining the purity of the camp (chap. 5), even to the point of settling marriage difficulties arising out of jealousy and suspicion.

The restrictions on those who took the voluntary vow of a Nazirite are given (chap. 6), and have particular interest for us since three of the best known biblical characters—Samson, Samuel and John the Baptist— seemed to be such from birth. They were to refrain from the use of alcohol in any form, from the cutting of their hair or beard, and from contact with dead bodies. The Nazirite vows were taken as an act of consecration to some special service to God. These vows are somewhat similar to the vow of fasting in the case of present-day believers. In this special connection, the well-known threefold benediction is uttered (6:24-26).

Chapter 7, the longest in the book, deals with the voluntary offering of the princes of Israel for the mainte- nance of worship. It is an almost monotonous recording of each man's identical offering. But the fact that it was so carefully chronicled indicates the interest of God in the individual's gift. The Levites then appear again, are separated from the rest of the people, cleansed, sprinkled, shaven, and finally presented to the Lord by Aaron. There is a clear analogy in this to the presentation of present-day believers before the Father by our great High Priest the Lord Jesus. He said of Himself, "I sanctify myself, that these also may be sanctified" (John 17:19, *KJV*). Thus we were separated by His death that we should be holy before

God. "Whatever you do in word or deed, do all in the name of the Lord Jesus" (Col. 3:17).

Three things yet remain to be set in order before the people begin their march from Sinai.

First, the Passover was kept for the first time after leaving Egypt. Gracious provision was made for the observance of it again one month later for certain ones who were unclean on the first occasion. This indicates some liberty in the observance of the Passover and perhaps helps with the problem in the Gospel of John, where it appears our Lord ate the Passover the evening before the rest of the nation partook of it.

The second thing to be done was to make clear the provision for guidance in the cloud and fire which rested over the Tabernacle. The people were not responsible to determine either the time or the direction of their march but were required only to be obedient to the divine signs. Sometimes the clouds tarried for two days, or a month, or even longer, and then, however difficult and dangerous was the location, there was no option but to remain encamped. Surely this is one of the most difficult lessons for believers to learn. "Wait" is the hardest word to learn in the vocabulary of spiritual discipline.

The third requirement before the cloud lifted as to learn the signals of the trumpets when they sounded. These signals clearly understood, the cloud over the Tabernacle was taken up and the people began their journey through the wilderness of Sinai. The account closes with the remarkable call of Moses to invite the presence of the Lord, both at their setting out and their resting, thus indicating that everything is centered in the presence and government of God.

THE PEOPLE'S REBELLION

Chapters 11-25 record the people's discontent with God's provision and care. The first complaint seems to be against the hardship of their circumstances, but when the fire of the Lord burned among them and Moses interceded on their behalf, the fire abated (Num. 11:1-3).

The next complaint arose over the monotonous diet of manna. All they could think of were the melons, the cucumbers, the leeks, onions, and garlic of Egypt. They forgot the bondage and misery of Egypt and remembered only its delights. Moses, in his complaint before Jehovah, comes perilously close to joining their murmuring; but God's answer is to appoint elders to assist Moses in the oversight of the people (vv. 16, 17). To the people God then gave quails in such abundance that they ate them for an entire month—and then began to complain about the abundance of meat!

These rumblings of discontent were followed by a mutiny in Moses' own family (chap. 12). Aaron and Miriam became upset at Moses' marriage to a woman from Ethiopia. Though the Lord directly explained to Aaron and Miriam that He had called Moses to a specialized ministry, nevertheless their jealousy continued and Miriam was punished with leprosy. Upon the intercession of Moses, and after seven days wait, Miriam was restored, for God is ever ready to pardon when evil is confessed and forsaken.

By this time the thousands of Israelites have reached Kadesh-Barnea, at the edge of the Promised Land. At the divine command, 12 spies were chosen to enter the land and view both its resources and its dangers (13:1-20). In comparing this with the first chapter of Deuteronomy it appears that the command to send out the spies was in response to the people's determination to do this. As they decided, so they were commanded to do; just another example of God's accommodation to man's weakness.

After 40 days the men returned, bearing with them, in the grapes of Eshcol, visible evidence of the land's fertility. But there is both a majority and a minority report. Ten spies compared themselves with the giants and were disheartened: the two spies compared the giants with God and were greatly encouraged. Upon hearing the majority report the people virtually mutinied and took action to return to Egypt. Though Moses and Aaron fell on their faces before the people, and Joshua and Caleb pled with them to act in faith rather than fear, the people responded by picking up stones to stone them.

At this, Jehovah's patience was exhausted and He threatened to cut them off and raise up another people through Moses. Once again, as in Sinai, Moses interceded with the people, pleading the honor of God and the gloating of the Egyptians should they hear that Jehovah was unable to bring His people into the land of promise (14:13). Again it is God's grace, working through His human instrument, Moses, to plead the cause of mercy.

The people were pardoned, but were sentenced to 40 years of wandering in the wilderness and exclusion from the land of everyone over 20 years of age. In a response of remorse rather than repentance, the people promised to go up to the land and attempted to do so in spite of the warning that their day of opportunity was gone. A defeat at the hands of the Amalekites and Canaanites was the result.

In seeming preparation for their 40 years of wandering, certain sacrifices and laws are repeated (chap. 15), with the explanation that they would be fulfilled when the people came into the Promised Land. What follows illustrates that they were not clear whether the laws were to be enforced in the wilderness. One man was found gathering sticks on the Sabbath and was put in custody until they determined the mind of God toward him (15:32-34). The people were immediately instructed to put him to death, according to the law, and when this was done they were all instructed to wear tassels on the corners of their garment. Into each tassel was bound a cord of blue, a symbol of the deepest truth in their life: that they were under the direct government of heaven.

Despite the divine warnings, rebellion continued to spread throughout the camp, and three men, Korah, Dathan, and Abiram, openly challenged the authority of Moses and Aaron (chap. 16). Korah, as a Levite, resented the fact that the priesthood was confined to the family of Aaron; while Dathan and Abiram, both Reubenites, were contemptuous of Moses' authority, and resentful of the circumstances into which he had brought them. Korah led 250 of the elders of Israel in seeking to offer priestly incense before the Lord, but the cloud of glory appeared to the congregation and the Lord warned all the camp to stand back from the dwellings of Korah, Dathan, and Abiram. As these men and their families stood at the door of their tents, suddenly the ground opened beneath them and they were all swallowed alive. Furthermore, fire from the Lord consumed the 250 elders (16:35).

On the morrow, in unbelievable stubbornness, the people yet murmured against Moses and Aaron, accusing them of responsibility for the death of those who had been punished. Immediately a plague from the Lord broke out among them, and 14,700 died before Aaron filled his censer with fire and made atonement for the people (16:47). Upon that, the plague stopped. To make an end of the spirit of murmuring, Jehovah commanded each of the heads of tribes to write their name upon an almond rod, along with that of Aaron, and leave them in the tent of meeting overnight. On the morrow Aaron's rod had budded, blossomed, and bore fruit (17:8), thus indicating that those who have the right to bear authority are those who walk in the fullness and fruitfulness of resurrection life.

Further regulations were then given for the sanctity of the priesthood and the work of the Levites, and provision was made for their support from tithes and offerings. The tribe of Levi was to have no part of the division of the land when they came into Canaan, for the tithe was to be their inheritance. The priests, likewise, were to have no inheritance, for the Lord Himself was their portion. All this has clear application to the universal priesthood of today.

Special provision for cleansing from defilement was made in the ordinance of the red heifer (chap. 19). With careful ceremony a red heifer was to be sacrificed, according to minute instructions, and its ashes were to be carefully gathered, mixed with water, and used for certain cases of uncleanness, particularly those involved with touching dead bodies. When it is remembered that on the average 82 people per day must have died during the 40 years wilderness wanderings, it is easy to see how necessary it was to have some provision for cleansing from such defilement. Nothing could more graphically portray the contagiousness of sin. There is unavoidable defilement involved in contact with those "dead in trespasses and sins" around us, but for this reason we must perpetually seek the fresh cleansing of the precious blood of Christ. As the book of Hebrews puts it, "If . . . the ashes of a heifer . . . sanctify for the cleansing of the flesh, how much more will the blood of Christ . . . cleanse your conscience from dead works to serve the living God?" (Heb. 9:13,14).

We now reach the record of events at the close of the 40 years, when the people were again at Kadesh-Barnea. Here Miriam, the sister of Aaron and the half-sister of Moses, died and was buried (20:1). Also, once again the people were without water. When they complained, God graciously sent Moses and Aaron with the rod to a rock to speak to it that the people may have water. But though God was gracious, Moses was ungracious, and in his irritation and unbelief he struck the rock twice. For this violation of type Jehovah told both Moses and Aaron that they would not be able to lead the people into the land. But, nevertheless, he caused the rock to bring forth water for the people's needs (20:11).

The enmity of Edom (the descendants of Esau) is indicated by their truculent refusal to let Israel pass through their land along the King's Highway. In circumventing Edom they came to Mount Hor on the border of the land of Edom. There Aaron died (20:28), after transferring his priestly garments to his son Eleazar.

On leaving Kadesh, the king of Arad, a Canaanite leader, attacked Israel as they called upon the Lord for grace, and was defeated. Immediately after their victory comes the incident of the fiery serpents sent among the people because of their murmuring and impatience against Moses (21:6-9). This is the incident referred to by the Lord Jesus in His nighttime talk with Nicodemus (see John 3:14,15). He pointed out its significance in that just as Moses lifted up a bronze likeness of the creature causing death, so Jesus, made in the likeness of sinful flesh, was lifted up to give life to all who would believe.

Chapters 22 through 24 tell the story of Balaam, that strange Gentile prophet who seemed to have a genuine knowledge of Jehovah and yet whose heart was filled with avarice and lusting for material advantage. He was hired by Balak, the king of Moab, to curse Israel, since Moab was next on their route of conquest. Told by God that Israel was only to be blessed, Balaam sent the Moabite embassy home with his refusal. But once again Balak sent princes to him to offer a huge reward if he would come and curse Israel. Evidently, Jehovah, reading the true intent of Balaam's heart, permitted him to go, though He was displeased with his motives. On his way, Balaam was confronted by an angel of the Lord—with drawn sword. However, only Balaam's donkey saw the angel. Three times the donkey turned aside to avoid the avenging angel. But when Balaam, in anger, struck the donkey, the Lord opened the animal's mouth to rebuke the prophet for his cruelty.

Three times Balak sought to have Balaam curse Israel,

and three times the prophet was unable to utter cursings but instead, in lilting poetry, predicted the sovereign call of Israel, their protection by the divine hand, and their ultimate conquering of the peoples around. When the furious Balak refused to pay him Balaam uttered an oracle of doom against Moab, Edom, and Amalekites, and the Kenites. In his final oracle he seemed to see even to the days of David, predicting "a star shall come forth from Jacob, and a scepter shall rise from Israel, and shall crush through the forehead of Moab, and tear down all the sons of Sheth" (Num. 24:17). In its ultimate fulfillment this reaches unto the Messiah Himself.

Though the Old Testament does not clearly describe Balaam's evil, the New Testament makes clear that the subsequent sexual immorality of the men of Israel with the daughters of Moab, and their consequent idolatry, was an outcome of the teaching of Balaam. When an Israelite man brazenly brought a woman of Midian into his tent for sexual purposes, Phinehas, the son of Eleazar, jealous for the honor of God, thrust his spear through both man and woman and by that terrible punishment stayed the plague which had broken out (Num. 25:6-9).

GOD'S PROTECTION

Chapter 26 begins the third and last movement of the book. Here we have the account of the second census taken of the men of war and their families. Instructions were then given to Moses concerning the division of the land when they came into Canaan. Of the original number that left Egypt, only two men were permitted to enter. These were Caleb and Joshua, the men of faith, who saw beyond the giants to the living God (Num. 26:65).

An interesting incident is related concerning the five daughters of Zelophehad. Left fatherless, they petitioned and were granted an inheritance in the land of promise (27:1-11). Typically, it established the principle that in Christ there is neither male nor female.

At this point, Jehovah informed Moses that the time has come for him to die, and at Moses' request for a successor, God appointed Joshua, the son of Nun (27:18,19). Joshua would not inherit the full authority Moses exercised, but that he would discover the divine will through the high priest by use of the Urim.

Following this, God repeated the various offerings and sacrifices to be given at the great feast days of Israel, already outlined in the book of Leviticus. Certain exceptions were then made to the general rule concerning vows. The vow of an unmarried daughter, living with her father, may be nullified if her father chooses to do so on the day she makes the vow as may that of a married woman by her husband (30:1-16). It is clear, however, that the men are involved only as the heads of households, otherwise single women were under the same solemn obligation to keep their vows as were the men.

The concluding chapters of the book, from chapter 31 through 36, are given over to an account of a holy war led by Phinehas the priest, against the Midianites, during which Balaam, the false prophet, is also slain. Here also, the two tribes of Reuben and Gad and half the tribe of Manasseh insisted unwisely on settling on the east side of the Jordan rather than in the land of promise. They were permitted to do so only by agreeing to join their brethren in subduing their Canaanite enemies.

After reviewing the route taken by Israel from Egypt to the Jordan, and giving directions for the division of the land when the tribes enter it, Moses then assigned certain cities as residences for the Levites, six of which are especially designated as Cities of Refuge (35:10-15) for those who killed as the result of an accident or a sudden flare of temper.

Historically, the book of Numbers closes where the last chapter of Deuteronomy begins, giving us the account of the actual death of Moses. Numbers is the record of the failure of the people in their perpetual stubbornness and foolishness, yet it is also the story of the unwearying patience and continual faithfulness of God. Thus it encourages those of us who have often found failure in our own spiritual life. We have come to learn, as the New Testament declares, "If we are faithless, He remains faithful; for He cannot deny Himself" (2 Tim. 2:13).

DEUTERONOMY

Deuteronomy is the last of the five books by Moses. It is a pastime of scholars today, and a supposed mark of intelligence, to raise the question of whether or not Moses actually wrote these books. Some maintain that the Pentateuch (the first five books of the Bible) was put together by some unknown editor who went through ancient books and abstracted various parts, and to which Moses' name was added to give it status. This is called the documentary theory of the Pentateuch. Anyone who studies comparative religion in high school or college will probably be exposed to it. But it is a theory that has been carefully examined and proved false by both Christian and Jewish writers. As one authority put it, "If the five books of Moses were not written by him, they must have been written by somebody else named Moses."

The book of Deuteronomy is made up of three great sermons, delivered by Moses shortly before his death. These were given to Israel while they waited on the east side of the Jordan in the Arabah, and after they had been victorious over Sihon, the king of the Amorites, and Og, the king of Bashan. At this time the multitude of Israelites were made up of a new generation who were but children when their fathers had been given the Law from Mount

Sinai, and many of them were not yet even born at that time. Now they are about to enter the land of Canaan, and it is essential that they thoroughly understand their history before they make such a venture.

REVIEW OF THE JOURNEY

Chapters 1-4 contain the first message, in which Moses reviews the journey from the giving of the Law at Mount Sinai until the people reach their present location in the land of Moab, at the edge of the Jordan River.

Moses' first task was to recite to the people the wonderful love and care of God, who led them with a pillar of fire by night and the cloud by day, and guided them through the trackless, howling desert. He reminded them how God brought water from the rock to slake their thirst in a vast and waterless area; how He fed them with manna that did not fail; and delivered them from their enemies again and again.

In chapter 1 he traced the movement of the people from the giving of the Law at Sinai (also called Mount Horeb) to the refusal of the people to enter the land at Kadesh-Barnea. In chapter 2, he reviewed the second movement from Kadesh-Barnea to Heshbon, around the land of Edom, and through the wilderness of Moab to their encounter with Sihon, the king of Heshbon. Throughout this passage, Moses emphasized the continual deliverance of the people by the hand of God from their enemies, despite their unbelief.

Continuing his discourse, Moses reviewed the conquest of the Jordan Valley as far north as Mount Hermon, and the decision of Reuben and Gad to settle on the east side of the river. In a note of pathos, he recalled his own eager desire to enter into the land when the people do, but also the divine denial of this to him, though he was permitted to view the land from the top of Mount Pisgah. Moses closed the historic review, in chapter 4, with an exhortation to the people to remember the greatness of their God and to be obedient from their hearts. He warned also against the danger of idolatry, especially in the making of graven images. He reminded them of their surpassing privilege of relationship with the living God above all other nations around them. He concluded the message with setting aside three cities of refuge on the east of the Jordan for the protection of those who accidentally kill another.

SECOND GIVING OF THE LAW

The second message of Moses covers chapters 5-26. This begins with a fresh recital of the Ten Commandments as God gave them to Moses on Mount Sinai. It is from this that the book gets its name, for Deuteronomy means ''the second (giving of) law.'' That has more significance than merely the historical account of the law's recital for a second time as we shall see before we finish the book. It must be understood that Deuteronomy is not merely a recital of the journeys of Israel, but it is also a divine commentary upon the significance of those journeys and their events.

In connection with the giving of the Law, Moses reminded the people that at that time they had promised to hear and to do all that God said. To this God had responded ''Oh that they had such heart in them, that they would fear Me, and keep all My commandments always, that it may be well with them and with their sons forever'' (Deut. 5:29). Moses then proceeded to give them the famous Shemah or ''Hear, O Israel,'' which devout Jews have used for centuries to summarize the central feature of their faith—the uniqueness of their God. In connection with this is given the divine requirement to observe these words, to teach them diligently to their children by means of talking to them when they were sitting in the house, walking by the way, lying down, or rising up. This is a great lesson on pedagogy, suggesting the utilization of "teachable moments," when truth could be imparted much better than in formal classroom situations.

Moses then began to review the conditions they would find in the land and the blessings that will await them there. He especially warned them to beware of three perils: that of *prosperity*, of *adversity*, and of *neglect to teach* their children. In chapter 7, Moses dealt with the danger Israel would face in confronting the corrupt nations already in the land. However tempted they might be to show mercy to them, they were commanded to thoroughly eliminate the inhabitants of Canaan, that no vestige of their idolatries and depraved worship should remain to turn the people aside from their worship of Jehovah. They were reminded that they were chosen because the Lord had set His love upon them and that He, Himself, would be their strength in subjugating the nations around. Their own prosperity and good health would depend on the faithfulness by which they carried out these instructions. They need not fear the people for God Himself would cast them into great confusion until they were destroyed.

Chapter 8 recalled to the people the lessons God had taught them in the wilderness; how they had been humbled, and fed with the manna, so that they might know that "man does not live by bread alone, but man lives by everything that proceeds out of the mouth of the Lord" (8:3). These were familiar words to Jesus who used them to good effect against the tempter in the wilderness of Judea centuries later (see Matt. 4:4).

When the people have entered the land and are feasting upon its richness, they are to beware lest they begin to feel self-sufficient and to take credit in their own heart for all that God has given them. They must not say to themselves that it is because of their own righteousness that the Lord brought them in; they must remember that they are basically a stubborn people, and their history is one of a continual provoking of the Lord to wrath. Moses then recalled the awesome scene at Sinai, when, in the very face of the demonstration of the power and might of God, the people sinned by making the golden calf, and Moses must intercede for them for 40 days and nights. At that time he also made the second tablets of stone, and later placed them in the Ark of the Covenant where they were at the very moment he is speaking to the people.

In a passage of great beauty and power, Moses reminded the people that God is not asking of them anything but to love Him and to serve Him with all their heart and soul, keeping His commandments and statutes for their own benefit. The central emphasis of all is that "the Lord your God is the God of gods and the Lord of lords, the great, the mighty, and the awesome God" (Deut. 10:17). Yet His actions toward them are those of infinite tenderness and love. God is not asking them to love Him, apart from their awareness that He has first loved them and tenderly cared for them and watched over them, delivering them from their enemies, and disciplining them that they may be strong and whole as a people. As they enter the land, therefore, they are promised rain from heaven to water the earth, grass in the fields for their cattle, power in their warfare to drive out great nations before them until the whole of the land shall be their possession. To remind them of the essential in all this, they are annually to recite the blessings on Mount Gerizim and the cursings on Mount Ebal, which faces the site of Jacob's well.

Chapters 12 through 21 constitute a series of statutes and ordinances which are given to the people for their government within the land. They must first destroy all the places of worship of the nations then in the land, tearing down their altars and burning their Asherim (phallic symbols). These were clear indications of the foulness of the worship in the land at the time.

God would then indicate, in due season, one place within the land where they must bring their burnt offerings and sacrifice and there they were to rejoice before the Lord. This was not fulfilled until the days of David and Solomon when the Temple was built, though a temporary provision was made when the Ark was located at Shiloh.

Further instructions are given as to the foods they may eat, avoiding always the eating of blood. They are then told how to tell false prophets from true. Even though the false prophet may be a wonder-worker, if, despite all his apparent power, he should suggest that they go after other gods, they were to stone him. Even if close friends or relatives should seek to entice them to idolatry, they likewise must be put to death. Even if a whole city should apostatize and begin to serve other gods, the inhabitants of that city were to be put to the sword, for "you are the sons of the Lord your God" (Deut. 14:1).

Once again the dietary laws are restated, and the tithes are required for the support of the Levites. The sabbatical years are reiterated as the solution to inequities in economic life, and periodic readjustment of the means of wealth. The three great feasts of Passover, Unleavened Bread, and Tabernacles, are once again required as the three times in a year when all Hebrew males must appear before the Lord at the Tabernacle.

Provision is then made for the functioning of judges to decide cases where the law had not specifically spoken; also for the choosing of a king, who must not be a foreigner, nor multiply horses, or silver and gold, but must carefully walk by the statutes of the Law and keep his heart humble before the Lord his God.

In chapter 18, there is the great promise given that "the Lord your God will raise up for you a prophet like me from among you, from your countrymen, you shall listen to him" (v. 15). In some measure this great prophecy was fulfilled by all the true prophets who would rise later in

Israel, but in its ultimate it looks forward to the coming of Jesus and His Moses-like actions in beholding the face of God, and uttering His word to all the people. This is the way Peter understood it in Acts 3:22. It is Jesus who perfectly fulfills the Old Testament ideal of priest, prophet, and king.

Again, three cities of refuge were chosen, this time on the west side of the Jordan. Those who were guilty of deliberate murder could find no sanctuary in these cities, only those who killed accidentally were to flee to them to escape the avenger of blood. Ancient landmarks must not be removed, and truth between man and man must be maintained at all costs.

It should be remembered that the Israelites were being sent into the land not only to gain it for their own possession but also to act as the instrument of God in exterminating a foul and corrupt people. In view of the warfare this involved, they were charged to keep before them the vision of their God and His power, and to eliminate from their armies any whose hearts were occupied with other matters, or who were fainthearted and fearful. Terms of peace were to be offered to every city they attacked, and if they were accepted, the inhabitants were not killed but put to forced labor. If the terms of peace were refused, the city was to be decimated.

Chapters 22-26 gather up various regulations for the life of the people within the land. They concern lost or stolen property, prohibitions against the wearing of the opposite sex's clothing, regulations of sexual uncleanness and sanitation, usury, vows, and divorce. Provision was then made for the punishment of theft; but excessive punishment was strictly forbidden—anything which humiliated or made an individual appear vile in others' sight. It was likewise forbidden to muzzle an ox as it tread out the corn. This is given a special spiritual significance by the apostle Paul in 1 Corinthians 9:8-10. The law of the kinsman-redeemer for those left without an heir, was again enunciated, and all weights and measures were ordered to be kept strictly honest.

The second message then concludes with the instructions of Moses on how the people were to worship in the new land. They must bring the firstfruits and offer them to God, with acknowledgements of His provision and grace, and this was to be followed with gifts given to Levites, to strangers, the fatherless and to widows. Upon the conclusion of this second message, Moses gave detailed instructions as to the impressive ceremony which was to be carried out upon the twin mountains of Gerizim and Ebal within the land. The Ten Commandments were to be given permanent display by being written upon plaster-covered stone monuments, and each year the sons of Rachel and Leah were to recite the blessings upon Mount Gerizim, and the sons of Jacob's concubines were to recite the curses upon Mount Ebal. The curses are detailed in chapter 27, and the blessings summarized in the opening words of chapter 28.

REVELATION OF THE FUTURE

The third message of Moses, chapters 27-31, is a great revelation of the future of Israel, both in terms of the possibility of blessing or of cursing. Chapter 28 is one of the most amazing prophecies ever recorded. It is as fully complete and remarkable in its detail as any other prophecy in all of Scripture, for it predicts the entire history of the Jewish people, even to the point where they cease to be a nation and are scattered over the face of the earth.

First, there is the prediction of the Babylonian dispersion, subsequent to the unbelief and disobedience of the people. This occurred eventually under Nebuchadnezzar, the Chaldean. Then there follows a prediction of their ultimate return to the land and that after several centuries they would again fall into the terrible sin of rejecting the great Prophet whom God would send. A strange nation would come in from the west (the Romans) who would be a hard and cruel people. They would burn the cities of Israel, destroy the inhabitants and once again disperse them to the ends of the earth.

Israel would then wander for many centuries as a people without a land, but God would at last gather them again, and there would be a final restoration. Upon concluding his great prophecy, Moses reminded the people that on this day they stand before the Lord their God and though there is much about the divine government which they cannot fathom, nevertheless the things that had been revealed to them in their past are given that they may take heed to their present and talk faithfully before their God. In graphic and vivid terms he described to them what would result if they turned from the living God to the gods of the nations about them.

In his closing word, Moses seems to look far into the future and see the people dispersed in lands of captivity. There he reminded them that if they will return to the Lord with all their heart and soul, God would forgive their sin, restore their fortunes, and gather them again into the land.

At this point, Moses uttered the great words which the apostle Paul quoted centuries later in his Epistle to the Romans, and which reveal the reason why Deuteronomy is called "the second law." Moses said to the people, "This commandment which I command you today is not too difficult for you, nor is it out of reach" (Deut. 30:11). This speaks of the divine provision by which the demands of the law might be fully met. "It is not necessary," Moses continued, "to go up to heaven and bring it down or to go beyond the sea and bring it back" (see vv. 12,13); but as Moses put it very plainly, "the word is very near you; it is in your mouth and in your heart, so that you can do it" (see v. 14).

In Romans 10:5 Paul declares that "Moses writes that the man who practices the righteousness which is based on the law shall live by that righteousness." Here he quotes the words of Moses concerning the Law given at Sinai, and taken from the book of Exodus. Then in Romans 10:6-9 Paul quoted this very passage from Deuteronomy 30, indicating that it refers to Christ, "But the righteousness based on faith speaks thus, 'Do not say in your heart, "Who will ascend into heaven?" (that is, to bring Christ down), or "Who will descend into the abyss?" (that is, to bring Christ up from the dead).' But what does it say? 'The word is near you, in your mouth and in your heart'— that is, the word of faith which we are preaching, that if you confess with your mouth Jesus as Lord, and believe in your heart that God raised Him from the dead, you shall be saved" (Rom. 10:6-9).

In this quotation from Deuteronomy 30, Paul is declaring that it is not necessary to bring Christ down from heaven (the Incarnation), or to bring Him up again from the dead (Resurrection), for this has already been done. It is only necessary that the heart believe and the lips confess that Jesus is Lord and risen from the dead. Thus "the second law," which Paul calls "the law of the spirit of life in Christ Jesus," fulfills, by another principle, the righteousness which the law demands. It is possible, because of this emphasis in Deuteronomy, that the book became Jesus' favorite.

Both of these principles are clearly taught to the people of Israel by Moses. He reiterates constantly the just demands of God expressed in the Ten Commandments. That is the first law. But, equally, he reminds them again and again of the gracious provision through the sacrifices and offerings by which the life of a living Lord can be their personal possession, to enable them to live at the level that God requires. The word "in the mouth" and "in the heart" would enable them to do all that God demanded.

As a consequence, Moses concluded his great address by saying, "See, I have set before you today life and prosperity, and death and adversity" (Deut. 30:15). And with earnest words he pleads with them to choose life "in order that you may live, you and your descendants, by loving the Lord your God, by obeying His voice, and by holding fast to Him; for this is your life and the length of your days" (30:19,20).

In the final chapters, Moses summoned Joshua before him and charged him to be strong and of good courage. Then Jehovah told Moses that the time had come for him to sleep with his fathers, and that despite his faithful warnings, the people he had led would fulfill all his solemn predictions and that God would necessarily visit them with the punishments announced.

Moses was then commanded to write a song which would remain in the memory of the people long after Moses himself had departed. The song dealt with the great themes of God's everlasting covenant with Israel, His mercies to them, their failures and the penalties which followed, and the promise of final deliverance.

Then, before Moses' lonely death, he announced a benediction, similar in its predictive insight to the blessing of Jacob upon his sons in Genesis 49. The great lawgiver concluded his benediction by reminding the people that "the eternal God is a dwelling place, and underneath are the everlasting arms" (33:27).

The final chapter is undoubtedly added by another hand, for it recounts how Moses ascended Mount Nebo to the top of the peak of Pisgah, and there, with his eye not dim nor his natural force abated, Moses laid down and died and the Lord Himself buried him in an unknown place in the valley of Moab.

The next glimpse of this mighty leader in Scripture shows him on the Mount of Transfiguration, along with Elijah the prophet, speaking to the Lord Jesus about His death which would soon take place at Jerusalem.

Though the people immediately rallied around Joshua and gave to him the obedience which they had shown to Moses, they knew that they would never see a man like Moses again, whom the Lord would speak to face-to-face, and through him manifest great and terrible deeds. It was not until the Messiah Himself should appear that the record of Moses would ever be excelled.

CHAPTER SIX

The Way to Victory

JOSHUA

The time had come for the people of Israel to enter into the land of promise. All those who left Egypt some 40 years before had perished in the wilderness, except for Caleb and Joshua. A new generation had grown up in the wilderness journey. Moses had fully instructed them in the laws and the sacrifices before he died, and Joshua had assumed the task of leading the people into the land.

Moses, the great lawgiver, was not permitted to take the people into the fulfillment of promise; rather Joshua (whose Hebrew name is the equivalent of the Greek name, Jesus) is given that privilege. This is surely an anticipation of the New Testament truth that the law cannot fulfill the promises of God, but they are all available to us through our heavenly Commander, Jesus.

Nevertheless, Joshua was instructed in the use of the law as necessary for meditation and a guideline to obedience. But the strength by which it shall be fulfilled lies in the great word, ''Be strong and courageous! Do not tremble or be dismayed, for the Lord your God is with you wherever you go'' (Josh. 1:9).

VICTORY IS POSSIBLE

After reminding the tribes of Reuben, Gad and the half tribe of Manasseh of their promise to assist their brethren in the conquest of the land, Joshua sent out his spies to view the situation. These go out as he himself went out, 38 years before, in confidence and faith that God intended to give them the land. They were simply attempting to see how that deliverance will be brought about.

With boldness they entered into the city of Jericho and were hidden in the house of Rahab, the harlot, who informed them that the people had for 40 years been afraid of the Israelites, having heard of their miraculous deliverance at the Red Sea and their conquest of the two Amorite kings, Sihon and Og. The giants which Israel feared at Kadesh-Barnea had themselves been afraid of the people of Israel for the whole 40 years' wandering!

Rahab's personal confidence that the God of Israel was the Lord of all the earth led her to hide the two spies and aid in their subsequent escape from the city, after having them promise that when the city fell she and her household would be spared.

Forsake Unbelief

After the spies returned, Joshua ordered the people to assemble for the crossing of the Jordan. The Ark of the Covenant leading the way would show the people that a living God was among them as He opened a way through the Jordan, just as He had once opened a way through the Red Sea.

Twelve men were chosen, one from each tribe, to memorialize the occasion. As the feet of the priests touched the edge of the Jordan, the waters began to recede, having been cut off far upstream near the little city of Adam.

The priests bearing the Ark of the Covenant remained in the middle of the river until all the people passed through. Then a monument of 12 stones was erected in the middle of the river and another similar monument at the river's edge. These were to be a memorial for the children to see, that they might ask and receive an explanation from their parents.

As we seek the significance of this event in the Christian life, we must remember that just as the crossing of the Red Sea meant the willingness to forsake the world typified by Egypt, so the crossing of the Jordan indicates a willingness to enter into all the promises which God has given the believer in Jesus Christ. It acknowledges the choice to forsake the unbelief of the wilderness and to fully lay hold of all that God has made available.

Some have seen in the two memorial monuments the Christian ordinances of baptism and the Lord's Supper, and surely these are designed as memorials to remind us of the basis upon which all of God's mighty promises rest. They too need to be explained to children so that they understand their full import.

Depend on God

Four significant events are recorded in chapter 5. First, all the males of Israel were circumcised at Gilgal. The name means "rolling away," for here the Lord said Israel had "rolled away the reproach of Egypt" (Josh. 5:9). Evidently the nation had forsaken this ritual during the wilderness wanderings; thus the mark of difference between them and the pagan nations around them had disappeared. Before the land is conquered they must again be seen as the distinct people of God. The New Testament speaks of a "circumcision of the heart" (see Rom. 2:29) which is the counterpart to this Old Testament ritual, and indicates a heart that is ready to forsake all dependence on the natural life and rely upon the strength of God alone.

The second event in Gilgal was the celebration of the Passover for only the second time since leaving Egypt. Then the day after the Passover the provision of manna ceased entirely, the third event of this chapter, and the people began to subsist upon the natural produce of the land of Canaan. This corresponds to our spiritual feeding upon the full potential of the resources we have in Christ.

The fourth event of chapter 5 was Joshua's encounter with the commander of the hosts of the Lord. Clearly it was not up to Joshua to plan the strategy of this campaign of conquest, but God Himself would do so, just as today it is not the church's task to develop the strategy by which it can overcome the world, but it is to obey the Word of the Lord and to obey the pattern of the church's function as given in the New Testament.

Release Worldliness

Both the foolishness of the Jericho strategy, in the eyes of the watching world, and its mighty power to conquer are revealed in the subsequent actions of Israel. Upon reaching the city of Jericho with its massive walls, the people were instructed to march once around the city in silence while the priests sounded trumpets. Each day for six days this was Joshua's command. Then on the seventh day the people were told to encompass the city seven times and, when the priests blew a mighty blast of the trumpets, the people were to shout and the walls would fall down.

To this apparently foolish behavior the people had faith enough to consent. And on the seventh day, exactly as predicted, the mighty walls tumbled down at the shout of faith. Rahab and her family were spared according to the prearranged provision, but the city was sacked and the rest of the inhabitants were put to the sword. A curse, involving the death of the firstborn and youngest son of any who would rebuild the city, was pronounced by Joshua. The fulfillment of this curse some two hundred years later is recorded in 1 Kings 16:34.

This curse indicates the symbolic meaning of Jericho in the life of the present-day believer. The death of the firstborn son links it with the final judgment of God that brought the Israelites out of Egypt. Jericho, therefore, like Egypt, is a type of the world. Christians are not to covet or to claim as their own the things of the world, but are to hold them loosely and use them for the Lord's purposes. They are likewise not to fight the world directly, but by faith to maintain an attitude of heart separation from the world, and thus it will lose its allurement for the believer who will find it open to conquest through the testimony of faith.

Battle the Flesh

Chapters 7 and 8 give us the bittersweet story of Ai, the next city in the line of conquest. It was such a small city and looked so easy to overcome that only a few thousand were sent to capture it. They suffered, however, a serious defeat, and about 36 Israelites were killed. As Joshua inquired before the Lord the reason for this, God told him that the defeat resulted from an incomplete obedience within the camp of Israel: one man, Achan, of the tribe of Judah, had disobeyed the instructions concerning Jericho and had hidden in his tent some silver, a wedge of gold and a garment from Babylon.

This helps us understand the symbolic significance of Ai in our own lives. It is a picture of the flesh, the natural humanity within us, inherited from Adam, which also loves the things of the world, and yet it appears to us to be of little consequence and easily overcome.

When the sin of Achan was discovered, apparently by the casting of lots, the seemingly harsh but faithful judging of the people by stoning Achan to death made possible a renewed attack upon the city of Ai, this time by the strategy of ambush. The city fell and all the inhabitants were put to the sword. Thus it is evident that the conquest of our enemy, the flesh within, is accomplished by our willingness to accept the judgment of death upon it, to take up battle against it by the power of the Spirit, for "the desires of the flesh are against the Spirit, and the desires of the Spirit are against the flesh" (Gal. 5:16).

Since Ai was the gateway to the west, its defeat left the entire central portion of the land of promise open to the Israelites. Joshua's first act was to fulfill the command of Moses and to build an altar upon Mount Ebal. There, as the law had carefully provided, the blessings were read from Mount Gerizim and the cursing from Mount Ebal, that Israel (and us) should forever remember the blessings that will follow the putting aside of the flesh and the cursings which will inevitably appear if we fail to accept the judgment of the cross upon our natural life.

Resist the Devil

The cities of the west along the coastal plain from Gaza in the south to Lebanon in the north met together to form a league to stop the Israelites' conquest (Josh. 9:1). One of the cities that lay in the immediate path of Joshua and his armies was the city of Gibeon, near present-day Jerusalem. Afraid for their lives, the Gibeonites resorted to a ruse to trick the Israelites into making a treaty of peace with them, which Jehovah had strictly forbidden should be done with any of the inhabitants of the land.

When later, upon attacking Gibeon, Joshua learned of their deceit, the worst he could do to them was to make them hewers of wood and carriers of water.

The kings of the Canaanite cities to the south now determined to combine their armies for a united attack on Gibeon. This large city, thus attacked by their own allies, immediately called upon Joshua for defense, in line with the treaty of peace he had made with them. By a forced march from Gilgal, Joshua and his armies traveled by night and took the enemy armies by surprise, throwing them into a panic. It was on this great occasion that Joshua prayed and asked for the lengthening of the day that they might have needed time to accomplish the routing of the enemy. It is recorded that the sun stood still over Gibeon and the moon over the valley of Aijalon for almost the length of a day. Accompanying this, huge hailstones fell from the heavens, killing more of the allied armies than even the Israelites themselves killed with the sword.

This event has been ridiculed by the critics for centuries, but impressive evidence now has been discovered that the earth has in times past shifted on its axis, and such a shift would account for the phenomenon recorded in Joshua.

Symbolically, the account pictures the ability of Satan to use circumstances in such a way as to harass and frighten the Christian, but when such circumstances are met by the unyielding heart of faith, the very circumstances are turned to the benefit of the believer.

Obey the Living God

After the battle of Gibeon the conquest of the south was soon accomplished. The cities were taken one by one and the inhabitants slaughtered in obedience to the command of God to eliminate the cities of the Canaanites in their entirety. Then the kings in the northern part of Canaan banded together under the leadership of King Jabin of the fortified city of Hazor. Joshua met them in battle at the waters of Merom and another great victory was accomplished, including the taking of Hazor.

On the defeat of the northern kings, the entire land lay under the control of Israel. Jehovah's promise to Joshua had been fulfilled that "no man will be able to stand before him." Thus we see the three great enemies of the believer—the world, the flesh and the devil—are overcome by the simple means of faith and obedience to the Word of the living God.

This first section of the book of Joshua is clearly designed to encourage us to understand that a complete victory is possible over these three fearsome foes—the world, the flesh and the devil. And though there are temporary failures (as at Ai) and partial compromises (as with the Gibeonites), God will give us victory just as He conquered the great giants who frightened the Israelites at Kadesh-Barnea.

THE CONQUESTS

The second section of the book covers chapters 12 through 21, and primarily consists of a listing of the enemies who were subdued under Joshua's first attack, in the first seven years after Israel had entered the land. Then we learn how the land was apportioned bit by bit to the various tribes according to the casting of lots. This device permitted the decision to be according to the divine mind and not according to man's wisdom. Thus each tribe would know that the portion of land given to them was given by God's own choice. We are reminded today that the circumstances in which we find ourselves are not of our own choosing necessarily, but the hand of the Lord has brought us to the place where, for the present at least, we are to be.

Though the major portion of the land promised to Abraham was now under Israel's control, still along the fringes there were unoccupied territories and within the land itself pockets of resistance remained. When Joshua allotted each tribe its own territory by casting lots, he reminded them that they were individually responsible to claim the territory which rightly belonged to them. There would be battles involved, but they were to be assured that the ultimate victory would be secure, for God had given His word.

Scattered within this section largely devoted to the distribution of the land are isolated stories which constitute beautiful illustrations of personal faith. One is the story of Caleb, who at 85 years of age was still willing to claim the inheritance promised to him when he was yet in the wilderness with Moses. In accordance with his request, Caleb was allotted the city of Hebron and its provinces as a permanent inheritance. But in order to conquer it he must drive out the giants who dwelt there.

The names of three of these giants, sons of Anak, are given: *Sheshai*, "who I am"; *Ahiman*, "what I am"; *Talmai*, "what I can do." These are clearly indicative of the believer's struggle to subdue the giants of self which oppose his progress.

This section also gives the account of the setting up of the Tabernacle at the city of Shiloh, the allotment of an inheritance to the daughters of Zelophehad, as Moses had promised them, and the designation of cities of refuge as the law had provided.

The Levites, of course, were given no inheritance within the land except for certain cities to dwell in, and they were reminded again that the Lord was their portion. As previously seen, the tribes of Reuben and Gad and the halftribe of Manasseh were given their part on the east of the Jordan, but the rest of the land was divided between the nine and one-half tribes.

THE CONSECRATION

The last portion of the book of Joshua, from chapters 22 through 24, include the account of the misunderstanding which arose between the tribes of Reuben and Gad and the halftribe of Manasseh east of Jordan, and closes with two addresses by Joshua to the people shortly before his death.

When the major portion of the land had been conquered Joshua permitted the two and one-half tribes to return to their homes east of the Jordan, but to the dismay of the other nine and one-half tribes, the eastern Israelites immediately erected an altar on the west side of the river. Remembering the sin of Achan and how God had punished the whole nation for the sin of one man, the western tribes gathered armies at Shiloh, under the leadership of Phinehas. They came to Gilead and demanded an explanation, reminding the eastern tribes that burnt offerings and meal offerings and other sacrifices were to be offered only at the Tabernacle in Shiloh.

The two and one-half tribes then explained that they had no intention of using the great altar for any such sacrifices, but had erected it as a memorial to teach their children that they too shared the inheritance of the Lord with the rest of Israel. These two tribes seem, therefore, to typify the Christians who still remain at heart committed believers, but who in their daily lives experience incomplete enjoyment of the full inheritance.

Aware of his advanced age, and knowing he will soon die, Joshua summoned Israel to Shechem and there he delivered two magnificent addresses which close the book. The first is a warning against turning to the idolatry of the surrounding nations and a solemn promise that if they do so, God will permit them to fall again under the power of their enemies. The second address is a marvelous review of the way the Lord has led them, from the plagues of Egypt to the conquest of the Promised Land.

Joshua ended his message with a magnificent summons to the people to make personal choice among themselves as to whom they will serve; but he warned again that such service must be from the heart and not from lips only.

Shortly after having recorded the promise of the people to serve the Lord, Joshua died at the age of 110. The close of this book looks back to the close of Genesis and records how the bones of Joseph were at last buried in the city of Shechem in the ground which Jacob had bought from the Hittites. Thus in the words appearing on the memorial to John Wesley in Westminster Abbey "God buries his workmen but carries on his work."

CHAPTER SEVEN

The Incomplete Victory

JUDGES

The book of Judges relates the history of Israel after the days of Joshua until the time of Samuel and the choosing of the first king over all of Israel. It is a record of alternating defeat and victory, corresponding to the experience of most Christians—especially in the early years of their Christian life when they alternate between succumbing to the enemies of faith and, upon confession and repentance, being restored again to a place of overcoming.

The book takes its name from the series of judges God raised up to deliver the people when they had fallen into the hands of their enemies. The repeated theme of the book is stated first in Judges 2:18,19: "When the Lord raised up judges for them, the Lord was with the judge and delivered them from the hand of their enemies all the days of the judge; for the Lord was moved to pity by their groaning because of those who oppressed and afflicted them. But . . . when the judge died, . . . they would turn back and act more corruptly than their fathers, in following other gods to serve them and bow down to them; they did not abandon their practices or their stubborn ways."

ISRAEL'S FAILURE

The first two chapters review again the situation in Israel at the death of Joshua. An account is again given of the conquest of Debir by Othniel. Though Judah and

Simeon joined together to subdue the Canaanites within their territory, they only succeeded in part. Some areas, especially the Philistine cities of the coast, remained unsubdued. Benjamin, Manasseh, Zebulon and Dan also failed to claim for themselves the full inheritance promised them within their allotted borders.

So once again, as within the wilderness, the angel of the Lord appeared to warn the people of the inevitable consequences of their unbelief and incomplete obedience (chap. 2). As we saw in Exodus, this promised angel of the Presence is a manifestation of a divine being. Though the people of Israel wept and apparently repented, their repentance was not long lived. Soon they were back again in their idolatries, bowing before the idols of their neighboring nations. Remember that the worship of these idols involved depraved sexual practices and even at times the sacrifice of living children.

Parallel to this in the Christian's life is the continual temptation to adopt the goals and standards of the world around him, and especially to seek the favor and approval of men rather than the approval of God.

In chapter 3 we are told that God used these remaining Canaanite tribes to teach the new generations within Israel how to make war—that is, how God, rather than man, makes war. As Paul will say in 2 Corinthians 10:4, "For the weapons of our warfare are not of the flesh, but divinely powerful for the destruction of fortresses."

DAYS OF JUDGES

When the Israelites fell into sordid idolatry, Jehovah allowed the nations around them and living among them to conquer them. They first fell under the rule of a king from Syria, to the north; but upon the repentance of Israel, Othniel, Caleb's nephew, rose in the Spirit of the Lord and led the forces of Israel against Syria and drove them from the land. For 40 years he ruled as the first judge of

Israel and the land had peace during that time.

Immediately upon his death, the people fell into sinful ways again and God allowed King Eglon of Moab to conquer a part of the country. For 18 years the Moabites held the people in bondage requiring heavy taxes from them annually. At last the people wearied of their bondage enough to turn again to the Lord and cry to Him, and in gracious response He raised up Ehud from the tribe of Benjamin, who was chosen to carry the tax money to the Moabite capital. There he tricked the king into receiving him in private, and when the two were alone Ehud drew from his belt a long dagger and thrust it into the fat king's belly (Judg. 3:15-23). Leaving King Eglon dead behind him, Ehud returned to Israel, blew the trumpet of assembly and mustered a large enough army to attack the Moabites, killing about 2,000 of their best warriors.

The land again enjoyed peace for about 40 years under Ehud, and apparently another 40 years under Shamgar, who is briefly mentioned (3:31), but who gained fame for killing 600 Philistines with an oxgoad. (It should be noted that the periods of relief under the judges are not to be taken consecutively, for some of them overlap, there being a judge in one part of the country and another ruling in another part.)

Deborah

In the north of Canaan, the Israelites fell under the hand of Jabin of the city of Hazor, who with 900 iron chariots made life unbearable for 20 years. The leader of faith in that part of Israel was a woman named Deborah, who judged Israel in the hill country of Ephraim (chap. 4,5). Through her God sent a command to one Barak in the tribe of Naphtali, who mobilized 10,000 men and led them against King Jabin.

Barak refused to go to battle with Jabin unless Deborah went with him. When she consented, 10,000 men assembled on the slopes of Mount Tabor and prepared to assault the armies of Jabin, led by his general Sisera.

When the Canaanite armies panicked before Israel, Sisera fled on foot and found what he thought to be a refuge in the tent of a woman named Jael. While Sisera slept in the tent, Jael took an iron tent peg and a hammer and drove the long spike through Sisera's head, ending his life and the power of the northern Canaanite tribes.

This use of two women, Deborah and Jael, again confirms the statement in Galatians 3:28 that in Christ "there is neither male nor female." Deborah seems truly to have fulfilled the office of prophet, while Jael is an instrument in the hand of the Lord to judge and remove the enemies of Israel.

The account is followed by the singing of a great song of triumph known as the "Song of Deborah," which recounts in poetic detail the story of the triumph of Deborah and Barak, giving credit to the God of Israel rather than the might of her armies.

Gideon

The 40 years of peace that followed was broken once again by the faithless idolatry of Israel. This time it was the people of Midian from the east of the Jordan who for seven years so harassed the Israelites that they were reduced to living in caves and dens of the mountains. The Midianites overran the land, claiming all the Israelites' sheep, oxen and donkeys for themselves and stripping the land of its fodder by enormous herds of camels.

Again Israel's deep trouble brought about their repentant cry for help, but this time they were warned by the prophet of God that what was happening to them was merely a fulfillment of what the Lord had predicted many years before through Moses. Nevertheless, in grace, God sent the angel of the Lord to appear to Gideon (chap. 6-8) who was threshing wheat in a winepress to hide himself from the Midianites. There, in an account similar to the call of Moses, Gideon pleads his low status in the nation and his inability to overthrow Midian.

As with Moses, God reassures him with, "I will be with you," and Gideon quickly returns to his home to prepare a meal for his strange visitor whom he has not yet recognized as the angel of God. When he spread the meat and bread upon a rock the angel touched it with his staff and the fire of the Lord consumed the sacrifice. That night Gideon pulled down the family altar to Baal and cut the wooden sex symbol of Asherah to pieces with an ax. When his neighbors discovered what he had done, they threatened to kill him for insulting their god Baal; but Joash, Gideon's father, defended his son by arguing that if the god Baal was truly a god he could defend himself. He thereby gained the nickname, *Jerubbaal,* which means, "Let Baal contend against him" (Judg. 6:32).

Soon after, the armies of Midian and other neighboring nations came with a great horde against Israel. God graciously strengthened Gideon's faith by twice giving him a miraculous sign involving the fleece of a sheep (6:36-40). So Gideon gathered 32,000 men of the northern tribes and assembled them beside the spring of Harod at the foot of Mount Gilboa. Across the valley, the Midianite hosts were encamped as numerous as a plague of locusts; but strangely, the Lord told Gideon that he had too many men. God wanted to be sure that Israel knew Who would defeat the Midianites.

When Gideon had sent home all the fainthearted, there were still 10,000 men of Israel left. Again, at the Lord's command, Gideon tested them at the brook and only 300 men remained. Putting torches within large earthen jars, and carrying trumpets along with their swords, the 300 divided themselves into three groups and surrounded the Midianite camp. There again Gideon's faith was strengthened when, waiting in the darkness, he heard a man of Midian recounting his dream from which he had just awakened. The other soldier interpreted it as an omen of the defeat of Midian, and when Gideon heard it he breathed a prayer of worship to God there on the spot.

Shortly after midnight, Gideon gave the signal and his men simultaneously broke the earthen jars causing the torches to flash out, and sounded the trumpets. Then they enjoyed the sight of watching the Midianite army destroy itself. In the subsequent confusion and panic the Midianites could not tell a friend from an enemy. The waiting troops of Naphtali, Asher and Manasseh then joined the fight, chasing the retreating Midianites to the Jordan River and capturing and killing their two generals, Oreb and Zeeb.

Gideon crossed the Jordan with his 300 men and fought all through the night. His men were weary and hungry and Gideon asked food both from the city of Succoth and the city of Penuel. He was rebuffed in both places and, vowing to remember their truculence, he pursued the Midianites until only 15,000 of their original 135,000 remained. On returning to Succoth and Penuel, he executed the promise of vengeance; then he took the two kings of Midian and put them to death because they had slain his brothers. Gideon refused the request of Israel to make him king, but foolishly he made a priest's garment for himself and decorated it with gold from the earrings of the Midianites. This soon became an object of idolatrous worship by Israel. But the land again had peace for 40 years while Gideon judged the nation.

Of the seventy sons Gideon fathered, one is especially marked out—Abimelech, the son of a concubine. Incredibly, as soon as Gideon was dead the Israelites began to worship again the idols of Baal. Evidently remembering that his father had almost become king of Israel, Abimelech sought the support of his Canaanite uncles in Shechem and with their help slew all 70 of his half-brothers, except for the youngest, Jotham, who escaped (Judg. 9:1-6).

When Abimelech was proclaimed king by the men of Shechem, Jotham stood on Mount Gerizim and, in Eastern fashion, recited to the men of Shechem the fable of the trees. The olive, the fig and the vine all refused to reign over the other trees. When they turned to the thornbush, it consented to be their king and warned them of a fiery destruction if they refused (9:7-20). By this Jotham indicated that Abimelech would destroy the leaders of Shechem and they in turn would destroy Abimelech. Subsequent events proved the accuracy of this prophecy.

When trouble arose between the men of Shechem and Abimelech, Abimelech led an army against the city, defeating and wounding many of the Shechemites. When he attacked also the suburb of Thebez, a woman on a rooftop threw a millstone which landed on Abimelech's head and in shame he bade his armor bearer to kill him, that it might not be said that a woman had slain Abimelech. Thus God punished both Abimelech and the men of Shechem, and Jotham's curse proved true (9:50-57).

Two judges next appear in brief account. One named Tola from the tribe of Issachar, who judged for 23 years. He was succeeded by Jair from Gilead who judged Israel for 22 years. As before, the people of Israel turned away from the Lord to worship pagan gods, and this time it is added that they ceased worshiping Jehovah at all. Since it is true that ''whatever a man sows that shall he also reap,'' it was not long before the Philistines and Ammonites were harassing and tormenting Israel again.

Jephthah

After 18 years, the Israelites pled for deliverance; but this time Jehovah sent them back to their new gods for help (10:14). In an amazing display of grace, when they had at last put away foreign gods, the heart of Jehovah grieved over their misery.

When the Ammonites on the east launched an attack against Israel, God laid hold of Jephthah (11:6—12:7), the son of a harlot (11:1). Jephthah's brothers had driven him away from their home that he might not share the inheritance with them. Under pressure of the Ammonite advance, the elders of Gilead, Jephthah's brothers, sent to him and asked him to lead the Israelites against Ammon. Jephthah attempted to negotiate with the Ammonites. In an interesting parallel to the present situation in the Middle East, where Arabs and Israelis argue over who properly possesses the land, Jephthah answers the Ammonite claim by reminding them that Moses had attempted to pass through their land peacefully, but when attacked he defeated their forces in battle and thereby won the right to inhabit the land.

Before the subsequent battle, Jephthah made a vow to the Lord that he would offer in burnt sacrifice whatever or whoever came out of his house to greet him on his return (11:29-31). Thus after the rout of the Ammonites, Jephthah returned and his daughter, his only child, met him at the door. Jephthah refused to break his vow, and the account says he "did to her according to the vow which he had made" (11:39).

This strange story has been the subject of much debate among Bible scholars. Did he actually sacrifice her, or not?

Since we have seen in Exodus that a provision was made to redeem all firstborn sons, who also were vowed to the Lord, by the payment of redemption money, so it is possible that this was done in this case also. Her sorrow then would be that she was to remain unmarried for the rest of her life.

Chapter 12 recounts the civil war which broke out between Abraham and the men of Gilead over the anger of the Ephraimites in not being summoned to battle with the Ammonites, though Jephthah explained that he had summoned them but they did not respond. Nevertheless, the Ephraimites continued their attack and a great battle ensued in which 42,000 of Ephraim were slain. Those who attempted to escape could not disguise themselves as Gileadites because they could not pronounce the word *Shibboleth* correctly.

Samson

After the death of Jephthah, a series of three little-known judges arose in various parts of Israel, judging for varying periods of seven to ten years each.

The record then focuses on the life of Samson (chap. 13-16), who is remarkable for being set aside before conception to be a Nazirite unto God for all of his life. Again in a time of decline, the angel of the Lord appeared to the wife of Manoah of the tribe of Dan, and announced that her barrenness was to end and she would bear a son who would be devoted to the Lord from his birth. Manoah seems to be a man of small faith, for it is not until the angel of the Lord ascends before him in the smoke of his offering that Manoah recognized the Divine Presence.

So Samson was born, like Isaac, a child of promise. When he grew to manhood, he manifested the presence of the Spirit of the Lord upon him in great deeds of physical strength. His one moral weakness seemed to be an attraction to the daughters of the Philistines. On the way to negotiate a marriage, Samson with his bare hands slew a lion that attempted to attack him (14:5,6). Later when he came to claim his wife he saw that the body of the lion had been inhabited by a swarm of bees and was filled with honey. While Samson waited, with 30 Philistine companions, for the negotiations to be completed, he put to them a riddle, promising each of them a new garment if they could solve it. The riddle was: ''Out of the eater came something to eat. Out of the strong came something sweet,'' referring to the honey in the lion (14:10).

For seven days they tried in vain to solve the riddle, and finally resorted to bribing Samson's new wife to extract the answer from him. When Samson told her, she repeated it to the Philistines. Samson paid his debt to them by killing 30 men of Ashkelon and giving their garments to his 30 Philistine companions. But angered at their deceit, he returned to his father's house and his wife was given instead to the best man (14:20).

When Samson went later to visit his wife, he learned that she had been given away. He caught 300 foxes, tied them together in pairs by the tails with torches between, and set fire to the Philistines' fields of grain. When the Philistines in revenge, burned Samson's wife and her father, Samson retaliated by killing many of them, and then went down to the rock of Etam (15:1-8). The Philistines demanded his return, and 3,000 men of Judah went to Samson and convinced him to allow them to deliver him bound with ropes into the Philistines' hands. When the Philistines came to take him, Samson broke the ropes and, seizing the jawbone of a donkey, he slew a thousand of the Philistines (15:9-17).

Thirsty after his exertions and finding no water nearby, Samson prayed to the Lord and He opened a spring of water before him at that place (vv. 18-20).

Then Samson became involved with a Philistine harlot. The Philistine men heard he was in Gaza and laid in wait for him. He arose at midnight, took hold of the doors of the city's gate and, pulling them up bar and all, he carried them on his shoulders to the top of the hill that is before Hebron (16:1-3).

The final incident of his life centered around a third Philistine woman named Delilah. The story of her attempt to discover the secret of Samson's strength has been told around the world. Three times he gave her false clues and three times the Philistines came upon him and he repulsed them. Despite her obvious disloyalty, he remained with her and when she nagged him unceasingly he finally told her the truth. Then, while he slept in her lap, she called a servant to shave off all of Samson's hair. When he awoke, it is recorded that "he did not know that the Lord had departed from him" (16:20). Since he was unable to resist, the Philistines captured him, gouged out his eyes and put him in prison in Gaza, forcing him to grind at the prison mill. Thus God's mighty man, wretched and blinded, stands as a continuing reminder to "abstain from fleshly lusts, which wage war against the soul" (1 Pet. 2:11). Left unjudged, these lusts will bring the mightiest saint into bondage and darkness.

But even in prison God's grace did not forsake Samson, His chosen servant. As the sightless Samson ground at the prison mill, his hair began to grow, and when after several months the Philistine lords gathered for a great sacrifice to their god Dagon, they called Samson before them to make sport of him. Samson asked the lad who led him to put him between the two great pillars that supported the house, and praying with earnestness to the Lord, he bowed himself mightily, pushed the pillars apart and the house fell upon the princes, crushing about 3,000 men and women to death. Samson, too, perished in the ruins (Judg. 16:28-30). His life testifies that even those of great and marked spiritual ability can fall from their place of usefulness; and although God in His faithfulness will not desert them, their spiritual effectiveness is far from what it could have been.

"Doing What Was Right. . ."

The strange story of chapters 17 and 18 is apparently included that subsequent generations might have a picture of the ignorance and unbelief which was quickly manifest among the people of Israel when they turned from the living God. A man named Micah in the hill country of Ephraim apparently stole 1100 shekels of silver from his mother, but when he confessed and restored the money, she took 200 pieces of silver out of which she had made one engraved metal image and one of cast silver. Micah's religious faith had evidently deteriorated to the level of mere superstition, for he took the two images and set them up in a house of gods, along with a priestly ephod and teraph. The explanation is given that this was a result of the lack of central authority in the land, and so "every man did what was right in his own eyes" (17:6). But what they thought was right was very wrong indeed.

When a young Levite from Judah came by Micah's house, needing a place of his own, Micah urged him to join the family circle and become the family's official private priest. This he did, and became to Micah as one of his own sons.

At that time, the tribe of Dan had been given a small inheritance near Judah's land, but recognizing its inadequacy, they sent five of their men toward the north to find new territory which they could subjugate and claim for themselves. On the way they stopped by the house of Micah. Finding the young Levite there, they urged him to inquire of the Lord whether their journey would be successful. Upon receiving his encouragement, they traveled north to the city of Laish, which is located near the foot of Mount Hermon. There they found people from the coastal city of Sidon, so isolated from their brethren they would be unable to defend themselves successfully. When they reported this to the Danites in Judah, 600 armed men went out to take the new land. When these came to the house of Micah, they enticed the young Levite to steal the two silver images, the ephod and the teraph, and to go with them to their new country as their official priest. Though Micah followed them to protest, he was unable to recover his lost treasures, and the Danites went on to capture the city of Laish and renamed it Dan. There they set up their graven images, and the young Levite, who turns out to be the grandson of Moses, becomes the head of a line of priests who served the city of Dan until the time of the Assyrian captivity.

The account explains the deteriorating moral condition which later permitted Jeroboam, the son of Solomon, to set up in the city of Dan the worship of the golden calf.

The final story of the book of Judges is likewise a flashback to the earlier days of conquest when Phinehas, grandson of Aaron, is still priest within the nation. It is one of the most sordid accounts in Scripture, and illustrates the ease with which even the most vile and repulsive sin can take root in the hearts of those who turn away from daily fellowship with the living God.

It concerns another Levite in the hill country of Ephraim whose wife had returned to her father's home in Bethlehem. When the Levite went to bring her back, his father-in-law received him warmly, and despite his repeated attempts to return home, persuaded him to stay for six days of feasting and drinking.

On the sixth day, having gotten a late start they found themselves at eventime near the Benjamite city of Gibeah. There they sought lodging, but no one would take them in, until at last an old man, finding them abandoned in the city square, took them to his own home. The subsequent account is reminiscent of the story of Lot in the cities of Sodom, for that evening certain men of Benjamin who had given themselves over to homosexuality beat upon the door of the house and demanded that the stranger be brought out for their sexual indulgence. Again, like Lot, the master of the house offered them his own virgin daughter and the Levite's wife instead. When they refused this offer the Levite forced his wife out the door and the men of the city took her and abused her all night.

At daybreak when the Levite prepared to go on his

way, he opened the door and found his wife lying dead on the threshold. He took her body to his home, and there with a knife he divided the body into 12 pieces and sent a piece to each of the tribes of Israel. This shocking deed so stunned the chiefs of the people that, in response, they gathered an army of 400,000 men and marched against Benjamin. They demanded that the guilty men within the tribe be given them for punishment, but the Benjamites refused. Instead they mustered an army of 26,000 men from the cities of Benjamin. The two armies met for battle before the city of Gibeon.

At this time the Ark of the Covenant was located at the city of Bethel before being removed to Shiloh, and the Israelites went to inquire of the Lord which tribe should lead into battle. Judah was chosen and when the battle had ended, 22,000 men from the Israelites had fallen. Shaken by this defeat, the Israelites inquired again of the Lord as to whether to continue the battle and were given command to go up again.

On the second day another great defeat followed and 18,000 Israelites were slain, all of whom were swordsmen. The double defeat indicated that other tribes were also implicated in the guilt of Benjamin. The whole army went up to the house of God and fasted and wept before the Lord, offering burnt offerings and peace offerings. This time the Lord commanded them to go up, but promised to deliver the Benjamites into their hands.

As in the battle of Ai, the Israelites resorted to ambush, and when they drew the men of Benjamin out of the city of Gibeon by feigning retreat, the men in ambush set the city afire. As the Benjamites turned and fled the men of Israel fell upon them and a total of 25,000 Benjamites were slain. A remnant of 600 fled through the wilderness to the rock of Rimmon for refuge.

This terrible civil war had taken a dreadful toll, for now the Israelites recognized that they had virtually eliminated one of the 12 tribes. They had vowed before the Lord at Mizpah that they would not allow any of their daughters to marry Benjamites; therefore it looked as though the tribe of Benjamin was doomed to extinction. Realizing what a breach this would make in their nation, they settled on a terrible remedy.

Learning that the city of Jabesh in Gilead had not sent any armed men to the conflict, they sent 12,000 of their men against that city and slew with the sword every male and every married woman in the city. They brought back with them 400 young virgins, and these they offered to the remaining 600 men of Benjamin for wives. To find additional wives for the remaining 200 men, they encouraged the men of Benjamin to lie in wait at the city of Shiloh and when the young women of the city came out to celebrate one of the annual festivals they were to fall upon them and take them for wives. By this bloody stratagem they preserved Benjamin as a tribe within the nation.

The book closes with the reminder that this was all the result of ''every man doing what was right in his own eyes.'' The terrible record of Judges is one of vile idolatry, treachery, betrayals, civil war and ruthless human connivance. It should be read frequently as a reminder of the fatal weakness which can permit the blackest of sins to take root when the heart no longer daily fellowships with God.

RUTH

The book of Ruth is universally recognized as a beautiful literary gem. On one occasion, Benjamin Franklin, then ambassador from the United States to Paris, read the book without comment to a literary circle in France whose members were largely made up of humanists and rationalists. When he finished the reading they were universally loud in their praise of such a perfect gem. When they inquired where he had found it, they were chagrined to learn it came from the Bible they despised.

The scene is set for us in the opening paragraphs, recounting the story of a man named Elimelech ("my God is King") who with his wife Naomi ("pleasant") and their two sons left Bethlehem because of a famine and went to live in the country of Moab. The story takes place in the days of the judges, and it is instructive to note that in Bethlehem ("the House of Bread") there was no bread, but a famine. The book of Leviticus has already told us that famine indicates a low level of spiritual vitality within the chosen nation.

In Moab, Elimelech died and his two sons, Mahlon and Chilion, married women of Moab, Orpah and Ruth. After 10 years, the two sons also died and Naomi was left with her two daughters-in-law.

On expressing her determination to return to Bethlehem, having learned that the famine was over, Naomi exhorted her daughers-in-law to remain in Moab and remarry there. Orpah is unwilling to leave her home for an uncertain life in Palestine, but Ruth refuses to stay in Moab, and in a plea of enduring beauty, declares her determination to identify herself with Naomi's land and Naomi's people. The deepest cause of her determination is seen in her statement in 1:16: "Your God [shall be] my God." This clearly represents her willingness to leave the idols of Moab for the worship of the living God of Israel.

So the two arrive in Bethlehem at the beginning of the barley harvest with a very uncertain future before them. The invisible hand of the Lord in caring for His own is apparent in the statement that Ruth went into the fields to glean, and "happened to come to the portion of the field belonging to Boaz" (2:3). This man, a close relative of Elimelech, Naomi's husband, appears in the story as a man of unusual character and sensitivity. He has heard the full story of Naomi and Ruth's return to Bethlehem. Upon meeting Ruth in his fields he commends her for her kindness to her mother-in-law, and especially for her faith in Jehovah the God of Israel, under whose gracious wings she has taken refuge.

Obviously attracted to the beautiful Moabite woman, and yet acting always with restraint and dignity, Boaz instructs his workmen to deliberately leave grain in the field for Ruth to glean. When she returns to Naomi in the evening with an unexpected abundance, she learns for the first time from her mother-in-law that Boaz is a possible kinsman-redeemer. Thus, at Naomi's instruction she continues gleaning in Boaz's fields through the barley and wheat harvest for approximately three months.

At the end of the harvest, when the winnowing of the grain took place, Naomi siezed the initiative provided by her relationship with Boaz and instructed Ruth on a stratagem that would combine both the law of redemption and the law of levirate marriage. By coming to the sleeping Boaz and lying at his feet, Ruth is following a custom in Israel by which she is essentially asking Boaz to fulfill the responsibility of a kinsman to marry her and raise up heirs to the deceased Elimelech. She does this so modestly that Boaz commends her for her action, and having now clearly fallen in love with her, he eagerly consents to take on the requested responsibility. He has evidently hoped that such a situation would occur, for he immediately informs Ruth that a closer kinsman is involved and his claim must be settled first.

In the morning he generously sends her back to Naomi with a gift of six measures of barley and Naomi wisely tells her that the matter will surely be settled that day.

That same morning, Boaz took his seat at the gate of the city where the elders gathered for the settling of lawsuits and the judging of other matters brought before them. When the closer kinsman came by, Boaz requested an informal court, and when all were seated he presented his case to the other relative. He declared that Naomi wanted to sell a piece of land which belonged to Elimelech, but if she did the next of kin would be responsible to care for the family, since they now would have no property. Seeing the possibility of obtaining a choice piece of property, the first kinsman declared his willingness to assume this responsibility, but then Boaz played his trump card. He informed him that the land was also encumbered by a levirate marriage, and that if he bought the property he would also have to marry the woman. This changed the picture for the first kinsman, since the land would then not belong to him but to whatever issue resulted from his union with Ruth. To symbolize his action, in the colorful custom of the East, the man removed his right shoe and handed it to Boaz in the presence of the witnesses. The shoe symbolized his right as owner to set foot upon the land. This right now becomes Boaz's and the coast is clear for him to take Ruth as his wife.

The account closes with the birth of a son to Boaz and Ruth, who brings great joy to the heart of his grandmother, Naomi, and grows up to be the grandfather of David, Israel's mightiest king.

The beautiful little story of Ruth not only provides a link between the days of the judges and the subsequent reign of David, but symbolizes in the figure of Boaz how Christ our great Kinsman-Redeemer overcomes the obstacle of our birth in Adam, as strangers and foreigners to the promises of God, and takes us to Himself in a union that will produce the fruit of the Spirit to the honor and glory of God. It is highly significant that in the genealogy of Matthew, Ruth is included as the ancestress of Jesus the Messiah.

CHAPTER EIGHT

The Flesh and the Spirit

FIRST SAMUEL

First Samuel is one of the key books of the Old Testament, forming a link between the decadence of the period of the Judges and the rise of the monarchy—first Saul and then David. It is the story of three men: Samuel the last of the judges and the first of the prophets; Saul the first king of Israel; and David the greatest of all of Israel's kings. These three men mark off the divisions of the book.

The first seven chapters give us the life of Samuel. Chapters 8-15 present King Saul who is seen as symbolic of the man of the flesh; for in him we see the ruin which is caused by the mind which is set on the flesh. By contrast, David is the man of faith, and is a beautiful illustration of the mind which is set on the Spirit, as Romans 8:6 puts it: "For the mind set on the flesh is death, but the mind set on the Spirit is life and peace."

SAMUEL: THE VOICE OF GOD

Samuel, who became the human expression of the voice of God to both Saul and David, was the chosen instrument of God to close the realm of the judges and to introduce the beginning of the prophetic ministry and of the monarchy.

The first chapter introduces another of the great women of the Old Testament. Like Sarah and Rachel, Hannah enters the biblical scene as a barren woman. She was the wife of a man named Elkanah, a Levite of Ephraim.

Though her husband loved her, Hannah's life was made miserable by Elkanah's second wife, Peninnah, who taunted Hannah because of her barrenness and boasted of her own fertility in having given her husband many sons and daughters.

The barrenness of Hannah, coming as it does at the beginning of this book, doubtless is introduced to illustrate the spiritual state of Israel. The people of God had fallen into a state of utter infertility and barrenness. The priesthood, which God had set up with the Tabernacle as a means by which the people would have access to Him, was beginning to disappear. It had degenerated to mere ritual and ceremony and was no longer a potent factor in maintaining the vitality of faith within the nation.

Hannah was a woman of quiet faith and godly character. In great distress, she took her problem of barrenness to the Lord at the Tabernacle in Shiloh. As she prayed, Eli the priest saw her lips move but heard no sound. So he thought she was drunk. When she was rebuked by Eli, Hannah explained that she had been promising God that if He would give her a son she would dedicate him to the service of the Lord all his life, as a Nazirite from his birth. Eli pronounced a blessing on her and she and her husband returned to their home. In due course, the promised son was given and Hannah named him Samuel, which means "asked of God."

True to her vow, when the child was weaned, probably about five or six years of age, Hannah brought him to the Tabernacle and left him in the care of Eli the priest to serve the Lord.

Chapter 2 records the beautiful song Hannah sang on this occasion. Within it she indicates the problem she herself has faced in the mockery of her rival, which was also the problem Israel faced as a nation at that time.

"Boast no more so very proudly, do not let arrogance come out of your mouth; for the Lord is a God of knowledge, and with Him actions are weighed. The bows of the mighty are shattered, but the feeble gird on strength'' (2:3,4).

The priesthood was failing in Israel not because there was anything wrong with the priesthood, but because the people, in pride, refused to bow before the Lord. Through arrogance they would not turn from their idolatrous worship and come before the Lord for cleansing. As a result, their access to God was cut off. Ultimately, in the contrasting lives of Saul and David, this book will describe the eternal conflict between the proud heart which finds confidence in itself and its ability to perform and the humble spirit which looks to God in utter dependence and thus receives all the fullness of divine blessing.

The state of spiritual decay in the priesthood was clearly visible in the lives of Eli's two sons. Contrary to the law, they forced the people to give them the best parts of their offerings. Also they openly lay with the women who served in the Tabernacle. This scandalous conduct was only mildly rebuked by their father Eli, and in due course Jehovah sent an unnamed man of God to Eli to announce that the priesthood would be taken away eventually from his descendants and given to another. This prophecy was fulfilled in the days of Solomon, when Abiathar of Eli's family was set aside and Zadok from another house within the tribe of Levi was given the priesthood. The promise of ''a faithful priest who will do according to what is in My heart and in My soul'' (2:35) seems to anticipate the coming of the Messiah and the eternal priesthood of the Lord Jesus.

The remarkable account of the boy Samuel being called by the direct voice of the Lord (3:1-18) is reminiscent of the appearing of God to Moses in the wilderness of Midian. The nature of Samuel's ministry as an authentic prophet of the Lord was indicated by God's revelation to him of the fate of Eli and his sons. As the lad grew to manhood, he became widely recognized as God's appointed prophet, so that "all Israel from Dan even to Beersheba knew that Samuel was confirmed as a prophet of the Lord" (v. 20).

Again the low state of Israel's faith was observable when, on the occasion of a military defeat at the hands of the Philistines, the people superstitiously demanded that the Ark of the Covenant be taken from the Tabernacle and accompany them in the renewed battle. Total disaster followed wherein thousands of Israelites were slain, including the two sons of Eli, and the Ark itself was taken captive by the Philistines.

When news of his sons' death was brought to old Eli, he fell over backward and broke his neck at exactly the same moment his daughter-in-law gave birth to a son. In view of the terrible circumstances, she named the child *Ichabod* ("the glory has departed"). Here Israel reaches one of the lowest states in its national history.

Though the Ark of the Covenant brought no victory to Israel, nevertheless, in the hands of the Philistines it proved to be a source of continual torment. The Ark was placed in the temple of Dagon, the Philistine fish god. On two successive mornings the Philistines found their idol, first lying on its face before the Ark and the second morning shattered to bits. Next a plague of tumors broke out among the people of the city of Ashdod, who hastily sent the Ark to Gath. There the tumors broke out again. The association of these tumors with mice (probably rats) has been understood by some scholars to indicate a form of the bubonic plague.

Finally, in desperation, the lords of the Philistines decided to return the Ark to Israel, along with an offering of five golden tumors and five golden mice. In order to determine whether God was actually behind the plague, the Philistines hitched two milk cows to a cart but shut up the cows' calves at home. Contrary to nature, the cows drew the cart away from their calves, directly to Bethshemesh, which was the first city within the border of Israel.

Here God taught the people a lesson in reverence, for when 70 men looked into the Ark out of curiosity, contrary to the Law, they immediately died. Frightened by this slaughter, the inhabitants of Bethshemesh appealed to the people of Kiriath-jearim to take the Ark into their city. There it was put into the care of Eleazar, a Levite, and remained for some 20 years.

Samuel seized the occasion of Israel's renewed fear to exhort the people to put away their idols and to serve the Lord only. The people gathered at Mizpah and confessed their sin. As Samuel was offering the burnt offering, the Philistines attacked but were routed by a mighty thundering from the Lord. The subsequent great victory over the Philistines was memorialized by a stone which Samuel erected and named Ebenezer, "the stone of help."

SAUL: THE MAN OF FLESH

Saul, the first king of Israel, begins his career with bright promise. But a shadow over his reign is seen from the very beginning when the people demand of Samuel a king "like all the nations" (8:20). This is a denial of their very purpose, for under Moses they had been called to be unlike all the nations, and were to be a people directly governed by God. Though in Deuteronomy provision had been made for a king, he was to be a king of humble spirit and obedient heart who would be the human instrument of the government of God. But as so many times before, God permitted them to have their way that they might learn from the sad results the nature of their folly. The principle of the flesh is thus seen at work in the nation of Israel to destroy its communion and enjoyment of God's blessing.

The same principle is interwoven in every Christian life. The desire of the flesh is to be religious in a manner acceptable to the world and to conduct its business along the principles of the world. Even within the church many are often uncomfortable with the idea of an invisible Head directing the affairs of the local assembly. They insist on making a pastor or some other leader the ultimate voice of authority in the church, and thus follow Israel in their folly.

The fascinating story of Saul follows. It is the story of a young man of handsome physique and apparently modest disposition, who nevertheless proves to have little real concern for the things of God, but rather is interested in pursuing his own endeavors (9:1,2). He is first found busy with his father in the donkey business. In the inscrutable ways of God, the donkeys strayed off and Saul was sent in search of them. After a long and fruitless search he ended up at the town where Samuel lived. Saul's servant suggested that they consult the prophet as to the location of the donkeys, but Saul was not anxious to do this for he wanted to return home. The servant prevailed upon him. So Saul went to Samuel and, to his amazement he found that Samuel was expecting him (9:18-20), for God had told Samuel that a young man from Benjamin would appear the next day and Samuel was to anoint him as king over Israel. The prophet had prepared a feast for Saul and symbolically set the shoulder of the roast before him, the portion of an offering always symbolic of government (9:22,23).

The next day, Samuel privately anointed Saul as the new king. He described three signs which would be fulfilled to assure him that this was a definite call of God (10:1-8). These signs were immediately fulfilled. In due course the people were called together at Mizpah for the formal presentation of their new king. On this occasion there was a manifestation of that weakness of character in Saul which eventually brought about his complete failure as a king; for despite the clear demonstration as to the will of God, he seeks to evade that responsibility by hiding among the baggage (v. 22). It appeared to be modesty, but in view of Saul's later character it seems more likely to be a stubborn spirit which found it inconvenient to do God's will.

As Saul stood among the people, they raised a great shout, for he looked the very picture of a king, towering head and shoulders above everyone.

The first test of his kingship came with an attack by the Ammonites against Jabesh-gilead in the north (chap. 11). Stirred by the Spirit of God, Saul sent word to the 12 tribes to gather an army, and 330,000 men responded. A great victory resulted and in the midst of it Saul manifested a spirit of fairness and mercy toward some who had refused to acknowledge his kingship. Responding to Samuel's call the people gathered at Gilgal and there renewed their vows to the Lord and offered peace offerings and burnt offerings for the new king (11:15).

On this occasion, Samuel delivered what was virtually a farewell address on his part (chap. 12), for though he would continue to serve as prophet it would be in a somewhat more private manner. He rapidly surveyed the history of Israel from the days of Moses and Aaron to the present moment, reminding them that deliverance had always come to them when they walked in obedience to God, but disaster had befallen them whenever they turned from Him. Now even though the Israelites' insistence on having a king meant a partial rejection of the government of God, the old prophet promised them that the Lord would not cast away His people for His own name's sake, and he, Samuel, would continue to pray for them and teach them.

Chapters 13 and 14 are a summary of Saul's wars with the Philistines. It is difficult to determine how long a period they encompass, but it was probably several years.

Saul first amassed a standing army of 3,000 men and

put part of it under his son, Jonathan, who defeated a garrison of the Philistines at Geba. This brought on a massive mustering of the Philistine army with some 30,000 chariots, 6,000 horsemen and troops like the sand on the seashore. This enormous army so frightened the Israelites that they fled before them, hiding in the caves and rocks of the mountains.

Meanwhile, Saul waited at Gilgal with his small army for Samuel to come and offer offerings for their success. When the prophet delayed beyond the seven appointed days, Saul took on himself the priestly office and, as he explained to Samuel when he came, "forced myself, and offered the burnt offering" (13:12). This self-dependent spirit was rebuked by Samuel with the announcement that, because of Saul's act, his kingdom would be taken away and given to another man.

While the people trembled before the oncoming Philistines, Jonathan and his armor-bearer manifested great confidence in the power of God to act on their behalf. The two men made a remarkable attack on the foe, resulting in the slaying of 20 men. This unexpected attack produced panic among the Philistines and, seeing it, the Israelites emerged from hiding to complete the rout of the Philistines.

Again Saul's weakness is shown as he laid a rash oath upon the people to refrain from taking food during the battle. This so weakened the fighting men that they were unable to accomplish as great a victory as they might have. It further imperiled the life of Jonathan, who had not heard about his father's order and had eaten of some honey during the battle. When Saul's intransigence threatened Jonathan's life, the people refused to allow him to be sacrificed but ransomed him, apparently by the payment of money (14:45).

God gave Saul one last chance to redeem himself as king. He commanded Saul, through Samuel, to launch an attack upon the Amalekites and utterly destroy them by the edge of the sword. Remember that Amalek was the people about whom Moses had said, "The Lord will have war against Amalek from generation to generation" (Exod. 17:16). Saul's campaign was victorious, but again he proved disobedient; for he spared King Agag of the Amalekites and saved the best of the sheep and oxen and the goods. His fleshliness is thus revealed, for he presumed to find something good in what God had declared utterly bad. This is a clear picture of what many Christians do today when they refuse to judge the manifestations of the flesh, but defend them and excuse them as part of their personality or temperament.

When Samuel came to Saul, having been told of his disobedience by the Lord, he was met by Saul's announcement that he has completely performed the commandment of the Lord. However his self-commendatory speech was interrupted by the telltale bleating of sheep and the lowing of the oxen which he had spared. Saul lamely excused himself as having saved them for sacrificial purposes, but Samuel bluntly interrupted his hypocrisy with the announcement that the Lord had rejected him from being king over Israel. In the course of his rebuke he reminded Saul that obedience is the first and greatest service to God, and that rebellion is like witchcraft and stubbornness like idolatry. Samuel then called for a sword and himself slew the Amalekite king. Then Samuel returned to his home, never to see Saul again. However, he grieved over the disobedient king.

The statement at the end of chapter 15, "the Lord regretted that He had made Saul king over Israel," is written from a human point of view. The eternal God, of course, does not change His mind, and He knows the end from the beginning, even before anything is brought into existence. But to one living in Saul's day it would appear that God had changed His mind. Thus the statement is recorded from the human perspective.

DAVID: THE MAN OF FAITH

The story of David is the story of the man after God's own heart. Jehovah sent Samuel to the home of Jesse in Bethlehem in order to choose a king from among Jesse's eight sons. When the seven eldest passed before Samuel, each one looked like a king in the making, but God said to Samuel of each, "This is not the one that I have chosen." At last David, the youngest, was brought in from the fields where he had been watching his father's sheep. Though David was young and handsome, nevertheless the choice was not made according to outward appearance, for God declared that He looked upon the heart. Before his anointing, the Spirit of God came upon David and remained with him throughout his life.

In the meantime, the Spirit of the Lord had departed from Saul, and we are told "an evil spirit from the Lord terrorized him" (16:14). This expression means that God had allowed evil spirits to have access to Saul's mind and heart, since he himself had chosen to reject the ways and resources of God. As the book of Ephesians warns us, to give way to the desires of the flesh is to give the devil an opportunity over us (see Eph. 4:17-27). The result in Saul's life was attacks of some mental disturbance, expressed in violent outbursts of rage. To calm him in these times a skilled musician was recommended, and in the providence of God David was brought from his father's home to play his lyre in the king's court.

It is evident that David was not to be set on the throne immediately, as was Saul, but he was tested and proved by struggle and adversity. This is the principle God often follows with the man who learns to walk by faith. He is put through a time of obscurity and adversity. Everything seems to go against him until at last he recognizes the great principle by which God's activity is always enacted—man can do nothing in himself, but only in complete and utter dependence upon the God who indwells him. Even as a shepherd boy, David had begun to learn this, for he could say, "The Lord is my shepherd, I shall not want. He makes me lie down in green pastures; He leads me beside quiet waters. He restores my soul" (Ps. 23:1-3).

In chapter 17 we have the famous story of the testing of David as he comes face to face with the giant Goliath. The armies of Israel were being mocked and taunted by this giant who paraded up and down morning and evening, mocking the impotence of the Israelites who did not dare to send a man into combat against him. When David came from his flock to bring food to his brothers he found the whole camp of Israel plunged into gloom and despair. While he was there the giant came again and mocked the men of Israel, daring them to meet him in combat. David's question to his brothers was, "Who is this uncircumcised Philistine, that he should taunt the armies of the living God?" That is always the outlook of faith. It is not shaken by circumstances, but looks beyond them to the God who is greater than all circumstances.

Word was brought to Saul of the young man who is contemptuous of the challenge of the Philistine giant. When Saul summoned him he did not recognize David, possibly because some time had elapsed since David had served in his court, or perhaps Saul's mental illness had erased David from his memory. When Saul saw how young David was he attempted to dismiss him; but David reassured him with stories of how he had killed both bears and lions when they attacked his father's sheep. Saul then consented to David fighting the giant and, thinking to be helpful, put his own armor on David. But Saul was a much larger man than David, and the young man found it impossible to use his armor.

Instead he went down to the brook and chose five smooth stones for his sling. It has been suggested that he chose five because later, in the book of 2 Samuel, we read that Goliath had four brothers. David was prepared to take on the whole family!

When the Philistine champion saw David coming, he cursed David for his youth and vowed to give his flesh to the birds of the air and the beasts of the field, but David calmly replied that "this day the Lord will deliver you up into my hands" (17:46). David's faith rested in the assurance that "the battle is the Lord's." Projecting a stone from his whirling sling, he struck the giant between the eyes and Goliath fell on his face to the ground. David ran and seized the giant's own sword and cut off his head with it. Thus he becomes a picture of the One who encountered the great enemy of mankind and met him face to face and slew him with his own sword. We read in Hebrews 2:14, by death Jesus "might render powerless him who [has] the power of death, that is, the devil." David becomes here a picture not only of Christ, but also of the believer who lives the life of Christ.

This event is followed by the story of Saul's great jealousy of David. Because of his great victory over Goliath David has now become the sensation of the nation, and Saul eyed him with increasing envy from that day on. Twice, in his madness, Saul sought to kill David with his spear, but both times David evaded him. In sharp contrast with this, Jonathan, Saul's son, openly sought friendship with David and it is recorded he "loved him as himself" (1 Sam. 18:1).

Saul's enmity toward David grew so fierce that he attempted to enlist Jonathan in a plot to kill David. Jonathan nobly defended David and gained a temporary reprieve for him from the king's wrath. Soon, however, Saul again attempted to kill David with a spear, and once again David escaped. The king then sent soldiers to

David's house to take him, but Michal, his wife, let David down through a window and, placing an image under the blankets on David's bed, reported to the messengers that David was ill (19:11-14). When her duplicity was discovered she excused it to her father by claiming David had threatened to kill her if she did not aid his escape.

David, however, fled to Samuel at Ramah, and there, when Saul sent messengers after him, was protected by a direct divine intervention in which the Spirit of God turned back three companies of soldiers by compelling them to prophesy. At last when Saul himself came to capture David, he too was seized by the Spirit of God and prophesied before Samuel, so that it was said throughout all Israel, "Is Saul also among the prophets?" (19:24).

From here to the end of the book, we have the story of the unceasing persecution of David by Saul. It is a living illustration of the principle Paul declares in Galatians 4:29, "He who was born according to the flesh persecuted him who was born according to the Spirit." The quote refers directly to Esau and Jacob, but the principle is reflected in various accounts in Scripture, and especially in this account of the persecution of David by Saul. It was during these days of constant flight that David wrote many of the psalms, those wonderful songs which speak of God's faithfulness in distressing conditions.

David returned to seek the intervention of Jonathan with his father, and the two young men exchanged vows of eternal friendship. Jonathan knew that God had chosen his friend to be king, but he was without jealousy and consented to the divine appointment, only asking David to promise that he would not cut off his friendship from Jonathan and his descendants after he became king.

When Saul noted David's absence from the royal table, Jonathan explained that he had given him permission to go to Bethlehem. Upon this, Saul fell into a great rage and threw his spear at Jonathan. Seeing the king's unreasoning rage, Jonathan warned his friend by an appointed signal that his life was in great danger. The two took their leave of one another in a touching scene of mutual grief (1 Sam. 20:42).

Through the painful persecution that David was now experiencing it is evident that God was preparing him for the work that lay before him. He fled first to Nob, the city of priests. There, needing bread, he was given the Bread of the Presence from the table of showbread in the Tabernacle (21:6). Centuries later, Jesus would refer to this incident and justify David's conduct as the actions of a man of faith. However, the next incident reveals David's occasional fear, for he sought refuge among the Philistines in the city of Gath. There he found his reputation as a valiant warrior had preceded him. To avoid being slain by the Philistines, he pretended to be mad, letting his spit run down his beard. It is sad to see the anointed of the Lord reduced to such tactics to save his own skin. The story stands as a continuing warning against taking refuge among those who are basically the Lord's enemies.

David now gathered about him a band of some 400 men and made his guerrilla headquarters in the cave of Adullam. There everyone who was in distress, everyone in debt, and everyone who was discontented gathered to him. When Saul was told by Doeg the Edomite (a descendant of Esau) concerning David's visit to Ahimelech the priest, Saul summoned the entire body of priests to his presence. There he accused them of harboring David and ordered them to be killed. When the king's soldiers refused to kill the Lord's priests, Doeg the Edomite fell upon them and killed 85 persons. One of the sons of Ahimelech, named Abiathar, escaped the slaughter and joined David in his hiding place (chap. 22). It is interesting to note that in his exile David the king had a prophet, Gad, and a priest, Abiathar, whose resources were available to him even though he was being hunted, ''just as one hunts a partridge in the mountains'' (26:20). So too when we find ourselves in trouble, unable to work out our problems ourselves, we can find in the Lord Jesus Christ, (who is our Prophet, our Priest and our King) all that it takes to bring us through the time of trouble to the place of reigning and triumph.

King Saul's relentless pursuit of David meant that the affairs of the kingdom were falling in great disarray. The Philistines took full advantage of this condition, and attacked the city of Keileh. It is David, rather than Saul, who responds. With 600 of his men he put the Philistines to rout and saved the city. When David learned that Saul had heard he was in Keileh and was sending an army against him, David consulted the Lord through his priest, Abiathar, and learned that the men of the city were ready to give him up to Saul's vengeance.

Again he fled, this time to the wilderness of Ziph. There Jonathan sought him out and encouraged his heart with reminders that God had determined to make him king over Israel. The Ziphites attempted to betray David into the hands of Saul, but David was spared when the Philistines launched another attack and Saul had to turn aside from his pursuit of David and go against the Philistines (23:15-29).

David's greatness of spirit is revealed by the account of Saul's renewed pursuit of him after returning from the battle with the Philistines. Saul unwittingly entered the very cave in which David and his men were hiding. While Saul was in there, David managed to cut off the hem of the garment he had laid aside. After Saul left the cave David came out and held up the piece of garment as proof that when he had him in his power he did not take vengeance but rather honored him as the Lord's anointed and spared his life. Saul seemed to be moved by this mercy on David's part and acknowledged that David would indeed be king some day. But since David and his men returned to their stronghold, it seems they attached little importance to Saul's words (24:22).

The death of Samuel at this point meant that Israel had lost a great voice for God and a great prayer warrior for the people.

We then in, chapter 25, have the account of Nabal (which means "fool") and his wife, Abigail. When this wealthy but mean-spirited farmer was shearing his sheep near Mount Carmel, David sent 10 of his young men to ask for a supply of food, reminding Nabal that the safety he enjoyed was due to the presence of David and his men. Nabal refused with unusual churlishness, and David, angered, gathered his men to wreak vengeance upon the foolish man.

When Nabal's wife Abigail heard that David was intent upon their destruction, she hastily sent David a generous present of bread, wine and sheep, clusters of raisins and cakes of figs. Mounting her donkey she went toward the men and met David on his way to revenge. There, with gracious words, she reasoned with him, reminding him that he was taking vengeance into his own hands and this would be evil in the eyes of the Lord. David courteously commends her for the service she has rendered him in preventing a bloody deed on his part.

When Abigail, the next morning, told her husband Nabal of his narrow escape from death, the shock brought on an attack, which 10 days later resulted in his death.

When David heard of Nabal's death, he sent his servants and claimed Abigail as his wife. We are also told that David took Ahinoam of Jezreel to be his wife as well, in place of Michal whom Saul had given to another. Here we have evidence of a weakness in David which would ultimately lead him into the most terrible sin of his life.

Once again the Ziphites attempted to betray David to Saul, and once again Saul pursued him with an army of 3,000 men. This time David and two of his men found

Saul sleeping at night in the midst of his camp, and, carefully stealing into the camp amidst the sleeping men, David took Saul's spear and water jar and left the camp. Then standing afar off he called out, waking the king and his men, and rebuked Saul's general, Abner, for his lack of care of the king. He again reminded Saul that he had had an opportunity to take his life but spared him because he was the Lord's anointed.

Once again Saul was moved with remorse and confessed to David, "I have played the fool" (26:21). But there is no attempt to restore David to his rightful place, and the account ends with Saul returning to his headquarters and David going his way into exile again.

This perhaps accounts for David's weary and despondent statement that he feels he must soon perish at the hand of Saul, and again David seeks refuge among the Philistines, asking of King Achish accommodation in the town of Ziklag (27:5-7). From there he carried out raids against other Canaanite enemies of Israel. But in his reports to Achish, David deceived him into thinking his attacks were directed against the cities of Israel. It is clear that when a believer takes refuge among those who are the enemies of faith he is in great danger of violating some fundamental principle of righteousness himself. Surely the God who had delivered David from the hand of Goliath could have kept him from the hand of Saul, without the necessity of resorting to a refuge among the Philistines.

This dallying with the Philistines resulted in David being compelled to join the Philistine army in preparing to launch an attack upon Israel (28:1). When King Saul learned that the Philistines were gathering against him he was afraid and sought the Lord for guidance, but the Lord refused to answer him in any manner. In desperation, Saul disguised himself and sought out a medium, though he himself had given orders long before that such mediums should be put to death. Saul asked the medium of Endor to recall Samuel from the dead to advise him. Evidently God overruled in this and sent, not an impersonating spirit as the medium expected, but the true Samuel who announced Saul's impending death on the battlefield the next day (28:13-19).

The scene changed then to the Philistine armies who were assembling for the battle. When the lords of the Philistines saw David among them, they protested to King Achish and forced David to turn back. When David returned to Ziklag he found that in his absence the city had been sacked by the Amalekites. He sought the guidance of God and set out in pursuit. He managed to overtake the raiders and attacked and destroyed them, recovering his two wives and great quantities of spoil. He insisted that 200 of his men who had been too exhausted to join him should share equally in the spoil with those who had gone with him; for he maintained that it was the Lord who had delivered the enemy into his hands and not those who fought.

The closing chapter of the book recounts the fulfilling of Samuel's prophecy; for when the battle was engaged between Saul and the Philistines, the Philistines overtook Saul and slew all his sons, including Jonathan, and wounded Saul. When his armor-bearer refused to kill him, Saul died by his own hand. The Philistines, finding Saul's body with those of his sons, cut off their heads and hung their bodies on the wall of the city of Bethshan, but the men of Jabesh-gilead recovered them by night and buried their remains in Jabesh.

So Saul joined Samuel in the life beyond, but as one whose earthly life was essentially wasted and whose opportunity for service in eternity was thereby diminished. His life recalls the words of Paul in 1 Corinthians 3:14: "If any man's work which he has built upon it remains, he shall receive a reward."

CHAPTER NINE

The King After God's Own Heart

SECOND SAMUEL

Since the books of 2 Samuel and 1 Chronicles cover the same period of time, even though from quite distinct viewpoints, and though they do not follow one another in the biblical order, they may be studied as one book. They both center upon the story of one man—David, the king after God's own heart.

Second Samuel falls into four simple divisions: (1) chapters 1-5 trace David's road from king over the tribe of Judah only, to total dominion over the 12 tribes of Israel seven years later; (2) chapters 6-10 highlight the themes of worship and victory—those two things that always go together in the Christian life; (3) chapters 11-20 record David's failure and God's forgiveness and the results of both in David's life; (4) chapters 21-24 comprise an appendix which sets forth certain important lessons learned by King David in the course of his reign.

In focusing thus upon the life of David there are two ways that we may view him. First, it is perfectly proper to see him as a picture of the Lord Jesus Christ, for Jesus Himself used this analogy. David was not only the forerunner and ancestor of Jesus according to the flesh, but in his reign he is a picture of the reign of Christ during the millennium. David went through a long time when he was rejected, persecuted and harassed; but during that time of exile he gathered men around him who later, after he was king, became his commanders and generals. Thus

David pictures Christ in His rejection—forsaken by the world but gathering in secret those who will be His commanders, generals and captains when He comes to reign in power and glory over the earth.

Second, David is also a picture of each individual believer; and it is only as we read these histories from that point of view that the books come alive and glow with truth for us. "These things . . . were written," Paul says, "for our instruction" (1 Cor. 10:11), that we might understand ourselves as we see events worked out in the lives of these characters in the Old Testament.

The story of David portrays what happens in a Christian's life as he follows God into the place of dominion and reigning. Every Christian is offered a kingdom, just as David was offered a kingdom. That kingdom is the believer's own life and it is exactly like the kingdom of Israel. There are enemies threatening it from the outside and there are enemies threatening it from within, just as there were enemy nations outside the boundaries of Israel and there were enemy tribes living amongst the people within the land. The enemies from without are representative for us of the world and the direct attacks of the devil upon us. The enemies within represent those internal enemies of the flesh that threaten to undermine and overthrow the dominion that God intends us to have as we learn to reign in life by Jesus Christ. We do not call them Ammonites, Jebusites, Perrizites, etc., as they are called in the Old Testament, rather we call them jealousy, envy, lust, bitterness, resentment, worry, anxiety, etc. But they are the same enemies and proceed in the same ways.

What an accurate picture all this is! David, in 1 Samuel 13:14 is called "a man after [God's] own heart"; but King Saul, the first king of Israel, is labeled "the king like the nations around." Thus, as we have seen in 1 Samuel, Saul represents the man of the flesh who tries in his own way to please God by good-intentioned, highly sincere but basically disobedient efforts to be religious. For him everything falls apart. We learn from Saul that the Christian life is not to be a shabby imitation of the life of Jesus Christ. It must be the real thing, with Christ Himself living His life in us. But as Saul is the picture of the flesh and its attempt to imitate reality, David is the picture of the man after God's own heart, the believer in whom the Spirit of God dwells and who is open to the instruction of the Spirit and is led by the Spirit.

FROM EXILE TO THE THRONE

Second Samuel opens with a second account of the death of Saul, the man of the flesh. David learns of Saul's and Jonathan's death from a passing Amalekite who boasts that he slew King Saul, took his crown from off his head, and brought it to David (2 Sam. 1:10). When we recall that an Amalekite is a descendant of Esau and one with whom God has said He is at war ''from generation to generation'' (Exod. 17:16), we can regard his tale as essentially a fabrication, for it differs in considerable degree from the account of the death of Saul in 1 Samuel. Without a doubt he found the dead body of the king and attempted to despoil it and use it for his own advancement. The whole story affords an accurate picture of how the flesh can steal away our crown and seek to turn it to its own glory. David however honors Saul as the Lord's anointed, and gives the Amalekite the ultimate penalty.

In a song of great beauty and power, David, ever the man of faith, extols both Saul and Jonathan as men used of God despite their weaknesses. The song closes with an eloquent expression of David's sense of loss at the death of his dear friend Jonathan (1:26).

David's first act after the death of Saul was to inquire of the Lord where he should establish his residence as king of Judah; God directed him to the city of Hebron (''fellowship''). Here David was anointed as king by his own tribe of Judah (2:4) and with true nobility of character he commends the men of Jabesh-Gilead for having recovered and buried the body of Saul. However, kingship over all 12 tribes was not to be easily gained, for Abner, the cousin of Saul and his leading general, took Ishbosheth, the 40-year-old son of Saul, and anointed him king over all Israel outside of Judah. This act precipitated warfare between David and the house of Saul, which broke out in immediate conflict between Abner and Joab, David's nephew and general over the fighting men of Judah. Both these men were strong and powerful leaders and remained rivals throughout their careers. In the first encounter, Abner killed Asahel, Joab's brother and Joab was never to rest until his vengeance was satisfied by Abner's death.

The warfare between David and the house of Saul continued for the duration of seven years. Matters were brought to a crisis by a quarrel that broke out between Abner and King Ishbosheth, the son of Saul. Abner felt that he was unjustly charged with taking to himself a concubine of Saul's and in anger he swore to transfer his loyalty to David and thus to carry out what he felt all along was God's purpose: to make David king over all Israel. But when Joab, David's general, learned that Abner, his hated rival, was about to become David's supporter, Joab lured Abner into a private conversation at the gate of Hebron and there slew him (3:30). King David promptly denied all complicity with this murder, openly praised Abner to the people, and followed his bier to the grave. This greatly pleased the people, and David steadily won his way into that respect and love which is the greatest support for the power of a king.

Chapter 4 recounts the bloody story of the murder of Ishbosheth by two men of the tribe of Benjamin. They brought the head of Ishbosheth to David in Hebron, thinking to gain his approval but he met them with the same treatment he had given the Amalekite who brought the news of Saul's death. Their immediate death at the hands of David's men demonstrated again David's unwillingness to make use of subterfuge and injustice to secure the ends appointed by God. Nevertheless, with the death of Abner and Ishbosheth, the warfare with the house of Saul is ended and the way is now clear for David to be king over all of Israel. In our lives, this depicts the time when we come at last to the full truth of the cross and what that cross has done in putting to death the old man within us, thus bringing an end to the reign of the flesh, as pictured by the house of Saul. When at last it breaks upon our astonished minds that God really means it when He says He has separated us from the life of Adam and linked us to the life of Jesus Christ, and thus our old man no longer has any right to live, then we are standing right in the same place David was when he saw the opportunity to ascend to the throne over all the united land of Israel.

The elders of all the tribes gathered at Hebron and there publicly acknowledged David as king over the entire land (5:1-3). His first act was to attack the city of Jerusalem, the home of the Jebusites, and by forcing an entrance through a secret water tunnel he gained control of the site and made it his capital. Following this, he built a magnificent house of cedar in Jerusalem with the aid of Hiram the king of Tyre. Here in 2 Samuel 5:13-16, a note of weakness interjects, for we learn of further wives and concubines which David added to his family and from which were born many sons and daughters.

His growing power as king was immediately manifest in a double victory over the Philistine armies.

WORSHIP AND VICTORY

With the borders of land secure and a standing army of 30,000 men, David felt the time had come to bring the Ark back from its long resting place in the city of Keriath-jearim, here called Baal-Judah. David built a new ox cart and set the Ark in the middle of it and started back to the city of Jerusalem with the people singing and rejoicing around the Ark (6:5). It was a time of enthusiastic, utterly sincere, and complete dedication and devotion to God. But then a terrible thing happened: as the Ark was going down the road the cart hit a rut and trembled and shook so that it looked as though the Ark was about to fall off the cart. A man named Uzzah, standing by the cart, reached out his hand to steady it and the moment his hand touched the Ark the lightning of God struck him dead. David was nonplussed and fearful, not knowing what to do.

Of course, it cast a pall of tragedy over the whole scene, and the rejoicing and merrymaking was abruptly stopped. David was so sick at heart that he turned the ox cart aside and put the Ark of God in the house of Obed-Edom. Then he returned to Jerusalem, bitter and resentful against the Lord for doing such a thing.

Although David was afraid of the Lord because of this event, the truth was that it was David's fault that Uzzah had died. In the book of Leviticus there were very specific and detailed instructions on how the Ark was to be moved. Only the Levites were to touch it. It was David's fault that the Levites had not been asked to move the Ark. He was presumptuous enough to assume that God was so strongly for him that he could get away with almost anything. David had to learn the lesson that sincerity in serving God is never enough. Things must be done God's way in accomplishing God's will.

Perhaps you have had some similar experience. You may have had some favorite project which you felt, in the earnestness of your heart, would be a wonderful thing to glorify God, and you set about it, determined to bring it to pass. But God failed to bless the project and the whole thing crumbled to pieces. The death of Uzzah stands as a constant testimony that it is not God's responsibility to carry out our program; it is rather our responsibility to be in such a relationship to Him that He may carry out His program.

After three months, during which the Ark brought great blessing to the house of Obed-Edom, David had recovered to the point where he was ready to bring the Ark into Jerusalem, borne properly upon the shoulders of the Levites. As he danced in joy before the Ark he drew the contempt of his wife Michal, the daughter of Saul, who looked out at him from her window. But David was able to ignore her reproach, for he knew that what he had done was proper and right before the God of Israel.

Before David brought the Ark back to Jerusalem he had brought the Tabernacle from Gibeon for the Ark to rest in. But now he found himself concerned that he himself was dwelling in a beautiful house of cedar, while the Ark rested in a lowly tent (7:1,2). It came into his heart to build a magnificent house for the Ark of God. When Nathan the prophet heard of this he encouraged David to fulfill his desire. But God sent a message to Nathan saying that it was not His will for David to build the Temple, since he was a man of war; only a man of peace could properly build the Temple of God. Surely this anticipates the New Testament truth that Jesus Christ alone, the Prince of Peace, is capable of erecting the Temple of God among humanity. Though God had rejected his plan to build the Temple, David, evidently learning the lesson of Uzzah, humbly accepted the divine will, and in a prayer of great beauty and humility praised God for His glorious leadership over himself and the nation, and accepted the reversal of his own plans with grace and patience (7:18-29).

The rest of this major section gives itself to an account of David's consolidation of his kingdom, conquering many of Israel's ancient enemies on every side, including Edom, Moab, the Ammonites, the Philistines, the Amalekites, and even the Syrians, far to the north.

A beautiful interlude is recounted of David's search for any remaining sons of Jonathan (chap. 10). Upon finding one named Mephibosheth, who had been lamed by a fall on the terrible day when Saul and Jonathan fell in battle, David brought him to Jerusalem, set him at his own table, and treated him as his own son. Thus he remembered his covenant with Jonathan to "show the kindness of the Lord" to his descendants. In all this he appears afresh as a man after God's own heart.

DAVID'S FAILURE, GOD'S FORGIVENESS

The next part of the story of David can be told in three simple sentences: he saw; he inquired; he took. It is the story of his tragic downfall and the entrance of sudden and terrible sin into David's life.

Walking on the roof of his house (when he should have been in battle), David saw a beautiful woman taking a bath. He sent and inquired about her, and then he took her. In those three statements we have a graphic tracing of the process of temptation. All temptation begins, first with a simple desire. There is nothing wrong with the desire, for it is awakened in us because we are human beings. It may be along any avenue, but whenever it appears it must be properly dealt with. Either it is to be put away, or it is to be formed into a proper intent. David saw the beautiful woman, desired her, and then began to work out a way by which he could take her, even though he knew it was wrong. This was followed immediately by an act of adultery, and David, "a man after God's own heart" is thus involved in deep sin.

When the act was accomplished he refused to face the music, as many of us do. Instead of openly confessing and acknowledging the wrong and trying to make it right, he committed another sin to cover it up. This is often the process of sin. Commit one sin and you must commit another to cover that one up, and 10 more to cover up the second. So when David found out that Bathsheba was pregnant, he sent for Uriah, the husband of Bathsheba, and tried to trick him into lying with his wife, thus covering up David's double-dealing. But Uriah, in simple faithfulness to his duty and to God, confounded David. The matter ended finally in the murder of Uriah at the hands of the Ammonites. Joab, David's ruthless general, became a conspirator with David in the plot, and Uriah was placed at the forefront of battle. Though slain by the Ammonites, it was really David who was the murderer. So, suddenly and appallingly, there breaks into David's life the double sin of adultery and murder.

Many have wondered how the man who is called "a man after God's own heart" could ever merit such a title after being guilty of such a sin. But if you want to see what God meant when he called David "a man after his own heart," look at what happens in David's life when God sent Nathan the prophet to him. Nathan told the king a parable, which caught him completely off guard; and when the king responded in righteous anger, Nathan charged him with having committed the sin he had just condemned. Immediately, David acknowledged and faced his sin; he no longer tried to justify it, but confessed his total wrong in this matter. It was at this point that David wrote Psalm 51. Many have turned to this psalm in times of guilt and self-condemnation, and have found in David's experience the grace to handle their own sin properly before God, and to know also the washing away of stain and ugliness in the ever-flowing stream of God's mercy.

Chapters 12 through 20 record the results of David's sin as they unfolded in his life. When Nathan the prophet came to David, he told him, "Thus says the Lord, 'Behold, I will raise up evil against you from your own household; I will even take your wives before your eyes, and give them to your companion, and he shall lie with your wives in broad daylight' " (12:11). This was to be literally fulfilled by Absalom, David's own son. Nathan had further said to the king, "However, because by this deed you have given occasion to the enemies of the Lord to blaspheme, the child also that is born to you shall surely die" (v. 14).

So it proved to be. The first result was that the baby born of this illegitimate union died, even though David pled with the Lord in a pathetic, poignant passage which reflects the tearing of his heart by grief. Then the predicted results in David's home, his family, and his kingdom began to appear.

Chapter 13 tells the dark story of Amnon, David's son, who sinned against his own sister, Tamar. This resulted in a black hatred born in Absalom, also David's son, against Amnon. In David's family, among his own sons, was spread a bitter spirit of rebellion and evil created by David's personal failure. The story of Amnon and his quarrel with Absalom, and finally the murder of Absalom at the hand of Joab, shows King David to be utterly helpless. He cannot even rebuke his own son, for Amnon simply follows in David's footsteps.

We are told next of the uprising of Absalom (chap. 15). This handsome, brilliant, gifted son of David fomented rebellion throughout the whole kingdom and secretly worked against his father in attempting to take the throne for himself. He was so successful that David, along with all his court, finally had to leave the city, fleeing as an exile. Weeping, David left the city, barefoot and with his head covered as symbolic of his penitent heart. He acknowledged the fact that these evil circumstances were the result of his own folly. But even in his humiliation and shame he had the presence of mind to send Abiathar and Zadok back into the city; he told his friend Hushai that he could serve him better by remaining behind, rather than acompanying him in his exile.

Further ignominy was added to the fleeing king when

Zeba, Mephibosheth's servant, met him with the false information that Mephibosheth had remained in Jerusalem with the expectation of seeing the house of Saul restored by Absalom (16:1-3). Also Shimei the Benjamite and a relative of Saul openly mocked and cursed King David. But when Abishai, Joab's brother, sought permission to kill Shimei, David, with great magnanimity of spirit, restrained him, remarking that perhaps the Lord had sent Shimei to humble David even further (16:5-12). Thus he showed himself, even in his humiliation, as a man after God's own heart.

Meanwhile, back at Jerusalem, Hushai had won the confidence of Absalom and was invited to act as one of his counselors. Ahithophel, formerly David's advisor, suggested to Absalom that he immediately pursue and kill his father. Hushai was able to turn Absalom from such counsel and advised him rather to wait until he could gather a large army from all of Israel and then go up against the king. In suggesting this, he was seeking to give David time to gather men.

Eventually the two forces came to battle in the forest of Ephraim, and a mighty conflict ensued, resulting in the death of over 20,000 men. When Absalom saw that his forces were defeated he tried to escape on a mule through the forest. He was caught in a branch of a tree and left hanging by the head in midair. When Joab heard of this, he immediately went to the spot and, taking three darts, thrust them into Absalom's heart, directly contravening the orders of David who had commanded his men to spare Absalom's life. When the news of Absalom's death was brought to David he was crushed with sorrow and cried, "O my son Absalom, my son, my son, my son Absalom! Would I had died instead of you" (18:33).

So distraught was David that Joab ultimately reproved him for his mourning and warned him that he was in danger of losing the support of his fighting men by apparently loving his rebel son above all his loyal supporters.

The section ends with the account of the return of David in triumph to Jerusalem. Again he showed magnanimity to the now remorseful Shimei, who formerly had cursed him, and was gracious again to Mephibosheth, who explained that David had been deceived by Mephibosheth's servant. David's return, however, was marred by the rebellion of Sheba, a Benjamite, who sought to exploit the situation by leading a break-away rebellion from David's authority. Abishai and Joab were sent to suppress the outbreak and on their way they met Amasa, formerly Absalom's commander, at Gibeon. Joab, knowing that David had offered to make Amasa commander in his place, treacherously greeted Amasa with an apparently friendly kiss, but instead stabbed him with his sword and left his body wallowing in blood on the highway. The strange ferocity of this man, coupled with his loyalty to David, was manifested clearly in this bloody deed.

The insurrection ended when a woman in the city where Sheba had taken refuge convinced the townspeople to save their city from siege by beheading Sheba and throwing his head over the wall to Joab. Thus, through much humiliation, shame and bloodshed David was restored to his position as king, and the affairs of the kingdom were once again set in order.

THE EPILOGUE

The epilogue to 2 Samuel, chapters 21 through 24, gathers up, though not in chronological order, some of the events and lessons which David experienced through his 40-year reign. The first is the story of the Gibeonites whom Saul had attacked, contrary to the covenant which Joshua had made with them when he first had conquered the land. The result of Saul's breech of faith was a continuing famine in that section of the country which could not be ended until expiation was made by handing over to the Gibeonites seven of Saul's sons or grandsons. The lesson of this incident is that the past must be reckoned with. If there are things in our past which can still be corrected, we have a responsibility before God to go back and set these things straight. Thus, in the account of David and the Gibeonites, a correction was made of something which occurred under King Saul, and as Saul's heir to the throne, David had to set it straight.

Chapter 22 records one of David's most beautiful psalms. It appears again as Psalm 18. In it is found David's own recognition of the things that made for greatness in his kingdom. He acknowledged God as the source of all human strength and the One who alone can bring deliverance. He stated that what a man is to God, God will also be to that man. If one is open and honest and forthright with God, He will also be open and honest and forthright in return. But if a man insists on being crooked and perverse and deceitful, God will cause the circumstances of his life to deceive him. This reflects the same truth that Paul declares in Philippians 3:12, in which he says, in essence, about Christ, ''what I am to Him, He will be to me.''

The final chapter gives the account of David's third great sin as recorded in this book—his sin of numbering Israel. Many have wondered why God would view this as sin, since He Himself had commanded Moses to number the people, as recorded in the book of Numbers. But David's numbering was done from a quite different motive, as seen in the rebuke of Joab to the king. Apparently the king began to reckon on his military might and the numbers of the people rather than wholly on the grace and power of God. For his sin, David was given a choice of three possible punishments; wisely, he left the matter in the hands of the Lord. To indicate the seriousness of reliance on human strength, the angel of the Lord was sent among Israel for three days, and a pestilence took the lives of 70,000 men. The prophet Gad was sent to the king to tell him to erect an altar on the threshing floor of Araunah the Jebusite, where the plague was stayed. This was later to be the site of the erection of the Temple in Jerusalem.

Thus 2 Samuel closes with the man after God's own heart turning from his sin to the worship of the living God.

FIRST CHRONICLES

It is clearly evident that 1 Chronicles was written after the return of Israel from their 70 years of captivity in Babylon. It was probably written by Ezra the priest, who also wrote the book which bears his name. Ezra was one of the great figures who returned with the captives to reestablish the Temple and the worship of Jehovah in Jerusalem.

Although 1 Chronicles covers much of the same period as 2 Samuel, it does so with a particular emphasis on the worship of Israel. This is evident in the opening chapters. The first nine chapters are given over to a long list of genealogies. This is not merely the stringing together of many names, but is a compilation of some of the most helpful material available to anyone working on the problem of biblical chronology. If we look at these names carefully and compare them with other accounts, we will see that God is selecting and rejecting, excluding and including and working toward an ultimate goal. These genealogies are given that we might see both the goal toward which the Lord works in human history, and the principle by which He includes or excludes events.

THE PROCESS OF SELECTIVITY

The genealogy begins in chapter 1 at the dawn of

human history, listing the sons and descendants of Adam—Seth, Enosh, Kenan, Mahalalel. We know that among the sons of Adam were Cain, Abel and Seth, but here Cain and Abel are excluded and there is no mention of them. The focus is upon the descendants of Seth, for from him eventually came the family of Abraham and the Israelites. Here is the principle of exclusion in evidence.

Then the line of Seth is traced down to Enoch and Noah. The three sons of Noah are listed as Shem, Ham and Japheth, but Ham and Japheth are dismissed with a brief word and attention is focused on the line of Shem. From Shem we trace on down to Abraham and his family. The constant narrowing process also excludes Ishmael, the son of Abraham, and Esau, the son of Isaac, and focuses on Jacob's 12 sons who became the fathers of the 12 tribes of Israel.

The genealogy continues and selects the tribes of Judah and Levi—the king and the priestly lines. It traces the tribe of Judah down to David, to Solomon and then through the kings of the house of David to the Babylonian captivity. The tribe of Levi is traced down to Aaron, the first of the priests, and then to the priests who were prominent in the kingdom at the time of David.

In all these genealogies there are interspersed brief reasons for the selections which are made, and certain isolated incidents are reported. One is found in chapter 4:9, where we read, "Jabez was more honorable than his brother, and his mother named him Jabez saying, 'Because I bore him with pain' " (Jabez means "pain"). The reference goes on to recite the brief prayer of Jabez in which he asks God to enlarge his borders and keep him from harm. God granted him what he asked. This apparently minor incident reflects the principle God follows in His process of selectivity. Wherever God can find an obedient heart, that individual is included in the account. In the case of Jabez, his native disabilities were cancelled out by his faith and he is immediately made an effectual instrument in the working of God through him in history. When God excludes a name, or turns from a line or family, it is always on the basis of repeated disobedience. This principle can be traced throughout the entire genealogical record.

Chapter 10 gives a brief account of the death of Saul, the first of Israel's kings. Verses 13 and 14 tell why Saul's kingship ended: "So Saul died for his trespass which he committed against the Lord, because of the word of the Lord which he did not keep; and also because he asked counsel of a medium, making inquiry of it."

GOD'S KING

The rest of 1 Chronicles is about David. The book emphasizes that from the moment he was anointed king, David was God's king. His first act after coming to kingship in Israel was to take over the pagan stronghold of the Jebusites, the city of Jerusalem—God's city. This was the place where God had chosen to put His name among the tribes of Israel.

Beginning with chapter 11:10, the account names those who were loyal to David during his exile, and the things they did that made them mighty. These were men of faith and passion, and were attracted to David by the character he displayed. These mighty men who shared David's exile eventually became the leaders in his kingdom. It is a beautiful picture of the glory we are promised to share with the Lord Jesus when He establishes His kingdom of righteousness over all the earth.

A second emphasis of the book is on the Ark of God. In chapter 13 we are told that David went down to the city where the Ark was situated and took it upon a cart to bring it back to Jerusalem. Evidently David knew that the law commanded that the Ark be carried only by Levites, but in the exuberance of his joy and his zeal for God's cause he attempted to do it another way. The result was the immediate death of Uzzah, who touched the Ark to steady it when it appeared about to fall. There is no incident in the Old Testament that teaches more clearly the importance of a careful, precise obedience to what the Word of God says. It also teaches that God is able to care for His own cause. Many today, like Uzzah, are seeking to steady the Ark of God which they feel to be in danger, but it is quite apparent from this incident that God is quite able to defend His own cause.

When eventually David does bring the Ark into Jerusalem, borne by Levites, he placed it in the Tabernacle which he had previouly brought up from the city of Gibeon. The restoration of the Ark to the Tabernacle was an occasion of great rejoicing and we have recorded in chapter 16 the great psalm sung on this momentous occasion. It is made up of parts of psalms 105, 96 and 106. It is a great declaration of the government of God, the majesty of God which draws forth the worship of His people, and a great expression of gratitude to God for what He is in Himself.

The account in chapter 17 of David's desire to build a Temple in place of the Tabernacle and God's rejection of that plan, with David's subsequent prayer of praise and worship, is almost identical to the account in 2 Samuel. Likewise, the story of David's victories over the nations surrounding Israel is, with slight variations, identical with 2 Samuel 8. These stories are beautifully descriptive of what happens in our hearts when Christ is crowned as King. There is immediately a subjugation of the dark enemies of our soul that created so much havoc in our lives.

It is remarkable that the double sin of David in taking the wife of Uriah the Hittite and arranging for the murder of her husband is passed over in this book in total silence. The only reference to it is the fact that "David stayed at

Jerusalem'' (20:1). That sin was one which grew out of his own foolish willfulness as an individual. It had nothing to do with his reign as a king; therefore it is omitted from this book which centers on his kingship. But David's action in numbering Israel is recounted in detail, as representing an abrupt departure from the principle of dependence upon the strength and glory of God. As king, David desired to see the number of people that were available to him, and thus to glory in the physical strength of his realm.

A problem arises in any Christian circle when men begin to depend upon numbers. One of the great principles which runs through the Bible, from beginning to end, is that God never wins His battles by a majority. When we begin to think that the cause of Christ is losing out because the number of Christians is decreasing in proportion to the population of the world, we have succumbed to the false philosophy that God wins His battles by numbers. In many instances throughout the Bible we are taught that God does not rely upon numbers but upon quality. There is the story of Gideon, with God's deliberate reduction of the number of men supporting him from 32,000 to 300. There is also the story of David and Goliath, the deliverance of Israel by a single shepherd boy with a single sling and a single rock from the brook. There is the story of Samson, who slew the Philistines with nothing but the jawbone of a donkey. Thus, all through Chronicles, the same principle is repeated as we find the emphasis upon God's method of the development of quality rather than quantity.

As the result of David's departure from this principle, and because the whole nation looked to him as king, God's judgment was exceedingly severe. The prophet Gad was sent to David to give him the three choices of punishment. When the angel of the Lord came into the midst of the people pestilence raged throughout the nation. David saw the angel with his sword stretched out over the city of Jerusalem, ready to slay there also, and David pled with God saying, "It is my fault; why do you take vengeance upon these others? I am the one to blame" (see 21:17). Then God instructed him to buy the cattle and the threshing floor of Ornan (spelled Araunah in 1 Samuel). On this spot David erected an altar and worshiped God. The altar was placed where the angel of God stayed his hand from judgment.

AUTHORITY OF THE TEMPLE

Chapters 22-29 tell of David's passion for the building of the Temple. Because he understood that a nation without a Temple could never be a proper nation, he longed to see the Temple built. A people without the living God in their midst would never amount to much. Though David knew that Solomon his son had been appointed by God to be the actual builder of the Temple, yet in grace God allowed David to do everything for the Temple but to actually build it. It was David who drew the plans, designed the furniture, collected the materials and made all the arrangements for ritual and ceremony. He brought down cedars from Mount Hermon and Mount Lebanon from the north. He dug up the rock and quarried the stones. He gathered in great quantities of gold, silver and iron, and when it was all ready, David commanded the leaders of Israel to help Solomon in his task. In order to give Solomon the prestige and power necessary to this work, David made him a virtual co-ruler with himself.

Careful detail is given as to the work of the Levites in carrying out the work in the Temple, and special attention is paid to the ministry of music for the services within the Temple. David's musical skill had played a great part in his life, and his interest in these musical arrangements was most natural and delightful. David's concern for every detail of the building of the Temple is evident in his care for the workers who labored in its building, and for the cultivation of crops and the raising of cattle and all that pertained to the welfare of his people in carrying out their central activity—the worship of the living God.

Chapters 28 and 29 recount the final charge of David to his son Solomon and his impressive recital of reasons for God's refusal to allow him to do the building and his choice of Solomon for that task. David then gave to Solomon the pattern of the house with all its detail. Then, standing among the people, David blessed the Lord in the presence of all the assembly, recognizing God's gracious gifts to them and the privilege of giving back to him the very best that men could give. He concluded with a great prayer for Solomon that God would preserve him in safety and grant him a perfect heart to fulfill the great work.

What is the ultimate message of 1 Chronicles? It is the supreme authority of the temple in our individual life. Central to all of life is the worship of the heart. Over the three great doors of the cathedral in Milan, Italy, are three inscriptions. Over the right hand door is carved a wreath of flowers and the inscription, ''All that pleases is but for a moment.'' On the left hand door is a cross, and over it is written, ''All that troubles is but for a moment.'' Over the main entrance are the words, ''Nothing is important save that which is eternal.''

This is the lesson of Chronicles, for it is in some sense the lesson of the whole Bible. ''Whatever you do in word or deed [i.e. in the temple of the body], do all in the name of [by the authority and by the ability of] the Lord Jesus [King in His temple]'' (Col. 3:17).

The Way to Lose a Kingdom

FIRST KINGS

In the Hebrew Bible, our books of 1 and 2 Kings are combined into one book simply called Kings. The present division was not made until the first century before Christ by the translators of the Greek version of the Old Testament, the Septuagint. Since 1 Kings and the first 26 chapters of 2 Chronicles cover the same period of time we will take them together in this study.

The unknown writer of the books of Kings has written not only a book of history, but has selectively chosen significant events from this history that would help his readers understand the internal meaning of the outward events, especially as measured against the covenants which God made with Israel centuries before at Mount Sinai.

First Kings begins with the reign of Solomon and carries us through the tragic division of the kingdom under Rehoboam, the son of Solomon. Then we are given summaries of the various dynasties within the Northern Kingdom of Israel, and the lives of the kings of the single dynasty of the house of David in the Southern Kingdom of Judah. In each case, the spotlight is always on the king, for it was what the king did in relationship to God that determined how the nation went. When the king walked with God in obedience and humility, God's blessing and prosperity and victory rested upon the kingdom. The rains came at the right time, the crops grew and the land flourished. There was victory over their enemies even though the enemies came in allied forces. But when the king disobeyed and allowed the people to fall into the worship of other gods, immediately famines broke out, plagues came, invasions occurred, and the land fell into difficult and serious conditions. The kings that walk in obedience become, as always, types of Christ, such as David, Solomon, Hezekiah, Jehoshaphat, and Josiah. But the kings who walk in disobedience become types or pictures of the anti-Christ, the man of sin who is yet to appear upon the earth.

The factor, of course, that makes even these historic books of perennial fascination to us is that the kingdom of Israel is an accurate picture of our own lives. It was for this purpose that God chose Israel to be a nation and gave it its unique laws and its unique government, in order to provide an example to all the world of what the living God is willing to be in any individual's life. Thus, as we read these books, we find ourselves also in the midst of the problems, the blessings, and the possibilities that are reflected in these books of the kings.

THE REIGN OF SOLOMON

First Kings opens with the last days of David. He appears here as a very old and feeble man, unable to discharge properly the duties of his high office. This feebleness created the opportunity for one of his sons, Adonijah, to foment a rebellion which would make himself the successor to his father. We can place the time of this rebellion as following that of Absalom recounted in 2 Samuel, and occurring just before Solomon was acknowledged openly as joint king along with David, his father. Though Adonijah obtained the support of Joab and Abiathar, the priest, his plans were thwarted by the intervention of Nathan the prophet who, through Bathsheba, David's wife and Solomon's mother, informed King David of the plot. Immediately David arranged for the public anointing of Solomon as king.

Adonijah, fearing Solomon, took shelter at the altar in the court of the Tabernacle and was spared for a season; however, he eventually was slain at Solomon's command. After David's death, Adonijah presumed to threaten the throne by seeking marriage with the girl who had been David's nurse during the closing days of his life.

Before David died, he called Solomon before him and solemnly charged him to walk in the ways of the Lord his God, and to teach his children after him, that the kingdom might endure in safety and prosperity forever (2:1-4). He left to Solomon's wisdom the fate of those men whom David had never fully trusted in his own time—Joab, his brutal and bloody general, and Shimei, who cursed David so violently on the day he fled from Absalom (vv. 5-9). David had kept his covenant with these men by sparing their lives; but they eventually paid for their treachery by death at the command of Solomon. He also deposed Abiathar, the priest, and substituted Zadok in fulfillment of the prophecy given to Eli many decades before.

The reign of Solomon appeared to hold much promise for it is recorded that he loved the Lord and walked in the statutes of David, his father (see 1 Kings 3:3). Soon after Solomon ascended the throne, the Lord appeared to him in a dream and offered him his choice of gifts. Aware of his own incapacities for the heavy demands of government, the young king asked for the gift of wisdom—the ability to distinguish between good and evil. God's answer was one of gracious and abundant mercy for He gave Solomon what he asked, but added also the riches and honor he might have chosen but wisely had passed by. It is clearly evident from this that wealth and fame are proper honors when God bestows them, but if sought for selfish purposes they frequently prove to be curses rather than blessings.

Solomon's gift of wisdom is immediately manifested in the famous story of his choice between two mothers who each claimed a certain baby as her own. When Solomon ordered the child divided by a sword and half given to each, the real mother quickly gave up her right in order that the child might live, though the other woman would possess it. Solomon promptly awarded that child to the first and proper mother. With this incident his fame spread throughout the kingdom.

Solomon's reputation for wisdom spread far beyond the borders of his kingdom, which now extended from the Euphrates in the north to the border of Egypt in the south, almost the entire extent which had been promised to Abraham hundreds of years before. A summary of Solomon's wise sayings included 3,000 proverbs and 1,005 songs (4:32). His fame spread widely, also, as a naturalist and philosopher.

Yet, despite this apparent magnificence a note of weakness is found in his marriage alliance with Pharaoh, the king of Egypt, by bringing Pharaoh's daughter to Jerusalem as his wife. As we have seen, Egypt in the Scripture is always a type of the world's allurement to the human heart. When Solomon brought Pharaoh's daughter into his court the door was open for alliances with other lovely maidens from the tribes around Israel. Soon he had 1,000 wives. And along with them came their idols. Thus, despite outward prosperity and glory, the kingdom began to deteriorate under Solomon because he allowed the world to entice and allure him and draw him away from his heart's interest in the Temple, where his worship should have been centered.

By the fourth year of his reign, Solomon was ready to begin the building of the Temple, 480 years after the Israelites left Egypt. They were now settled in the land of promise, enjoying a season of rest from warfare, and unusual prosperity. In preparing materials for the Temple,

Solomon enlisted the aid of his father's friend, Hiram the king of Tyre, from whom he obtained massive quantities of cedar and cypress wood as well as skilled workers in bronze and gold (5:1-12). The stones for the Temple were quarried out beneath the Temple mount and were finished within the quarry so that "neither hammer nor axe nor any iron tool [was] heard in the house, while it was being built" (6:7). This remarkable sentence finds its parallel in Paul's statement in Ephesians 2:20-22, concerning the building of the church. It is "built upon the foundation of the apostles and prophets, Christ Jesus Himself being the cornerstone, in whom the whole building, being fitted together is growing into a holy temple in the Lord; in whom you also are being built together into it a dwelling of God in the Spirit." Without noise or fanfare the Spirit of God has for 20 centuries been constructing a glorious temple, from living materials, to be a habitation of God through the Spirit.

Solomon built the Temple along the same pattern as the Tabernacle in the wilderness, though it was double the size and was characterized by a greater magnificence and durability. Like the Tabernacle, the Temple was most beautiful from within, for almost everything was covered with pure gold.

In the midst of the account of the building of the Temple, which took a period of seven years altogether, the chronicler interjects a brief account of the building of the palace for Solomon and adds this significant statement: "Solomon was building his own house thirteen years" (7:1). The significance of this is seen in the insightful comment of Dr. G. Campbell Morgan, "If the time and possessions devoted to our own comfort be greater than those devoted to the service of God, it is sure proof that the master passion is self-centered rather than God-centered."

The furniture of the Temple likewise duplicated that

of the Tabernacle except it was of far greater magnificence. When all was finished the solemn moment for the dedication of the Temple arrived. In an impressive ceremony of solemnity and beauty, the Ark of the Covenant was brought from its place in the Tabernacle and installed within the Temple. When the priests came out from the holy place after installing the Ark in the holy of holies, a cloud of glory from the Lord suddenly filled the Temple, and when Solomon saw this evidence of God's immediate presence with His people, he uttered a cry of rejoicing and arose to bless the people (8:15-21).

Then kneeling (v. 54) before the altar of burnt offering and raising his outstretched hands, Solomon uttered a moving prayer of dedication, recognizing the faithfulness of God and the peril of departing from the ways of God (vv. 22-53). His understanding of God's transcendent majesty was manifest in his words, "Behold, heaven and the highest heaven cannot contain Thee, how much less this house which I have built!" (8:27). In prophetic vision he outlined the many circumstances that might arise in which the people would turn, temporarily, away from the ways of God, but from which they might recover when they turned again with repentant hearts to the presence of God, as symbolized by the Temple.

Rising from prayer he pronounced another blessing upon the people, and followed this with the offering of thousands of sacrifices (8:54-64). At the close, the joyful people returned to their dwellings, having participated in the greatest moment of glory the nation was ever to know from the days of Moses and until the time of the Messiah.

After the dedication of the Temple, Jehovah appeared again to Solomon in a dream (9:2-9) and assured him that his prayer had been heard. He told Solomon that His divine promises to David his father were renewed, upon the condition that Solomon and his descendants would walk faithfully before the Lord. If they failed to do this, the beautiful Temple would be torn down and the people would be driven from the land and become a byword and a proverb among the nations.

As we read the account, we know the terrible fulfillment of this in history, for the conditions were not kept either by the king or the people, so that the penalty was fulfilled in precise detail. Again, the parallel to the individual life is self-evident.

Solomon's present of 20 cities in Galilee to King Hiram of Tyre is recorded in 9:10-14. His establishment of various storehouse cities and military barracks throughout the land, and his creation of a commercial navy are detailed in verses 15-28.

At this time, the apex of Solomon's prosperity, the famous visit of the queen of Sheba occurred (10:1-13). Sheba was located in what is now southern Arabia, but even at that distance its queen had heard the fame of Solomon and especially of his noted wisdom and blessing from the Most High God. She came to Jerusalem with a great caravan to see for herself whether what she had heard was true. When Solomon showed her the magnificence of his palace and of his kingdom, she reported that even the half had not been told her, but in words of great insight she expressed clearly that the secret of his greatness lay in the centrality of the government of God.

A further description of Solomon's astounding wealth is given in verses 14-29, in which it is noted that he made silver as common in Jerusalem as stone, and cedar as plentiful as sycamore wood. The wealth of all the nations around seemed to pour into Jerusalem as a result of the blessing of God upon Solomon and his kingdom. Yet the luxury with which the king surrounded himself reveals a love of indulgence which, expressed in many ways, would soon result in widespread dissatisfaction within the nation and ultimate division and decay.

In chapter 11 the writer of Kings unveils in detail the

degeneration within Solomon's heart which was soon to result in the division of his kingdom. The point where evil first took hold was in Solomon's love for women. His commercial enterprises brought him into contact with many surrounding nations, and there he let his heart go after women from nations which the Lord had forbidden the Israelites to enter into marriage with. Soon he built temples for these women to practice their own degraded worship within, and eventually he joined them there, actually bowing down himself to the abominable idols of his pagan wives. For this "the Lord was angry with Solomon because his heart was turned away from the Lord, the God of Israel" (11:9). For the third time He appeared to Solomon, perhaps again in a dream, but this time to announce to him that the kingdom would be torn from him and given to another; yet for David's sake it would occur after Solomon died, during the lifetime of Solomon's son. Immediately we read of several adversaries rising up against Solomon, including Hadad the Edomite on the south, Rezon in the land of Syria on the north, and from within the kingdom itself, Jeroboam the son of Nebat, an Ephraimite who lifted up his hand against the king.

The prophet Ahijah was sent by God to meet Jeroboam outside of Jerusalem. Divesting himself of the new garment he wore, Ahijah tore it into 12 pieces. He handed Jeroboam 10 pieces, symbolizing that Jeroboam would be given 10 of the 12 tribes, while only two—Judah and Benjamin—would remain with the house of David. The promise given to David of divine blessing was extended to Jeroboam if he, too, would walk in the ways of God and keep His commandments as David had done. When Solomon heard of this he sought to kill Jeroboam, but he fled into Egypt and remained there until Solomon died.

After 40 years of unprecedented magnificence and

prosperity, Solomon died and was buried in the city of David, his father, a sad and tragic close to a life which had begun with great promise and possibility.

The life of this man clearly indicates the importance of the will. In the kingdom of your life the human will is the king, and nothing can take place in that kingdom except as it is allowed by the choice of your will. Therefore, what your will does determines what your life will be like. If, willingly and obediently, you yield yourself to the influences of the Holy Spirit dwelling in your human spirit, you are like the kingdom when David walked with God and the land flourished, and the influence of the kingdom reached to the uttermost parts of the earth. But if, like Solomon, you begin to walk in disobedience, if your will is defiant and set upon the things of the flesh rather than the things of God, then evil invasions will begin in your life. You will no longer have strength to repel inward corruptions that ruin and take their toll upon you; thus the kingdom of your life will fall into ruin as well.

THE DIVISION OF THE KINGDOM

When Rehoboam, Solomon's son, came to Shechem to be anointed king, the people, led by Jeroboam who had returned from Egypt, asked that the new king would grant them relief from many of the burdens which Solomon had placed upon them. These included forced labor, unnecessary extravagance, and heavy taxation. The king sent them away for three days and consulted with both the old men who had advised his father and the young men with whom he had grown up. His own pride and despotism was revealed when he chose the advice of the young men. He told the people that their burdens would be increased (12:1-15). This announcement became the signal for widespread revolt. The 10 tribes chose Jeroboam to be their king, fulfilling the decree God had made to Solomon.

Jeroboam set up his capital at Shechem and, fearing that if the people continued to worship at Jerusalem they would eventually return to the authority of Rehoboam, he introduced the great sin for which the Northern Kingdom was ever after to be noted. Making two calves of molten gold, he set one up at the city of Dan in the far north, and another at the city of Bethel, at the border with Judah. Summoning Israel he said to them, "Behold your gods, O Israel" (v. 28). This was a harking back to the sin of Aaron at the foot of Mount Sinai, when he made a calf of gold which the people began to worship. They called that calf, Jehovah (Exod. 32:5), not intending to deny that Jehovah was their God, but foolishly misrepresenting Him as no more than the gods of the nations around.

The parallel in our lives is that *form* of godliness which denies the power of God. It is an outward conformity to Christian faith which lacks the inner response of the Spirit. It means to conform outwardly to everything Christian, but inwardly there is no true worship at all. This is the fatal sin which Jeroboam, the son of Nebat, introduced to the Northern Kingdom.

From this moment on in Israel's history, David and Jeroboam became representative of two spiritual principles that are traced throughout the kingdoms. They became the standards of measurement for the kings that followed. In Judah a good king is said to "walk in the ways of David, his father," and to serve the Lord his God by tearing down the false and abominable worship that Israel had fallen into; but in the Northern Kingdom, the evil kings are said to "walk in the ways of Jeroboam, the son of Nebat, who caused Israel to go awhoring after the gods that he had set up." It is significant that in Israel, the Northern Kingdom, there are no godly kings at all. There is but a continual succession of kings who walk in idolatrous ways and who frequently gain the throne by murdering their predecessor. Despite this, God in grace often intervenes by sending prophets to arrest the decay and fall of the Northern Kingdom.

In Judah, the Southern Kingdom, there were a few godly kings among many who were evil, but these godly men stand out like lights in the darkness. The primary ones were Asa, Jehoshaphat, Joash, Hezekiah and Josiah.

In an attempt to give Jeroboam opportunity for repentance, God sent a prophet to him, warning him of his evil by predicting the immediate overthrowing of the altar. When Jeroboam stretched out his hand to order the prophet's arrest his hand was withered and he could not draw it back. When he begged the prophet for healing, the hand was restored, but it represented no real repentance on Jeroboam's part (13:1-6).

A solemn lesson follows when the prophet attempted to return to his home. He disobeyed the expressed word of the Lord and entered into another prophet's house to eat and drink with him after the man lied and told him God had sent him. There it was predicted that the man of God would die as a result of his disobedience. On the way home a lion met him and killed him. Though no excuse can be made for the prophet who lied to him, nevertheless the account indicates that when God gives a direct command, it must not be disregarded, even though an angel from heaven or another prophet suggests a change.

Further judgment fell upon Jeroboam in the sickness of his son. Ahijah, the prophet, sent word to Jeroboam through his wife that the same God who had exalted him to power and made him king over Israel would now, because of his sin, remove him from the throne. The sign of it would be that his son would die. As Jeroboam's wife brought the news to her husband the child died. Nothing further is told us concerning the 22 years of the reign of Jeroboam except to record his death and the fact that his son, Nadab, reigned in his stead.

Meanwhile, things were going no better in the Southern Kingdom under Rehoboam (14:21), whose 17-year reign also was characterized by the introduction of idolatry and the reappearance of homosexual prostitutes within the land. The result was an invasion by the king of Egypt, who carried away the treasures of gold from the Temple and the king's palace. The substitution of bronze shields and vessels for the golden ones was God's reminder to the king of the deterioration of the worship in the land. A border war raged continually between Rehoboam and Jeroboam, and ultimately it is recorded that Rehoboam, too, slept with his fathers and was buried in the city of David, and Abijam, his son, reigned in his stead.

Abijam lasted three years as king of Judah before he died and one of the good kings, Asa, began a 41-year reign. Asa's reforms included the elimination of homosexual prostitutes and the removal of idols, even that belonging to his mother, the queen, whom he removed from her office because of her idolatry (15:9-13). This partial reform under Asa undoubtedly preserved Judah, for the time, from the decay and corruption which was evident in the Northern Kingdom.

The Northern Kingdom suffered under the rule of a series of evil kings who all walked "in the way of Jeroboam." All this time, God tried to reach His people in Israel. When the most evil of all the kings of the Northern Kingdom ascended the throne, we meet a man whose name rings through history as a prototype of John the Baptist.

ELIJAH: THE PROPHET OF FIRE

Ahab not only adopted the idolatry of Jeroboam but in addition married Jezebel, the daughter of the king of Sidon, and thus introduced the worship of Baal into Israel. It is recorded that "he did more to provoke the Lord, the God of Israel, to anger than all the kings of Israel who were before him." It was during the reign of this evil pair that Elijah, the prophet, made his appearance. This is in line with the declaration of the New Testament, "Where sin increased, grace abounded all the more" (Rom. 5:20). The account of the conflict between Ahab and Jezebel with Elijah occupies the next four chapters, from chapters 17 through 20.

The sudden appearance of Elijah in the account is dramatic and startling. He came from Gilead, east of the Jordan, but not much more is known of his nationality or parentage. He suddenly confronted Ahab with the announcement that the living God was about to bring a drought upon the land, which would not be relieved until Elijah gave the word. The drought began immediately and was very severe. To protect him from the wrath of Ahab and Jezebel, Elijah was sent first to the brook Cherith where he was fed by ravens, and then to the land of Sidon on the coast, where he lived with a widow and her son.

After three years Elijah was sent back to confront Ahab, who greets him with the words "Is this you, you troubler of Israel?" (18:17). Elijah responds that it is the king who, through his vile idolatries, has troubled the land, and challenges him to a contest between the prophets of Baal and the power of God, to be held on Mount Carmel. There follows a familiar story, full of drama and majesty. On one side are 450 prophets of Baal and 400 prophets of Asherah. On the other side stands Elijah alone, crying out, "If the Lord is God, follow Him; but if Baal, follow him" (v. 21). There is a sardonic humor in the description of the Canaanite prophets calling out in vain for their god Baal to burn up the sacrifice that waited on the altar. Elijah mocks them by suggesting that perhaps the god is asleep, or has gone on a journey, or even has gone to the bathroom to relieve himself.

Finally, it was Elijah's turn, and after drenching his sacrifice with water he prayed a mighty prayer of faith, and God answered by devouring the sacrifice by fire from heaven. When the prophets of Baal had been proved to be false prophets, they were put to death. Then, in answer to the prayer of Elijah, the rain, which had not fallen for three years, now came in great torrents.

The fury of Jezebel was awakened by the destruction of her prophets. She sent a message to Elijah threatening him with immediate death (19:2) and, surprisingly, the prophet who stood with great courage against 850 adversaries on Mount Carmel, now fled for his life from a single woman. But God, with great patience and tender care, met first his physical need and then sent him to Mount Horeb where He gave him a great revelation of Himself through "a still small voice." That quiet voice then rebuked him for his lack of faith and revealed to him that there were yet 7,000 within the nation who had not bowed the knee to Baal. He was then sent back to anoint Hazael to be king of Syria, Jehu to be king of Israel, and Elisha to be prophet in his own place (vv. 9-18). The obedient prophet returned to the land and, finding Elisha plowing with oxen, cast his mantle upon him. After offering a sacrifice, Elisha took up his new role as servant to the old prophet.

Despite the wickedness of Ahab, God's patient mercy was extended to him on the occasion of an attack upon Samaria by the king of Syria, Ben-hadad (chap. 20). With arrogance Ben-hadad demanded the surrender of the city but, through an unnamed prophet, Jehovah announced the defeat of the Syrians at the hands of Israel.

Again the Syrians came against Samaria the following spring. Once again Israel won by the mercies and grace of God. But in the moment of his triumph, Ahab made a covenant with Ben-hadad whom God had clearly devoted to destruction. For this, God sent a prophet again to the king to announce his doom. Characteristically, Ahab returned to his house, "sullen and vexed" (20:43).

The terrible struggle between good and evil in the

heart of King Ahab seems to reach its crisis in the account of his selfish longing to possess the vineyard of his neighbor, Naboth. Thwarted by Naboth's unwillingness to sell, the king behaved with such petulance that his wife, Jezebel, offered to obtain the vineyard for him by an evil ruse. Falsely charging Naboth with having cursed God and the king, Jezebel obtained his death by stoning at the hands of the citizens of the city. But when Ahab went to the vineyard to take possession he is suddenly confronted by the rugged prophet, Elijah. Upon hearing from Elijah that his dynasty would end, Ahab tore his clothes and, with fasting and sackcloth, expressed his repentance before God. It was enough to obtain a temporary reprieve. God announced that "I will bring the evil upon [Ahab] in his son's days" (21:29).

The final chapter in both Ahab's life and the book of 1 Kings details the story of the visit of Jehoshaphat, who ascended the throne of Judah, to establish an alliance with King Ahab of Israel. Planning war against Syria, Ahab invited Jehoshaphat to accompany him, and the two kings, through 400 false prophets attached to Ahab's court, sought the mind of God as to the outcome of the battle. Their prophecies promised success, but Jehoshaphat insisted upon consulting Micaiah, a true prophet of God in Israel. At first he gave an ironic confirmation of the prediction of victory, but when pressed gave the true word of the Lord, predicting the death of Ahab during the battle.

By a cowardly ruse Ahab placed Jehoshaphat of Judah in a conspicuous place during the battle, hoping that he would be mistaken for himself and be killed. But an arrow shot into the air (by chance) by a warrior on the opposite side, found its way through Ahab's armor and into his heart. God is the God of circumstances, and even the God of accidents! Ahab's body was brought to the capital where his bloodstained chariot was washed, and the dogs licked up his blood according to the prophecy of Elijah. The final account of the book briefly summarizes the reign of Jehoshaphat of Judah, who walked in the godly ways of his father Asa. This story is picked up and continued in the second book of Kings.

The stories covered in this first book of Kings highlight the great truth declared in Proverbs 4:23, "Watch over your heart with all diligence, for from it flow the springs of life." The picture drawn for us, in our individual lives, reveals that nothing we face in terms of outward pressure or circumstances can ever succeed in dethroning us. Such dethronement will only come as we permit some rival worship to enter the heart and replace the living God. When we become emotionally attached to some place or someone that is a rival to the worship of God, then our kingdom's days are numbered.

SECOND CHRONICLES 1—20

Since the first 20 chapters of 2 Chronicles cover the same chronological period as 1 Kings and, for the most part, in somewhat briefer style, it will not be necessary to cover it in detail. There are, however, certain omissions and also certain additions which merit comment, and it may be helpful to point out additional factors that would apply in the parallel experiences of our own spiritual journey.

The first nine chapters recount again the story of the reign of Solomon. His humble request for wisdom from God's hand, his building of the Temple and construction of its furniture, and the solemn and impressive ceremonies of the Temple's dedication, are detailed. The visit of the queen of Sheba is also recorded here.

It is the nature of Chronicles, as different from Kings,

to give us more of detail of the worship of Israel and Judah and their kings than it does on historical matters. The transference of the worship of the nation from the Tabernacle at Gibeon to the Temple in Jerusalem symbolizes the growth of a Christian. From his early up and down experience, like Israel in the wilderness of wandering, a Christian grows to a more settled condition where he recognizes the Lord Jesus as King and Ruler and walks consistently in the light of God's settled presence.

In building the Temple, Solomon is the type of Christ as the Prince of Peace, who has the honor of building the true temple of the Holy Spirit, the human body. In Hebrews we are told that Moses had honor in God's house (the Tabernacle) as a servant, but Christ had more honor for the builder of the house has more honor than the house itself (see Heb. 3:5,6). Christ is the One who has made the temple of our body, which contains the sanctuary of the Spirit.

All this is pictured in the physical temple, described in 2 Chronicles. What a beautiful place it must have been! It was small, as temples go, but incomparably beautiful. The entire interior was completely lined with gold. It has been estimated that the value of it was some $10,537,000. The furniture of the Temple, except for the Ark of the Covenant, was rebuilt completely. The Ark, which symbolized the initial meeting place of God and man, needed no duplication, for the new birth can never be repeated. But in other ways, the Temple represented a new beginning. This parallels the experience of many Christians who, often after years of a vacillating experience, come to a place where, intelligently, conscientiously and with permanent intention, they yield themselves anew to the Lordship of Christ. Emotionally, it is almost like being born again. That is what is depicted in the new beginning of the Temple.

The response of God to Solomon's dedication of the

Temple, recorded in chapter 7, is given in somewhat fuller detail than the account in 1 Kings. Here the well-known promise is found in verse 14: If "My people who are called by My name humble themselves and pray, and seek My face, and turn from their wicked ways, then I will hear from heaven, will forgive their sin, and will heal their land" (2 Chron. 7:14).

The story of the visit from the queen of Sheba to Solomon is a wonderfully illustrative picture of the means by which God intended the whole earth to know the story of His grace. Jews of the Old Testament were never sent into the whole world, as we are commanded to do now in the Great Commission. God's grace was rather displayed by the building of a land and a people so wondrously blessed of God and so obviously different from all other nations around, that word of it would spread to the uttermost parts of the earth. People would then come to Jerusalem from all over the earth to learn the secret of God's blessing.

In the New Testament, God's supreme method of evangelism is that every believer is to be walking in obedience to the Spirit of God who inhabits the temple of his human spirit, and his life is to so manifest the victory, the rejoicing, the blessing, the prosperity, and the joy of the Lord, that people around will ask, "What is the secret of this life?" As 1 Peter 3:15 puts it, "Sanctify Christ as Lord in your hearts, always being ready to make a defense to every one who asks you to give an account for the hope that is in you, yet with gentleness and reverence." That is God's most effective method of evangelism.

An additional note is given in 2 Chronicles 11 covering the reign of Rehoboam, the son of Solomon. Despite the personal weakness of the king there was considerable spiritual vitality within Judah, and the secret of it is given to us in verses 16 and 17: "And those . . . who set their hearts on seeking the Lord God of Israel, followed them to

Jerusalem to sacrifice to the Lord God of their fathers. And they strengthened the kingdom of Judah and supported Rehoboam the son of Solomon for three years, for they walked in the way of David and Solomon for three years.'' Rehoboam misunderstood the secret of his strength and, it is later recorded (12:1): "He and all Israel with him forsook the law of the Lord." In consequent judgment, the king of Egypt, Shishak, came against him and carried off the treasures of the house of the Lord.

It is noteworthy that in 2 Chronicles, only the kings of Judah are reported in detail. The northern kings are passed over except as they had contact with the kings of Judah.

The obscure prophet Azariah, the son of Oded, is introduced during the days of Asa, the king of Judah (15:1). His ministry is revealed as having a part in the godly reign of Asa. Further detail is also given in Chronicles regarding the reign of Jehoshaphat of Judah. Upon returning from the disastrous battle of Ramoth-gilead, where Ahab of Israel was slain, Jehoshaphat was rebuked by the prophet Jehu for having made an alliance with Ahab. The king's response of turning back to God brought immediate reactions for good among the people. Jehoshaphat set judges over the people and reminded them that God was no respecter of persons, and they, too, would be accountable before Him.

Soon after, Judah was threatened by a powerful invasion of the united armies of Moab, Ammon, and certain Edomites. The response of the king was to lead the nation in prayer before the Temple. Confessing their powerlessness and their ignorance of what to do in the situation, but pleading with God for His intervention, the answer was immediate, for the Spirit of the Lord came upon a Levite and he prophesied that Israel need only take their position before the enemy but would not need to fight, for God would fight on their behalf. With music and singing the people went out to meet the foe; and Jehovah sent such confusion and terror among the enemy that they turned upon each other and their vast army was completely destroyed.

Yet, in his closing years, Jehoshaphat made another foolish alliance with Ahaziah, king of Israel, joining him in a naval expedition which met with disaster. Shortly afterward, King Jehoshaphat died, ending a reign of 25 years during which he had, for the most part, walked in godly ways, though it is recorded (20:33): "The high places, however, were not removed; the people had not yet directed their hearts to the God of their fathers." One of the outstanding highlights of his reign had been the sending out of bands of Levites, headed by the princes of Judah, to teach the law of God among the cities of Judah. As a consequence, the fear of the Lord fell upon all the lands around and they made no war against Jehoshaphat until the final invasion of the Edomite host. Thus, God was with the man who was with Him, and honored him with a protracted period of peace.

CHAPTER ELEVEN

Light and Shadow

SECOND KINGS

Since the two books of Kings in our present Bible were originally one book, 2 Kings continues on in the account of the kings of Judah and Israel where 1 Kings ends.

Second Kings opens with the closing incident of the life of Elijah during the reign of King Ahaziah of Israel, the son of Ahab. Ahaziah reigned for only two years and the last word we read of him in 1 Kings was that he "provoked the Lord, the God of Israel, to anger in every way that his father had done." Perhaps for this, he fell through a lattice window and, while lying injured, sent to inquire of the pagan god, Baalzebub, as to whether he would recover. For this he was severely rebuked by Elijah the prophet, who informed him that he would die.

When the king sent a band of 50 soldiers to capture him, Elijah called down fire from heaven to consume them. Another band of 50 men met with a similar fate, and when the third band of 50 came, the captain entreated Elijah to spare him and his men, and the prophet went with him to the king to convey personally his sentence of doom. When the king died his brother Jehoram succeeded him, for Ahaziah had no son.

Here a certain degree of difficulty enters in keeping straight the two lines of kings in Israel and Judah, for when this Jehoram had reigned for seven years in Israel another Jehoram, the son of Jehoshaphat, began his reign in Judah. The problem is further complicated by the fact that a shorter spelling, Joram, was used for both kings at various times. A similar confusion later exists with Kings Ahaziah and Joash.

Elijah's last moments on earth and his triumphant and miraculous translation into heaven without dying is next related in careful detail. When the faithful Elisha refused to leave him until his moment of translation, the mantle of Elijah fell upon him. He had been promised a double portion of the spirit of Elijah and this became evident immediately in the first two incidents of his ministry. There was the punitive character of Elijah in the story of the she-bears who came out of the woods to destroy those youths who jeered at him, in mockery of Elijah's translation (2:24). But there is also clearly evident the spirit of grace and kindness when he made the bitter watters wholesome by throwing a handful of salt into them (2:20,21).

These two men, Elijah and Elisha, both portray the future ministry of the Lord Jesus Christ. Elijah pictures His attitude toward official Israel, reflected in Christ's two cleansings of the Temple with the whip of cords and with flashing eyes, while Elisha pictures the ministry of Jesus to individuals, filled with compassionate tenderness and helpfulness.

During the reign of Jehoram of Israel, the nation Moab rebelled against Israel's control and Jehoram joined with King Jehoshaphat of Judah and the king of Edom to suppress the rebellion. The allied kings found themselves in the desert with no water. They sought the counsel of Elisha who promised that the valley should be filled with water, though no rain would fall, and that their attack upon Moab would be successful. Evidently a flash flood from some considerable distance did indeed fill the valley with water without any rain falling on the spot, and their campaign was successful, as the prophet had predicted.

Chapters 4-8 contain a series of incidents from the life and ministry of Elisha, which are given in a somewhat jumbled chronological order but are presented together in this way to indicate the ministry of mercy extended to individuals while the judgments of God ground out the ultimate overthrow and exile of the nation. In these miracles Elisha provided a continuous flow of oil to a poor widow until she had enough to pay her debts; he healed the barrenness of a wealthy woman of Shunem who had been kind to him; she later bore a son and he raised this same child from the dead when he succumbed to a sudden fever; he rendered harmless a pot of poisonous vegetables by casting in a handful of meal; he fed several hundred men with only 20 loaves of bread; he healed the Syrian general, Naaman, from leprosy by having him dip seven times in the Jordan River; he caused a lost axehead to float on top of water; he opened his servant's eyes to see the Lord's chariots of fire that were protecting them when the Syrian army was besieging them; he rescued the city of Samaria by making the attacking Syrian army hear sounds of a great army which frightened them away; he predicted to Hazael, the Syrian general, that his master, Ben-hadad, king of Syria, would recover from his sickness but would be murdered by Hazael who would then proceed to bring much distress upon Israel. This insight caused Elisha to weep, much as centuries later Jesus wept over the coming destruction of Jerusalem.

In 2 Kings 8:16 the chronicler returns to the history of the Southern Kingdom of Judah, giving a brief account of the reign of Joram, the son of Jehoshaphat, who married the daughter of Ahab of Israel and "walked in the way of the kings of Israel, just as the house of Ahab had done" (v. 18). As a result of his evil the land of Edom revolted from the rule of Judah as did the city of Libnah. Joram was succeeded by his son Ahaziah (v. 24) who joined with King Joram of Israel to war against Hazael, king of Syria.

During the battle Joram of Israel was wounded and returned to Jezreel to recover. While Ahaziah of Judah was visiting him Elisha sent one of the young prophets to anoint Jehu, the general of Israel to be king in Joram's place. Immediately Jehu mounted his chariot and, driving furiously, headed for Jezreel.

Learning that Jehu was on his way, the two kings, (Joram and Ahaziah) set out to meet him and came upon him at the vineyard, formerly belonging to Naboth. There the prophecy of Elijah to Ahab was fulfilled when Jehu drew his bow and slew Joram, leaving his body in the vineyard of Naboth. As Ahaziah fled, he was shot by Jehu's men and, wounded, fled to Megiddo, where he died.

Coming back to Jezreel, Jehu saw Jezebel, Ahab's widow, looking at him from her window. Jehu called to her attendants to throw her down from the window. When they did so her body was eaten by dogs, again according to the prophecy of Elijah.

Jehu then became a terrible scourge in the hands of God. But he himself did not turn from the sins of Jeroboam and "was not careful to walk in the law of the Lord, the God of Israel, with all his heart" (10:31). As a consequence, parts of Israel fell into the hands of Syria and after a reign of 28 years, Jehu died and his son Jehoahaz reigned in his stead.

When the queen mother, Athaliah (daughter of Ahab and Jezebel) learned that her son, Ahaziah, was dead, she seized the throne of Judah for herself, murdering the entire royal family (her own grandsons), except for an infant named Joash, who was hidden by his sister in the Temple. Like her mother, Jezebel, Athaliah was a devotee of Baal worship, and for the six years of her reign she did her best to introduce the worship of this male sex god to Judah, installing a priest named Matten to officiate at her altars.

During this six year period, the boy king, Joash, was still hidden in the Temple, as evidence of the divine overruling of human events. But in the seventh year, Johoiada the priest, the husband of the woman who had hidden Joash, organized a plot to put Joash on the throne. With the support of the army and the priesthood, he brought the seven-year-old boy out and publicly anointed him as king. Athaliah was slain and the temple of Baal destroyed (11:13-18).

Joash (also spelled Jehoash) reigned for 40 years in Judah; and it is recorded he "did right in the sight of the Lord all his days in which Jehoiada the priest instructed him" (12:2). The major event of his reign was the repairing of the Temple, which had been neglected for many years. This was accomplished by special offerings which the king himself oversaw. The close of his reign was shadowed by an invasion from Syria which Joash, in cowardice, averted by surrendering the treasures of the Temple to the king of Syria. Soon after this, a conspiracy was plotted by his servants, and Joash was slain in Jerusalem and his son Amaziah ascended the throne.

Turning again to Israel the Northern Kingdom, we find Jehoahaz, the son of Jehu, upon the throne. He continued the evil of the kings before him and in consequence the Syrians, under King Hazael, reconquered great portions of the land, and left Jehoahaz with an army of only 50 horsemen and chariots and 10,000 soldiers. Seeing the low state of Israel, the king turned to the Lord and besought His help. In response, "a savior" was granted to Israel. We are not told who this was, but it is very likely that it refers to an incident with Elisha the prophet, which immediately followed (13:14-19).

After a reign of 17 years Jehoahaz died and his son, Joash (not to be confused with the Joash of Judah) reigned. During his reign Elisha died and was buried, but even after his death miracles followed him. A group of men seeking to dispose of a body were suddenly surprised by a mob of bandits. They threw the body into the tomb of Elisha and when the body touched the bones of Elisha the man sprang back to life. Thus the entire ministry of Elisha seems to typify the ministry of the Spirit of Christ in bringing life out of death.

Turning briefly to Judah we are told that Amaziah, the son of Joash, "did right in the sight of the Lord, yet not like David his father" (14:3). Still the high places were not removed and worship continued there instead of at the Temple in Jerusalem where it belonged. Amaziah won a great victory over Edom and, emboldened by this, he challenged the power of King Joash of Israel. They met in battle and Amaziah was captured and a portion of the wall of Jerusalem was broken down and the Temple entered and sacked. Though Amaziah was permitted to reign 15 years after the death of Joash of Israel, eventually a conspiracy was made against him and he was slain in the city of Lachish. His son Azariah, who was only 16 years old, was made king in his place.

In Israel Jeroboam II, who followed his father Joash to the throne, had reigned for 41 years. During this time he reconquered all of Israel's territory from Syria and even brought Damascus and Hamath of Syria under tributary to Israel. The prophet Jonah (famous for his escapade with a fish) ministered in Israel during the days of Jeroboam II, also the prophets Amos, Hosea and Isaiah. Yet despite this gracious touch from the Lord, Jeroboam walked in evil ways and after his long reign, was replaced by his son Zechariah (15:8).

Azariah (15:1) is known as Uzziah in the book of 2 Chronicles (26:1-3) and also in the prophecy of Isaiah (6:1). It was during his long reign of 52 years that Isaiah began his great ministry. Azariah followed in the footsteps of his father, Amaziah, but like him did not remove the high places nor interfere with the worship that went on there. In 2 Chronicles 26:16 we are told that "when he became strong, his heart was . . . proud" and sought to offer incense himself upon the altar in the Temple at Jerusalem. For this he was smitten with leprosy and remained a leper until his death. His son Jotham shared the regency with him and succeeded to the throne upon Azariah's death.

Meanwhile in Israel, things were rapidly sliding into chaos. Zechariah, the son of Jeroboam, only reigned for six months and was slain by Shallum who thus ended the dynasty of Jehu in the fourth generation, as had been predicted. Shallum was only on the throne one month, and was succeeded by Menahem, who slew him and reigned for 10 evil years, characterized by cruelty and extortion. During his days the land was invaded by the new world power of Assyria to the north. Menahem was forced to pay tribute to Pul (otherwise known as Tiglath-pileser).

Menahem was succeeded by his son, Pekahiah, who reigned for two brief, evil years (2 Kings 15:23) and was slain by an army captain named Pekah. During Pekah's reign of 20 years, Tiglath-pileser of Syria invaded the northern portion of Israel and carried off captives from Galilee. Pekah later was slain by Hoshea, who had the support of Assyria. This murderous state of affairs in Israel was testimony to the persistent evil of king and people, in turning from the living God.

Things were not much better in Judah, for though Jotham, the son of Amaziah, walked before the Lord in some degree of righteousness, nevertheless, during his 16-year reign, the kings of Syria and Israel threatened the land of Judah, sent, as we are told, by the hand of the Lord as a judgment against Judah.

Jotham was followed by his son Ahaz, who likewise reigned for 16 years in Jerusalem. During the reign the nation sank to a new low, for the king himself practiced the abominations of the Canaanites, even offering his son as a burnt offering to the god Moloch. When the combined armies of Syria and Israel came against him he sought help from the king of Assyria, offering to be his vassal. He followed this idiocy by constructing a heathen altar in the actual courts of the Temple, commanding the priests to offer sacrifice on it (16:10-16). Further, he desecrated some of the holy furnishings in the outer court of the Temple. Yet during his reign, Isaiah and Micah, the prophets, carried on a faithful ministry of testimony to the truth.

In chapter 17 we have the record of how God's long patience with Israel was at last exhausted, and the divine stroke of judgment falls. During the nine-year reign of Hoshea, the last king of Israel, Shalmaneser V of Assyria, invaded Israel and besieged Samaria. After three years the city fell and the Assyrian king systematically deported the Israelites into various cities of Assyria and Media.

Careful assessment is made of the reasons for this overthrow of the people of God. Their persistent sins of pride, evil practices, and public idolatry are detailed, and especially set against the patient love of God who had warned them repeatedly through prophets and seers.

When the 10 tribes had been deported, the Assyrian king attempted to repopulate the land of Israel with people from Babylon and other countries, who brought with them their own idols. Experiencing some difficulty in settling in the land, they blamed it on their ignorance of the God of Israel, and it is recorded that they "feared the Lord, and served their graven images" (17:41, *KJV*). This attempted religious mixture probably contributed to the enmity between the Jews and Samaritans which, centuries later, was recorded in the New Testament (see John 4). This is clear testimony to the folly of trying to mix the religion of man with divine revelation. The result is corruption worse than anything else. The Christian church can provide many examples of this principle.

While Israel was collapsing in the north, Hezekiah, the son of Ahaz, began his reign in Jerusalem (chap. 18). His father had been an ungodly king, but Hezekiah, perhaps warned by the fate of Israel, began to walk wholeheartedly before the Lord. It was said of him "after him there was none like him among all the kings of Judah, nor among those who were before him" (18:5). The kingdom had fallen into such decay that when he came to the throne his first act, as we learn from 2 Chronicles, was to cleanse the Temple. It took the Levites 16 days to carrry out all the rubbish which had collected (2 Chron. 29:17). Hezekiah also reinstated the Passover in Israel and dstroyed the great brazen serpent which the people had been worshiping (2 Kings 18:4). This was the serpent God had used for their blessing when Moses erected it in the wilderness. It had become a souce of idolatry just as many things which once blessed our lives become idols if we begin to hold them in too high regard.

When Hezekiah had been on the throne for 14 years, the Assyrian king Sennacherib, who had replaced Shalmaneser, invaded Judah and took certain of their fortified cities. Frightened by this, Hezekiah offered to pay tribute, and was forced to strip the gold from the Temple to meet the payment required. Undeterred by this, the Assyrian king sent his general Rabshakeh, to besiege Jerusalem. With terrible arrogance and scorn, the Assyrian general challenged, not only the might of Israel, but the power of their God to deliver them.

In desperation, Hezekiah turned to his old friend, Isaiah the prophet, who reassured the king that God was yet in control and would turn the Assyrian hosts aside, by causing them merely to "hear a rumor" (19:7). When Rabshakeh returned to learn Hezekiah's answer, he found that Sennacherib had been diverted by rumors of an attack from Ethiopia. A letter was sent to Hezekiah to warn him that the Assyrians would return, and nothing could save him from their wrath. Hezekiah spread the letter before the Lord in the Temple, and in a moving prayer, called upon God for His deliverance (19:14-19).

Apparently when the Assyrians returned to the attack, Isaiah the prophet sent word to Hezekiah announcing that the Lord held Assyria and its armies in utter contempt, and by His own mighty hand would turn them back upon the way they had come. That very night an angel of the Lord entered the camp of Assyria and slew 185,000 men (19:35). Secular history records this as a great plague which swept the camp. With the remnant of his army Sennacherib departed for Nineveh, where, according to the prophecy of Isaiah, his sons slew him in the temple of his gods.

When King Hezekiah fell sick and was told he would die, he wept bitterly and besought the Lord for a reprieve (chap. 20). In response to this, his life was extended for 15 years, and as a sign, the shadow on the sundial turned back 10 degrees. In those 15 years, however, Hezekiah had a son whom he named Manasseh, who became the worst king Judah ever had. His was the longest reign of any of the kings, extending for 55 years of ungodliness. Some have said, therefore, that Hezekiah was "the man who lived too long," for had he accepted the word of the Lord about his death, Israel would have been spared the terrible days of Manasseh. Also during these 15 years, Hezekiah received the envoys of the king of Babylon and showed to them all the treasures of the house of the Lord. For this he was severely rebuked by Isaiah, who prophesied that the things which the envoys had seen would ultimately be carried to Babylon. In due course Hezekiah died and Manasseh became king.

Manasseh's long reign of 55 years is covered in brief account, for it is said, "he rebuilt the high places which Hezekiah his father had destroyed; and he erected altars for Baal and made an Asherah . . . and worshiped all the host of heaven and served them'' (21:3). His reign is summarized in these words, ''Manasseh seduced them to do evil more than the nations whom the Lord destroyed before the sons of Israel'' (v. 9). His son, Amon, followed him to the throne, to reign for two years. He was killed in a conspiracy and his son Josiah was made king in his stead.'

Josiah was eight years of age when he came to the throne (22:1). His reign marked the last attempted reformation before the kingdom would be carried into captivity. The evil state of the nation after Manasseh and Amon is seen in the fact that when King Josiah attempted to clean out the Temple and repair it a book of the Law of Moses was found within. Incredible as it may seem, neither the king nor the people seemed to know of its existence. The sacred writings had been so neglected that the actual Temple copy was lost. When this book was read to the king, his sensitive conscience was greatly distressed, and he turned for counsel to the prophetess Huldah. She responded that it was too late to save the nation from its fate, but that the reforms which the king would effect would delay the judgment of God until he had gone to his grave.

With great enthusiasm the king began his reform, first reading the book of the Law directly to the people and then making a personal covenant to walk before the Lord and keep His commandments with all his heart. The Temple was cleansed of all idolatries of the false cults, and throughout the country idolatrous priests and altars were put away (chap. 22). The reform extended even to Bethel in the north, which had been part of Israel, and the altar at Bethel which Jeroboam had erected was torn down and ground to dust.

Following this the Passover feast, which had long been neglected, was observed again in moving ritual and power (23:21-23). Homosexual prostitutes, wizards, mediums, and other abominations were swept from the land. But despite King Josiah's sincere efforts at reform,

· the heart of the people was not truly repentant, and when Josiah was slain in battle with Pharaoh Neco of Egypt and his son Jehoahaz succeeded him, the nation immediately returned to evil ways.

After a brief reign of three months, the king of Egypt deposed Jehoahaz and set his brother Eliakim, whose name he changed to Jehoiakim, upon the throne.

For 11 years Jehoiakim reigned, first as a tributary to Egypt and then for his last three years, under tribute to Nebuchadnezzar, king of Babylon (24:1). During these years the land was torn by raiding bands of Chaldeans, Syrians, Moabites and Ammonites, for the long patience of God was now ended.

Jehoiakim was succeeded by his son Jehoiachin, but after a brief reign of three months Nebuchadnezzar came against the city, besieged it, and eventually overthrew it and carried off to Babylon both the people and the treasures of the city. Jehoiachin was carried to Babylon as well and his brother, Zedekiah, was set upon the throne as a vassal king in Jerusalem. In his ninth year he attempted to rebel against Babylon, and again Nebuchadnezzar came against the city and besieged it. In Zedekiah's eleventh year a breach was made in the city wall. The king was captured and blinded and sent to Babylon in chains. The house of the Lord was burned, the walls of the city broken down, and a governor was appointed over the land. When the governor was later murdered, the remnant of Israel fled to Egypt (25:26). Thus the nation which God had called and delivered from the power of Egypt, returned to that land as a scattered and suffering people.

Yet a touch of grace closes the book, for after 37 years of imprisonment in Babylon, Jehoiachin was released by Evil-merodach, king of Babylon, who showed him great kindness and permitted him to feast from the king's table for the rest of his life.

We remember that the book of Kings began with the

wonderful scene of Solomon, his kingdom at peace, kneeling in his royal robes, praying to the God of heaven. Contrast this with the final scene when the Temple lay in ruins, the city was destroyed and the people were slaves and bondservants in a foreign country. In this contrast we have a vivid picture of what happens in the human heart when it disobeys God. God's loving warnings are ignored for so long that God's patience draws to an end and disaster follows.

SECOND CHRONICLES 21—36

Since the record of 2 Chronicles chapters 21-36 cover the same events that we have just covered in 2 Kings it is unnecessary to repeat the story in detail. Though in general the accounts are briefer than in 2 Kings, the author of Chronicles gives more understanding of the reason events occurred. Greater detail is given of the reformation under King Hezekiah and King Josiah than in Kings, and we learn from Chronicles that Manasseh, the most wicked king of Judah, after he had been taken captive by the Assyrians and sent to Babylon, repented from his evil and turned with a whole heart to God. He was restored to his throne and in the closing years of his life accomplished certain reforms within Jerusalem. But although the king's personal repentance was genuine, and met with the gracious restoration of God, nevertheless his long years of evil had so affected the people of the nation that when his son Amon came to the throne, the evil ways of Manasseh broke out in full force again throughout the land.

The closing days of Judah and the exile into Babylon are traced in much briefer detail than in Kings, and in the closing paragraphs we learn that the reason for the 70 years of exile was in order to permit the land to enjoy its

Sabbath; the nation for 490 years failed to keep the sabbatical year of rest.

An additional note of hope is struck at the very end of Chronicles when the writer recounts how the Spirit of the Lord stirred up Cyrus, the king of Persia, after the years of exile, to issue a decree to build again the house of God in Jerusalem. This lays the groundwork for the record in the books of Ezra and Nehemiah and suggests perhaps that the writer of Chronicles was Ezra, the priest.

As we contemplate in these historical books the sorrowful record of the decline of the nation from its days of glory in the time of Solomon to the awful record of the exile, there are many valuable lessons to draw in the parallel experiences of our individual lives. Certain steps can be traced in the downward path of the nation.

THE PATH TO DESTRUCTION

First, there was the *self-indulgence* of Solomon, which weakened the spiritual strength of the people. Following him, Rehoboam his son turned a deaf ear to the advice of his older counselors and, it is recorded that when he was strong, "he forsook the law of the Lord." As a result, the kingdom was invaded by the Egyptians. So in our lives the moment there is a turning away from obedience to the voice of God there is an immediate weakening of the defenses of life and the enemies begin to invade.

When Jehoram followed his father Jehoshaphat to the throne, a spirit of *jealousy* in the royal family enters, and it is recorded that Jehoram slew all of his brothers with a sword and also some of the princes of Israel. Further he made high places in the hill country of Judah and led the inhabitants of Jerusalem into unfaithfulness. This too was quickly followed by invasion and by plague.

In Israel, King Ahaz introduced directly the *worship of the Baals* with their despicable practices of vile and sexual nature. Ahaz further burned his sons as offerings;

immediately invasion followed from the king of Syria. We sometimes wonder why we fall prey to afflictions and oppressions, to nervous reactions, and depressive -neuroses. Sometimes these are from physical causes, but often it is because the defenses of our temple are destroyed. Some inner idolatry is weakening us, and we find ourselves defenseless against the invaders of the spirit that bring on depression, frustration, defeat and darkness. So the awful account goes on, set against the continual efforts of a patient God to awaken the consciences of evil kings and correct the practices of a stubborn and rebellious people.

THE GRACE OF GOD

By contrast, the good kings of Judah reflect the grace of God in cleansing and restoring the land and the people. There are five great reformations recorded during which God sought to arrest the deterioration of the nation and restore it to the place of glory and blessing as in the days of David. With each one, certain principles of reformation are revealed which have also application to us.

The first of these periods of reformation was under King Asa. He not only took away the foreign altars and high places, broke down the pillars, and hewed down the Asherim (a sex symbol), but also "commanded Judah to seek the Lord God of their fathers and to *observe the law and the commandment*" (2 Chron. 14:4, italics added).

It is not surprising, therefore, that when he was attacked by the Ethiopians with an army of a million men, the prophet Oded met him and said to him, "The Lord is with you when you are with Him" (15:2). Thus in Asa we find a determination to obey the Lord as an important principle in reformation. The way to return ends in renewal of the vow, a renewal of the determination and hunger to walk before the Lord. Immediately, there is a return to rest.

King Jehoshaphat during his reign also cleaned out the idols from the land, but in 17:7-9 a second principle of restoration is stated: "In the third year of his reign he sent his officials . . . *to teach in the cities in Judah; . . . having the book of the law of the Lord with them*" (italics added). Here the great principle is that of study and teaching of the law and the Word of God.

Under King Joash we have the third principle of reformation. The main accomplishment of Joash was to *restore the Temple, and to do it required the collection of long-neglected taxes.* If, as we have seen, the Temple represents the human spirit, then the repairing and restoring of it is a picture of the strengthening of the spirit. This is often accomplished by the process of restitution—the paying of that which we owe. It may be an apology to someone, or the restoring of something wrongfully taken, or putting back something which has been wrongfully used. No matter—it is an important principle of return.

In Hezekiah's reign, a fourth principle is seen in the *cleansing of the Temple*. The Temple was finally cleansed after 16 days of clearing out rubbish. The worship was restored and a Passover celebrated. This clearly pictures the cleansing of the Temple of our spirit by putting away the filth which has accumulated. It is to turn away from wrong ideas and concepts and attitudes to which we have given ourselves and to turn back to the cleansing of the Lord and the renewing of our minds with truth.

Then, in Josiah, the last good king of Judah, we find the final principle of restoration. His attempts to restore the worship of the Temple resulted in finding anew the book of the Law which had been lost. Josiah himself publicly read this book to the people and made a covenant to walk before the Lord and obey His commandments. Thus the final principle of restoration is a *return to the hearing of the Word of God and a determination to daily walk in its light and understanding*.

Let us never forget that as we read these books we must bear in mind the words of Paul in 1 Corinthians 10:11: "Now these things happened to [Israel] as an example." We have noted specific details of these from the various incidents we have covered, but even in the total picture there is a remarkable parallel.

From the very beginning of the monarchy there were two divisions within the nation. Even under David this was true, for David was king only of Judah for seven years and it was only during the last 33 years of his life that he reigned over all 12 tribes. Thus a division between the 10 tribes of the north and the two tribes of Judah and Benjamin in the south existed from the start. But though there were two sections within the nation they were intended to worship only at Jerusalem and to be under the authority of only one king. Taken as a whole, therefore, it is evident that the nation of Israel represents the divisions of our humanity.

There are clearly two divisions in us: the outer man, consisting of the body, and the inner man, consisting of soul and spirit. But in the capital city of Jerusalem the very essence of the nation was vested in the Temple wherein the living God dwelt. We know from the Scriptures that in the human life there is not only body and soul but within the soul, so closely linked with it that only the Word of God can divide between soul and spirit, is the spirit, the dwelling place of God. Thus the temple of the Spirit was in Jerusalem and all the worship of the kingdom was to be there.

In this picture, then, the 10 tribes of the north represent the body, while the two tribes of Judah and Benjamin in the south represent the human soul, and linked to the soul is the temple of the spirit where the Spirit of God Himself dwells. This is surely what the Lord Jesus had in mind when He said to the woman at the well of Samaria, "God is spirit; and those who worship Him must worship *in spirit* and truth'' (John 4:24, italics added). We find many who worship him in soul, that is mere emotional worship. But God is not interested in that. He is looking for that worship which is centered in the deepest part of our nature—in the spirit.

In line with this, it is instructive to note that when the nation began to disintegrate, it was the 10 tribes of the north which fell apart first. It is amazing how early marks of sin begin to appear in the body when there is a dissolute and debauched way of life. Coarseness and vulgarity soon begin to mark the bodies of those who give themselves to overindulgence in food and drink and a debauched lifestyle. The body is the first to deteriorate, as Israel was the first to go in this record.

But Judah (depicting the soul, the personality), was next, arrested temporarily by the reformations we have noted. Ultimately the kingdom declined until Judah too was carried away into captivity. For a few years the Temple remained in Jerusalem, but in the end it too was stripped and burned. Thus the whole record is a picture of a wasted life. It is the picture of an individual who is a Christian but who has built upon the foundation of Christ with only wood, hay and stubble. Eventually the test of fire comes and only that which cannot be burned survives.

CHAPTER TWELVE

The Way Back

EZRA

The books of Ezra and Nehemiah (one book in the Hebrew Bible) trace the story of the return of the people of God to the land of Israel after the 70-year captivity in Babylon. Scholars differ as to the chronological order of the books, some maintaining that the events of Nehemiah occur before those of Ezra. Other historians place the return under Zerubbabel (recounted in the first six chapters of Ezra) as the earliest return, dated approximately 537 B.C., with Ezra and Nehemiah leading later returns in that order. Be that as it may, we shall follow the biblical order so that we might learn the meaning of these events in the spiritual parallel of our individual lives.

The book of Ezra begins with the same words which close the book of 2 Chronicles. They recount the decree of Cyrus, king of Persia, to reestablish and restore the house of the Lord at Jerusalem. This gives us our clue to the meaning of Ezra, for it is a book which recounts the method of God in restoring a heart which has fallen into sin.

The book divides naturally into the ministries of two men: Zerubbabel, chapters 1-6 and Ezra, chapters 7-10. Both of these men led expeditions of Jewish captives back to Jerusalem from Babylon. Zerubbabel was a descendant of David and thus of the kingly line. Ezra descended from Aaron and is therefore a priest. This suggests immediately that in the work of restoration both a king and a priest are needed. The work of the king is to build, or in this case, to rebuild. The work of the priest is to cleanse. Restoration in an individual life always requires these two ministries. There is need to rebuild the character through a recognition of the kingship and lordship of Jesus Christ in the human spirit. Such building involves the recognition of God's right to own and direct us and to change us according to His will.

But restoration also involves cleansing. The spirit and the soul are to be cleansed by our great High Priest, who is able to wash away our guilt, tidy up our past and restore us to a place of fellowship and blessedness before God.

ZERUBBABEL

Under Zerubbabel an early return takes place. This kingly descendant led about 50,000 people from Babylon back to Jerusalem. This is far fewer in number than those who have returned to the land in our own day, but the biblical record attaches great importance to this first return. Cyrus, the king of Persia, may have known of Isaiah's predictions concerning his instrumentality in the hands of God, for he gave willing aid to the Jews who returned, putting in their hands again the vessels of the Temple and giving them goods and animals (Ezra 1:7).

When they came to Jerusalem it was the seventh month of the year and they arrived in time to celebrate the Feast of Tabernacles. This feast (also called the feast of ingathering) was the time when Israel dwelt in booths to remind them of their pilgrim character. This feast also looks forward to the eventual regathering of Israel from their vast worldwide dispersion to celebrate the personal reign of Messiah upon the earth in great power and glory.

The careful list of those who returned, given in chapter 2, indicates that not only did various families and clans go back but also a company of priests, a smaller number of Levites, certain servants who were to assist the Levites in their service, and a number of people whose genealogy was somewhat uncertain.

Their first act upon return was to build an altar on the original Temple site, in the midst of the ruins. Under the open sky they erected an altar to God and began to worship and offer sacrifice as the Law of Moses had bid them. This is most significant, for the first act of a heart that really desires to return from wandering in darkness and the ways of the world to real fellowship with God is to erect an altar. The altar is the symbol of divine ownership and involves sacrifice, worship and praise. The sacrifice is that of our right to run our own lives; worship is the enjoyment of the restored relationship where the heart is ministered to by the only One who can fully meet its needs; praise is that of a rejoicing heart.

The second thing they did was to lay the foundation of the Temple (3:10). This work when finished was met with mixed feeling, for some of the people shouted with a great shout of joy and others, including those who had seen the first Temple built by Solomon, wept with a loud voice, so that it was impossible to distinguish the shouts of joy from the sounds of weeping (3:13). Perhaps you too may have felt this way. Have you ever returned to God after a time of coldness and withdrawal, with a great sense of joy as the foundations of fellowship were relaid by the Spirit, yet with regret for the loss of wasted years? This is what is portrayed here. Tears of joy mingled with tears of sorrow as the people saw the Temple being rebuilt.

The third factor in the return of Zerubbabel was the immediate opposition which developed to the restoration of the Temple. Here we see portrayed the force at work in every human heart which immediately rises up to oppose everything God attempts to do. There is a great lesson here in how this force reveals itself. The opposition first appears as friendly solicitude. The people of the land approached Zerubbabel and said, "Let us build with you,

for we like you seek your God; and we have been sacrific-
ing to Him since the days of Esar-haddon king of Assyria,
who brought us up here'' (4:2). This apparently friendly
and openhearted desire to participate in the work marked a
very subtle attack upon the returning exiles. It is not
difficult to say no to an enemy who breathes fiery threats
of slaughter, but when he comes dripping with solicitude
and offers to help with your project it is difficult to say no.

But this Zerubbabel did, for he declined their offer of
help and stated the Jews would do the work alone. It may
have seemed a bit churlish, but it was not mere caprice,
for God had commanded Israel not to fellowship with
other nations or engage with them in joint enterprises
concerning faith. It meant simply that God rejects utterly
the philosophy of the world in carrying out His work in the
world. There is a worldly religion and a worldly
philosophy which tries to interject the concepts and
methods of the world into the lives of God's people. God
has made it clear that these are to be rejected. The thinking
of the world reflects the spirit of the devil, who is the god
of this age. His philosophy is, ''Advance yourself; do this
for your own glory. Use religious ways to advance your
own purposes and thus win admiration, power and
fame.'' But God rejects this principle in its totality.

When the offer of friendship was rejected, it quickly
turned to hatred. The people of the land began to mock
and taunt the Jews, thus discouraging Israel from doing
the work that God had commanded. These so-called
''friends'' even used legal means to undermine Israel's
authority and right to build, for they obtained from Artaxerxes, the king, a decree to stop the rebuilding of the
Temple in view of the rebellious history of the Jews. The
work was stopped for a period of six years and the Temple
lay with only its foundations completed, overrun with
weeds and grass (4:24). It was during this period that,
according to the prophet Haggai, the people turned in-

stead to building their own homes with many luxuries and comforts. Those who attempt a return to fellowship with God may often find that the record of their past rises again to haunt them and impede their progress, but a determination to go on with God would overcome even this handicap.

To aid the people, God sent two prophets, Haggai and Zechariah, who proved to be God's instruments to turn the people back to their work (5:1). God also moved the heart of Darius the king to search for the original edict of Cyrus which allowed the restoration of the Temple. When it was found a decree was sent to Israel to permit the rebuilding to continue.

At last the work was finished, and in chapter 6 we read of the celebration of the Passover, marking the beginning of their new life under God. Since the Passover pictures the conversion of a Christian, it is clear from this that our new birth will never be a source of delight to us until we are restored in the temple of our spirit to fellowship with the living God. Unless we are enjoying the glory and the light of heaven upon our hearts we have nothing for which to give thanks, nothing to celebrate.

EZRA

Chapters 7-10 concern the ministry of Ezra the priest. He too led a band of captives back to Jerusalem, though the exact dates are difficult to determine. It is said of him that ''he was a scribe skilled in the law of Moses, which the Lord God of Israel had given; and the king granted him all he requested because the hand of the Lord his God was upon him'' (7:6). What kind of a man is this whom a Gentile king regards so highly that he will give Ezra anything he asks? The secret is given in 7:10, ''For Ezra had set his heart to study the law of the Lord, and to practice it, and to teach His statutes and ordinances in Israel.'' He was not only a Bible reader; he was also a

Bible doer. As a result, Ezra could ask anything of the king and it would be granted.

Ezra's specific assignment by Artaxerxes the king was "to adorn the house of the Lord which is in Jerusalem" (7:27). To achieve this Ezra gathered a great company about him, taking special care to include among them a company of Levites. After prayer and fasting they set out on their journey, committing themselves to the overruling providence of God to keep them safe on their way. In due time they arrived in Jerusalem and there Ezra found an incredible condition. The Jews and the Levites had again begun to marry with their ancient enemies, the Canaanites, the Hittites, the Perizzites, the Jebusites, the Ammonites, the Moabites, the Egyptians and the Amorites.

Centuries before, God had given specific orders that the Israelites were not to intermingle with these tribes. Now they were starting the whole wretched mess over again. It was this intermarrying which had broken the strength of the nation before. It had undermined the power of God among them and finally divided the people, broken up the tribes and separated them into two nations. At last, as they succumbed to the idolatrous practices of those whom they had married, God delivered them into the hands of their captives. Now it appears that after 70 years of captivity they had not learned a thing. This is a vivid reminder that the flesh within us never changes. No matter how long we may walk in the Spirit, we will never arrive at a place where we cannot revert to the worst we have ever been, if we depart from dependence upon the Spirit of God.

When Ezra heard that the people had disobeyed God in intermarrying he tore his garments, pulled the hair from his head and beard, and sat appalled until the evening sacrifice. It was unbelievable to him. But as the book nears its close Ezra prayed to God and confessed this great sin of the people. In graciousness God moved the hearts of the people and the leaders came in brokenhearted contrition to Ezra and acknowledged their wrong. A great proclamation was issued and the people assembled together. It happened to be a day when it was raining, but despite the rain the people stood, thousands of them, in front of the Temple and confessed their guilt and agreed to put away the wives and children they had acquired outside the will of God (10:9-17).

This was not an easy thing to do, but it is surely what Jesus meant when He said, "If anyone comes to Me, and does not hate his own father and mother and wife and children . . . he cannot be My disciple" (Luke 14:26). It does not mean that a man must put away his wife today, for this is symbolic teaching. It means that we are to put away whatever comes from the flesh (which is always pictured by the Canaanite tribes).

The book closes with a listing of the men in Israel who were faithful to the Word of God, and obeyed Him in this painful matter. Thus the work of Ezra was completed and the task to which he had been assigned, that of beautifying the Temple, went forward. So it is also in the parable of our lives.

NEHEMIAH

As the book of Ezra recounts the building of the Temple, so the book of Nehemiah gives us the story of the rebuilding of the walls of Jerusalem. This is a significant order, for always the way back to God after a period of declension and captivity to evil must begin within the human spirit—the temple of man. But the next step is to begin a reconstruction of the walls, since walls are universally the symbol of strength and protection. This is a clear picture of the process of rebuilding the defenses of the spiritual life to protect against the attacks of any enemy. Many human derelicts drift up and down the streets of our cities, hopeless and helpless, because their defenses have crumbled away; but frequently God in grace reaches them, against all the expectations of those who have known them, and their walls of defense are rebuilt again. This is the story of the book of Nehemiah.

REBUILDING THE DEFENSES

The first step in this process is given in chapter 1 where a report is brought to Nehemiah in the city of Susa concerning the ruin and decay of Jerusalem. When Nehemiah heard these words he wept and mourned for several days, fasting and praying before the God of heaven (1:4). *Thus the first step in rebuilding the defenses of any life is to become greatly concerned about the ruins*. Have you ever taken a good look at the ruins of your life? Have you ever stopped long enough to assess what you could be to God, compared to what you are? Have you looked at the possibilities that God gave you and seen how far you have deviated from that potential? If you have, then like Nehemiah, you have received word in some form or other of the desolation and ruin that is present. If you will begin to be concerned and weep over those ruins, you will have begun the process of rebuilding.

This mourning is immediately followed by confession (1:5-9). Nehemiah prays a great prayer in which he acknowledges the sin of his people and the justice of God in having fulfilled the words of Moses, given in warning centuries before. Also in Moses' words, recorded in Deuteronomy, was the promise that when anyone, even in a distant country, would begin to pray to God, a recovery and restitution to the place of blessing would begin.

The prayer of confession is followed by a great commitment (1:10,11). Nehemiah asked for divine success to be given him, for a plan is already forming in his mind even while he has been in prayer. He has something definite which he wants to ask and he prays that God will grant him mercy in the sight of the king.

Here is a man who, out of his concern and after the confession of his heart, commits himself to a project. Invariably in an enterprise like this there are factors over which man has no control and God must arrange them. So Nehemiah prays about his appearance before the king.

When, in his work as cupbearer, he comes before the king (2:4-8), his face shows concern over the city of his fathers. At the king's request he makes known to him what is troubling him. The account especially notes that the queen was sitting beside the king. Our Bible scholar has identified the king as Ahasuerus who appears also in the book of Esther. If this is the case the queen here is Esther herself. The names Artaxerxes and Ahasuerus are not proper names but are really titles meaning *the great king* (Artaxerxes) and *the venerable father* (Ahasuerus). If Esther is the queen then it would explain why the king in Nehemiah is willing to restore Jerusalem; for Queen Esther is also a Jewess.

The next need in rebuilding the defenses of a city, or of a life, is that of *courage to face the opposition that immediately arises*. Encouraged by the king, Nehemiah returned to Jerusalem (2:8) where he found certain Canaanite leaders who were greatly displeased that someone had come to seek the welfare of the children of Israel. Whenever a man like Nehemiah says "I will arise and build," Satan always says, "Then I will arise and oppose."

Such opposition requires not only courage but caution. Nehemiah rode out around the city of Jerusalem by night (2:15), surveying the ruin that was there and taking careful note of what needed to be done. He made an honest survey of the facts and then began to lay his plans. There was no public announcement of what he intended to do, for that would have stirred up even further opposition. But without conceit or ostentation he began his work.

PRINCIPLES OF RECONSTRUCTION

If the walls of your life are broken down or your defenses have crumbled so that the enemy is getting at you on every hand, and you easily fall prey to temptation, it would be well to pay special heed to the principles of reconstruction set forth in chapter 3 of this book. We learn, first of all, that the people were willing to work. Second, that they became personally involved and began right where they were. Each began to work on the part of the wall that was nearest to his own house, and so called forth the deepest of personal involvement on his part.

It is noteworthy that the reconstruction of the walls centered about the 10 gates of the city. Again, in one of the marvelous hidden revelations of truth which is frequently found in Scripture, the names of these 10 gates, in the order in which they appear, is most instructive.

First, there is the Sheep Gate (3:1). Through this gate the sacrificial animals were brought into the city to be offered on the altar. This clearly pictures the Lamb of God, whose blood was shed on the cross for us, and therefore stands for the principle of the cross. That is always the starting place to regain strength in your life. You must recognize anew that the work of the cross is to cancel out your selfish ego and put to death that which is for your own glory and advancement.

The account then moves to the Fish Gate (3:3). When we remember that Jesus said to His disciples, "Follow Me, and I will make you to become fishers of men" (Mark 1:17), this gate suggests the witness of a Christian. Every Christian is called to be a witness. If you can never give an account of what the Lord has done for you, then this wall is broken and the Fish Gate needs to be rebuilt.

In verse 6 the Old Gate (3:6) represents the unchangeable truth of God upon which everything new must rest. As someone has well said, "Whatever is true is not new, and whatever is new is not true." In many places today the old truth is being forsaken, but if you allow this old truth to go you will find that the wall crumbles and enemies outside gain access to your soul.

The next gate is the Valley Gate (3:13). This suggests the place of humility, the place of lowliness of mind and humbleness of heart. On almost every page of Scripture God speaks against the pride of man. He looks always for the lowly, the humble, the contrite and those who have learned that they are not indispensable. This gate seems to be frequently in need of repair with many of us. But we need to be reminded that "God is opposed to the proud, but gives grace to the humble" (Jas. 4:6).

Next in order is the Dung Gate (3:14). This is not a very beautiful name but it represents an essential process in life: you need to eliminate that which is corrupt and defiling. No life can be strong or healthy that does not have an often used elimination gate within it.

The Fountain Gate is mentioned next (3:15). This name reminds us instantly of the words of Jesus to the woman at the well: "The water that I shall give [you] shall become in [you] a well of water [a fountain] springing up to eternal life" (John 4:14). This speaks of the Holy Spirit who is to be like a river of life in you, enabling you to obey God's will and His Word. To drink from that flowing fountain is to be refreshed in spirit, and to find power to do what God requires.

The Fountain Gate is followed by the Water Gate (3:25,26). Water is always, in Scripture, the symbol of the Word of God. The interesting thing about this Water Gate is that it did not need to be repaired. Evidently it was the only part of the wall that was still standing. The people who lived near it are mentioned, but nothing is said about its repair. Thus the Word of God never breaks down nor does it need repair, it simply needs to be reinhabited.

The eighth gate is the East Gate facing the rising sun (3:29). This is, therefore, the gate of hope, anticipating that which is yet to come when the trials of life and the struggles of earth end, and the glorious new sun rises on the day of God. This gate needs to be rebuilt in many of us who fall under the pessimistic spirit of this age and are crushed by the hopelessness of our times.

The ninth gate is the Horse Gate (3:28). The horse in Scripture is the symbol of warfare, that is, the need to do battle against the forces of darkness. It too is often in need of repair. As the apostle Paul says, "For our struggle is not against flesh and blood, but against the rulers, against the powers, against the world-forces of this darkness, against the spiritual forces of wickedness" (Eph. 6:12).

The final gate is the Muster Gate (Neh. 3:31). The Hebrew word means literally "the examination" gate. This is evidently the place where judgment was conducted, and speaks of our need to take a good look at ourselves now and then and evaluate what we are doing.

That brings us around again to the Sheep Gate (3:32), the gate of the cross. The cross must be at the beginning and end of every life.

PRAY AND WATCH

The derision and scorn of their Canaanite neighbors continued to mount, and threats were made against the lives of Nehemiah and other leaders. In response, Nehemiah did two important things: He went to prayer, and set up a guard. From then on, the workers labored with their weapons beside them, keeping watch and building at the same time (4:16). It was a practical demonstration of, "Praise the Lord and pass the ammunition."

Seeing his persistence, his enemies tried various approaches to stop the work. Nehemiah retained a single eye to the work to which God had called him. The end result was the finishing of the wall and the gaining of the respect of surrounding nations when they saw the hand of God at work.

When the walls were completed the people were encouraged to move back from the suburbs to homes within the city walls (chap. 7). The register of peoples is almost identical to the list in Ezra, which lends confirmation to the theory that it was Nehemiah who first returned from Babylon and Ezra who came later. This also is strengthened by the fact that it is only at this point in Nehemiah that Ezra appears in the book.

When the walls were completed, the time came to reaffirm the spiritual strength of the nation. In a great gathering of the people, the Law was read to them anew, accompanied by exposition given by Ezra the priest (chap. 8). It is especially significant that when the people were convicted by the reading of the Law to the point of weeping, Ezra and Nehemiah comforted them with reassurances that the Lord Himself had made provision for their forgiveness, and that "the joy of the Lord is your strength" (8:10).

Chapters 11 through 13 conclude the book, with first a recognition of certain gifts among the people. Levites, gatekeepers, singers and various other ministries were recognized. This is similar to the New Testament which sets the church to discover the gifts of the Spirit that are given among them, and put them all to work. In chapter 12 is the story of the dedication of the wall. The people gathered and marched around the wall with instruments, singing and shouting, playing and rejoicing.

During the reading of the Law, it was learned again that the people of God should give no official place to either an Ammonite or a Moabite. Nehemiah, who had gone back to Persia and apparently had returned for the dedication of the walls, reminded the high priest that Tobiah was an Ammonite and had been given a place to live within the very Temple itself. This is the Tobiah who had done so much to hinder the work of building the wall. To correct this, Nehemiah went in and threw Tobiah's furniture out into the street. Further, he found that the priests and Levites had been cheated, so he restored the money that belonged to them. Then discovering that the people were violating the Sabbath, he commanded that the doors of the city should be shut when the Sabbath began and kept shut until it was ended. Finally, he dealt with some violence with the problem of intermarrying with forbidden races again. When he learned that one of the priests was the son-in-law of Sanballet, who had done so much to oppose Nehemiah's work, he chased the young man from his presence.

To us it may appear that Nehemiah was overly severe with these violations, but here is a man who has learned that there can be no compromise with evil. He manifests one of the greatest lessons the Spirit of God can ever teach us: to say no when it needs to be said and to say it with firmness and determination. Those who have made a mark for God throughout the history of the church have been those who have learned to say no at the right times.

Thus the book of Nehemiah has given itself to a clear demonstration of how to rebuild the walls of strength in our individual lives, and to maintain those walls in strength by unceasing resistance to allurements and attacks which attempt to force us to compromise. How important it is to be ruthless against the forces that undermine and sap the vitality of our lives in Christ.

ESTHER

The book of Esther is an historical incident that occurred during the days of Jewish captivity in Babylon.

Some Bible scholars feel that the Persian king, Ahasuerus in the book, is Xerxes the Great; one great Bible scholar, however, identifies him with Astyages—also called Artaxerxes in Nehemiah and Ezra—the father of Cyrus the Persian.

Esther doesn't appear to be a religious book because nowhere does the name of God appear—nor any mention of heaven or hell. However, the name *Jehovah* does appear four times in the original Hebrew in a hidden way: in the form of acrostics. It is interesting to note that Jehovah declared in Deuteronomy 31 that if His people forsook Him He would hide His face from them.

As in our study of other Old Testament events, the greatest lesson in the account of Esther is in its spiritual parallel to man himself. This pattern appears in the Tabernacle, is repeated in the Temple, appears in the three-fold division of the nation Israel and now is the key to the book of Esther.

Ahasuerus, the king, depicts the soul of man, comprising mind, emotions and, especially, will. His capital city, Susa, is the body in which all his decisions and actions will be most immediately felt. His empire is the sphere of influence which each one of us exerts on all whom we contact. His queen is the spirit of man, closely bound to the soul in such a way that no division or separation can be felt. The queen, bound in marriage to the king, depicts the place of fellowship, refreshment and communion with God which is intimately related to our soul.

Ahasuerus's empire was in a time of peace and blessing, fullness and fruitfulness. No enemy threatened his kingdom from the outside; there was nothing to do but display the lavish glory of his kingdom. Unfallen Adam, in parallel, was just such a king. His whole empire, the Garden of Eden, lay at rest and he was free to do nothing more than manifest the riches, fruitfulness and glory of his kingdom while enjoying unhindered communion with God.

During a six-month long feast, which began in joy and merrymaking but ended in tragedy, the king was lifted up in pride and sought to disgrace his queen. Her refusal to submit to his demands resulted in her being deposed from the throne. This decree became a law which could not be changed. When Adam chose to assert the desire of his will over what he knew in his heart that God wanted, he laid the groundwork for the eventual fall of the entire race. His disobedience caused him and all his descendants to enter a fallen state, losing communion with God, which they were helpless to change.

In his loneliness, Ahasuerus sought a new queen. Esther, one of the Jewish captives, who was under the control of her cousin Mordecai, was chosen and was exalted to second place in the kingdom. In the spiritual parallel of our life, fallen man, in loneliness and restlessness, also searches for a new place of communion and fellowship with God, even though he himself hardly knows what he is looking for. The new queen depicts our moment of conversion. At this moment we receive a new spirit who, though we do not yet understand it, is under control of another—the Holy Spirit. Throughout this book, "the little man," Mordecai, is the power behind the throne, thus depicting the humility and self-effacement of the Spirit of Christ.

When Haman, a descendant of Amalek—who always pictures the aspects of the flesh—convinced Ahasuerus to decree that the Jews should be destroyed, Esther risked her life to save her people. She told the king that his decree would mean her death as well as her people's death. The king, in consternation, had Haman hanged; Mordecai is exalted to a place of power and instantly everything begins to change. Another decree by the king removed the threat of death from the Jewish captives and allowed them to kill their enemies, just as in Romans 8:2 Paul tells us that ''the law of the Spirit of life in Christ Jesus has set you free from the law of sin and of death.''

The book ends with the establishment of the feast of Purim as an enduring memorial to the events of this story. There is a tradition among the Jews that the feast of Purim is the only feast that will be observed after the Messiah comes. This reflects the truth that to walk in the Spirit is normal for both time and eternity. It is the greatest lesson which God wants us to learn.

In this book we have the same king and the same kingdom at the end as we do at the beginning. The only difference is that Haman is out and Mordecai is in. But what a difference! Just as the king and kingdom remain the same, so the Christian remains the same person when the Spirit is given the place of control in his life. Personality does not change, but it is cleansed and enhanced by the presence of the Spirit. So Paul can say, ''I have been crucified with Christ; and it is no longer I who live, but Christ lives in me'' (Gal. 2:20). The person remains the same; the principle upon which he lives and acts is entirely different. That is the secret of the Spirit-filled life. As Mordecai, through the will of the king, brings power and peace to the kingdom, so the Holy Spirit, through our human will and never beyond it, brings peace and prosperity into our lives.